Benjamin Franklin

His Life As He Wrote It

The 'Gray Coat' portrait by Duplessis

Benjamin Franklin

His Life As He Wrote It

Edited by
ESMOND WRIGHT

HARVARD UNIVERSITY PRESS
Cambridge, Massachusetts
1990

This book is printed on acid-free paper, and its binding materials
have been chosen for strength and durability.

Library of Congress Cataloging-in-Publication Data

Wright, Esmond.
Benjamin Franklin : his life as he wrote it / Esmond Wright.
p.   cm.
Includes bibliographical references.
ISBN 0-674-06654-5 (alk. paper)
1. Franklin, Benjamin, 1706–1790.   2. Statesmen—United States—
Biography.   3. Printers—United States—Biography.   4. Scientists—
United States—Biography.   I. Title.
E302.6.F8W88   1990
973.3'092—dc20
[B]
89-39795
CIP

CONTENTS

ILLUSTRATIONS

EDITOR'S NOTE

In preparing this volume, I have relied in large measure upon *The Papers of Benjamin Franklin*, 27 volumes thus far, which bring the story to 1778 (New Haven: Yale University Press, since 1959, ed. L. W. Labaree, W. B. Willcox, Claude-Anne Lopez, Barbara Oberg et al.); upon A. H. Smyth's edition of *The Writings of Benjamin Franklin* (10 volumes, New York: Macmillan, 1905–1907); upon the Yale edition of *The Autobiography* (1964), its impressive scholarly apparatus and biographical notes; and upon the resources of the American Philosophical Society in Philadelphia. I am also indebted to the following for permission to quote from documents in their possession: the American Academy of Arts and Sciences, the Boston Athenaeum, the British Library, W. G. Drummond Moray, Abercairny, Crieff, Scotland, the Harrowby MSS Trust, Stafford, Eng., the Trustees of the Henry E. Huntington Library and Art Gallery, the Library of Congress, the Massachusetts Historical Society, the Pierpont Morgan Library, the New York Public Library, the Scottish Record Office, and the Yale University Library.

I am grateful to a number of scholars of eighteenth-century America and France, particularly those fellow-workers on the Franklin Collection at Yale, whose own writing and whose counsel have been of such help over the years: Alfred Owen Aldridge, Whitfield Bell, Jonathan Dull, Leo Lemay, Claude-Anne Lopez and Catherine M. Prelinger.

See also Carl Van Doren, *Benjamin Franklin* (New York: Viking Press, 1938); Alfred Owen Aldridge, *Franklin and His French Contemporaries* (New York: New York University Press,

1957); J. A. Leo Lemay, *Benjamin Franklin, Writings* (New York: Library of America, 1987); Claude-Anne Lopez, *Mon Cher Papa: Franklin and the Ladies of Paris* (New Haven: Yale University Press, 1966); Esmond Wright, *Franklin of Philadelphia* (Cambridge, Mass.: Harvard University Press, 1986).

May I add my thanks to Sheila Thompson for her skill as editor, her patience, and her ability to decipher Franklin's 'scribblings' and—much more difficult—my own.

A certain amount of editing of the text has been undertaken in the interests of consistency, but Franklin's use of italics and his sometimes idiosyncratic spelling have been retained.

Omissions within the text are marked by ellipses (. . .).

Benjamin Franklin

His Life As He Wrote It

INTRODUCTION

Benjamin Franklin's is probably the best known story, now thick with legends and anecdotes, in American history. The tenth and youngest son in a family of seventeen children (he was the fifteenth), he was born in colonial Boston in 1706. His father was a tallow-chandler and soap-boiler who had left England twenty-three years before.

With little schooling behind him, beyond what he acquired in the course of an apprenticeship to one of his brothers, Benjamin ran away from home—first to New York and then to Philadelphia, where, after an eighteen-month spell in London, he finally launched himself as a printer. He then married and embarked upon a hectic round of civic activities, becoming an Assembly-man and politician, interesting himself in the nature of electricity, and founding a hospital, a college, a library, a fire company and a fire insurance system. One can understand the fashionable Philadelphian view that Franklin was born in Philadelphia at the age of seventeen (or perhaps one should say 'born again') for, from that age the city became his base for a host of enterprises: continental postmaster; colonial agent in London; envoy to France to secure, first, an alliance in the War of Independence, and then a Treaty of Peace guaranteeing it; and, in the end, establishing himself as Founding Father Extraordinary.

But it was at Twyford, six miles from Winchester, that he began what he referred to as 'a little scribbling'; and this was the work that later became the first part of the most famous autobiography in American history.

The form of the book—a memo and conduct-book ostensibly

written for his son—was not new. Only seven years before Franklin began his memoirs (he himself never described them as an *Autobiography*), Horace Walpole had published on his private press the autobiography of Lord Herbert of Cherbury. As an apprentice-printer in Boston, Franklin had been fascinated by the work of Bunyan and Defoe, and, four years after his arrival in Philadelphia, he read William Penn's *Fruits of a Father's Love*. As a young man he had read Plutarch's *Lives*, and knew that the best guide to character-forming, and to good conduct and decorum, was the study of the lives of the great men of the past; though for him, as for others of the enlightened eighteenth century, Bacon, Locke and Newton were the most admirable mentors, and Cato was preferred to Caesar.

The form deceived no one, least of all the son to whom it was addressed. William was illegitimate, but had been brought up quite openly by his father and his wife Deborah. Educated at the Middle Temple during his father's first mission in London (1757–62), he had been by 1771 (when he was forty) for nine years a Royal Governor of the province of what is now New Jersey, but was then known as the Jersies, East and West. William had married the daughter of a wealthy West Indian planter, lived in style in Burlington and needed, it seems, few instructions in decorum or gracious living.

The passages of explicit preaching on morals on which many of Franklin's critics have seized occur not in Part I, but in Part II of the *Autobiography*, written in 1784 at the urging of his Quaker friend Abel James and his English friend, Benjamin Vaughan. He lists the virtues he admired and describes his method of attaining them by keeping and tabulating the score almost by calendar. He wrote this Part in 1784, aged seventy-eight, in his French rural retreat in Passy, after the War of Independence was won and the Treaty of Peace was signed. There is evident recognition on his part that he is now a public figure, a symbol not only in Paris but in America too; and he writes with coolness and irony, however earnest the exhortations. He was, moreover, remote from his own books and records, even from the first Part of his story which, along with his papers, he had left for safe-keeping—or so he thought—with his friend and former political colleague, Joseph Galloway, at his home at Trevose outside Philadelphia. Galloway had, however, become a Loyalist in 1778, when Lord Howe's forces occupied Philadelphia, and had moved to London: Grace Galloway was forcibly evicted from their Philadelphia townhouse at 6th and Market Street by a group led by the artist-patriot Charles Willson Peale, and the house later became the residence of President Washington. As a result, the 'Franklin Papers'—so the news reached Passy—had been scattered to the winds.

Inevitably, therefore, there was some duplication in the writing at this stage. Clearly, he drew on a project he was nursing, the never-written *Art of Virtue*, for it is a moralist Father Abraham who appears with a plan for moral algebra as a response to Abel James's call 'to promote a greater spirit of Industry and early attention to Business, Frugality and Temperance into the American Youth'. And, at least at the age of seventy-eight, he recognized that too careful a keeping of the score of success or failure would result in 'a kind of foppery in morals'. Part III, and the very brief Part IV, giving an account of his scientific experiments and his public activities, including the supply of equipment for Braddock's unsuccessful campaign to capture Fort Duquesne (Pittsburgh) were both written in Philadelphia, when he was eighty-two.

What was distinctive about the *Autobiography* was less the form of its four different Parts than the style—and the contents. Franklin's prose is remarkably lucid, terse, and deceptively simple. He always honoured his own prescription in the *Pennsylvania Gazette* (2 August 1733) that good writing should be 'smooth, clear and short'. In retrospect, he recognized that it was his skill with words that had been 'a principal means of my advancement'. Hardly any club or society that he joined failed to elect him, often at once, as secretary and/or keeper of minutes and/or deviser of agenda. By the time he began his *Autobiography*, Franklin had drafted legislative papers, and the replies to many of them; had edited his *Gazette* for three decades; and had produced his annual almanac, *Poor Richard*, full of wise—and earthy—saws and modern instances, many of them the product of his own roguish invention and, in Woodrow Wilson's phrase, 'racy of the soil'. He was a master raconteur, adept at making up a story on the many occasions when news as such was thin, in a century of erratic communication, of primitive news-gathering and even many weeks of total isolation from London or Boston 'truth'. He drew on his own local world, and made it live. His addiction to parables and aphorisms echoes Bunyan and Defoe, Cotton Mather and the 'hell-fire club' of the 'Honest Wags', his fellow-apprentices in his brother's print shop in Boston. The wit usually deflates, the scorn is sharp for the humbug and pomposity of proprietors or Quakers or the 'wealthy and powerful', or of 'the men of the black gown'. As Leo Lemay has stressed, even the lay-pulpit style of Part II, however well-intentioned, is also satirical; moral perfection is to be sought, but Franklin was a journalist—he was always aware of and prompt to reveal his own remissness, and the similar *errata* of others. His is never the style of an evangelist or of a crusader for causes; it is closer to Voltaire than to Rousseau, neither poetic nor Utopian; he sounds no call to high endeavour. The message is simple: always let your conscience be your guide. The moral preceptor, however, was franker than his predecessors in this autobiographical genre—Cellini, perhaps, apart—in revealing his *errata*, hinting at indiscretions in his exchanges in the 1750s with the virginal Catherine Ray of Block Island; hinting at (and hoping for?) indiscretions in his gallantry with the ladies of the *salons* in Paris in his *bagatelles* of the 1780s—when he was seventy-five or more. And to check his pride, did he not add humility as the thirteenth of the virtues he ought to cultivate?

All of which was not only distinctive for its day, but uniquely American. The tone and the content speak of a New World, filled with leather-aproned men, mechanics and farmers, with their own shrewd wisdom; the style in its Biblical resonance is earthy and unbookish. The preoccupations are of the ordinary world: stoves and smoky chimneys, fire hazards, insurance and libraries, schools, hospitals and the postal service. There are parallels with Defoe, not least in humbleness of origins, in the Puritan adages, in the journalistic skill and in the fertility of proposals for civic improvement. However, by contrast, Defoe suffered imprisonment and persecution, and ended his life in obscurity; whereas Benjamin Vaughan, in urging Franklin to tell his story, stressed that one of the merits of the *Autobiography* was that it 'was connected with the detail of . . . a rising people'. Franklin lived on a continent where literacy was ever expanding, where the inventor and the scholar were esteemed (despite Dogood's scorn for Harvard), and where letters and learning were rapidly being democratized.

Journalist, civic planner, political agent, diplomat, entrepreneur: even this list is not complete. When he describes his electrical experiments, as in his correspondence with the English Quaker scientist Peter Collinson, Franklin's writing is not only limpidly clear and expository but sophisticated. Much of it went promptly into print in London to win him, in 1756, his Fellowship of the Royal Society, and to be translated into French and earn him that European reputation as scientist that would be of incalculable benefit twenty-five years later when he appeared in Paris as political envoy and negotiator. He could be cosmopolitan as well as plebeian, pious when appropriate, jocular and ribald and a teller of tall tales when relaxed, but precise, analytic and humble in describing his experiments. And all his inventions were for use, and free. His *errata* were numerous, but pride, greed and exploitation were not among them.

Franklin's range was—for any century—extraordinary. In one month (January 1766) he wrote at least eleven letters, nine essays for English periodicals, and drafted a long pamphlet against the Stamp Act. One one day (22 August 1772), he wrote at least seventeen letters to as many people on topics as diverse as canals, anti-slavery propaganda, finding workmen for a glass factory, silk culture, rhubarb cultivation, books for the Library Company, post office accounts, and the investments in London of the Pennsylvania hospital. Nor did this activity prevent notes of political assessment, a glass or two of Madeira of an evening in a coffee house on the Strand with his Dissenter and Scottish friends, and the pondering on a literary hoax to entertain, enliven—and occasionally frighten—the readers of the London press. He was many-sided, ever-enquiring, lively and gregarious.

Nor were his private letters (which, as the years passed, were, he knew, handed round, talked of and often printed and published) the hurried effusions that serve today. With each correspondent Franklin sought to establish a special relationship: flirtatious with Katy Ray, Polly Stevenson or the ladies of the *salons*; warm and avuncular to his sister Jane; genial and relaxed with his fellow-printer Strahan; captivating with the Shipley girls; politically wise to Richard Jackson or Governor Shirley; meticulous and precise with Collinson; scientific-philosophic with Cadwallader Colden or Lord Kames; bitter in rebuke to Arthur Lee; admonitory to John Paul Jones; encouraging to George Washington; firm, even expressing a stern personal declaration of independence, to Lord Howe in 1776. Throughout, his tone was urbane and warm. Mather Byles, the Boston poet, thanked him for 'the easy and gay light in which you view our leaving this little earth', and the botanist John Bartram said that his letters had 'a magical power of dispeling melancholy fumes and chearing up my spirits'.

There has been a considerable literature of comment and assessment of the *Autobiography*, as a work of art and artifice, and on its historical or political significance. There are those who see it as a picaresque adventure-story, almost a novel with its varied characters, their actions and interactions, with Governor Keith as villain, Keimer as *braggadocio*, and the temptations of London that tested the pilgrim on his travels. To others it is a fable, a secular *Pilgrim's Progress*, with every adventure preceded or followed by a moral. To many in the late nineteenth century it tells of the climbing of the industrious apprentice, one of the seventeen children of a Boston candle-maker, who talked to kings and dined with one of them, and then defied them to found a republic. Others noted that despite all his Yankee counselling—work hard and count your pennies, 'the sleeping fox catches no poultry', 'keep thy shop and thy shop will keep thee'—he practised thrift only as long as he had to, and not a moment longer; indeed, that he practised it primarily to be seen doing so, to attract customers and praise, *and* that he retired from his newspaper business at forty-two.

'In order to secure my credit and character as a tradesman, I took care not only to be in *reality* industrious and frugal, but to avoid all *appearances* of the contrary. I drest plainly; I was seen at no places of idle diversion; I never went out a fishing or shooting; a book, indeed, sometimes debauched me from my work; but that was seldom, snug, and gave no scandal . . . Thus being esteemed an industrious thriving young man, and paying duly for what I bought . . . I went on swimmingly.'

He told his daughter Sally, when the war came, to avoid luxuries and fripperies, but his own wine-cellar in Passy was well-stocked. His contemporary John Adams could deplore (and probably envy) the praise lavished on him in France, and his apparent enjoyment of it, and note his departure from Puritan or Quaker decorum. D. H. Lawrence later disliked his mean maxims, his absence of poetic turbulence, his ultra-rationalism of mind, and his unheroic view that honesty was admirable because it was the best policy, and that discretion was the better part of virtue. Others could be struck, however, by the sparkle and irony in the man, as when he told Madame Brillon that we give the name of sin to many of our pleasures 'so that we might enjoy them the more', and that he had not visited her that evening because he was waiting till the 'nights are longer'.

'I am consulting you on a case of conscience. I will mention the opinion of a certain father of the church which I find myself willing to adopt though I am not sure it is orthodox. It is this, that the most effectual way to get rid of a certain temptation is, as often as it returns, to comply with and satisfy it.

  Pray instruct me how far I may venture to practise upon this principle?'

What is striking in Franklin is that a man who apparently speaks so openly of himself and of his *errata*, even perhaps embroidering and inventing them, nevertheless retains a certain reserve—or, as Poor Richard might say, 'If you would keep a secret, keep it secret'. The most chatty and irreverent of journalists could follow the golden rules of diplomatic negotiation: never write it if you can say it, never say it if you can nod your head.

  The facts are that in a long and extraordinarily varied career, or many careers, Franklin is many-sided, a man of many paradoxes: on the one hand, the enquiring journalist, the sceptic, the critical experimenter skilful with his hands, the self-analyst; and on the other, a devious political operator, a Deist to whom God is at least the Supreme Clockmaker, and a good self-advertiser. He can be affable, but he is also a scholar, warm at one point, sardonic at another. This master of words was also a skilled manufacturer of fresh and human characters: Silence Dogood, the country widow who was 'a friend of virtue', and Poor Richard and Father Abraham 'serving scraps from the table of wisdom', Polly Baker, defending her right to bear illegitimate children, and in the end himself, 'Benjamin Franklin of Philadelphia, printer, Minister Plenipotentiary of the U.S. to the court of France, and President of the State of Pennsylvania'.

This single-volume edition of Franklin's writing is, like all its predecessors, inevitably selective. The Yale edition of his *Papers*, the most full and scholarly ever attempted, began appearing in 1959: thus far twenty-seven volumes have been published, at approximately yearly intervals, and yet it has only reached 1778. The editors may need another thirteen—or more—volumes to cover the key years of his French mission, and of the making both of the Treaty of Alliance of 1778 and of the Treaty of Paris 1782–3, editorial patience and stamina (and financial resources) permitting. The Yale edition is dauntingly comprehensive; it rigorously excludes any letter or document where there is any suspicion that it is the work of other hands, but includes all the letters to as well as from Franklin. There are over 30,000 items in it, and Franklin's correspondents in the end number more than 4000.

It is not least the depth and range of the Yale *Papers* that make it possible in this volume to 'fill out' the *Autobiography*. That memoir, in itself, is incomplete: it stops at 1757, just as Franklin's London enterprise is beginning and before his twenty-five years of hectic foreign service: it plays down his scientific interests and, of course, omits the 1774 negotiations, in England, and all the years and trials of his embassy in France. It was written over a period of nineteen years, but in short spells of hurried creativity. It also omits all the pseudonymous writing to which he was addicted from the age of sixteen, especially in his London years, and his role in Passy where he was buyer of supplies, propagandist, negotiator, spymaster, abettor of John Paul Jones's piracies on the seas, and planner of the invasion of Britain in 1779—when, happily, as in 1588, God blew and the fleets were scattered. It omits the evidence for the father's cooling relations with his son, which became a total break when William became a Loyalist. The accounts of Benjamin Franklin's involvement in public affairs, in London, Philadelphia and Paris, clearly intended as material for future additions to his *Autobiography*, could no longer be cast in the fashionable form of a letter to a son.

The public man of the *Autobiography* is the civic do-gooder, the private man is cast as a moralist, in quest of virtue. In fact, the whole man is more than these, and more than the innocent and unsophisticated pilgrim recounting the trials of his voyage. So varied and fascinating is he that Carl Van Doren described him as 'a tradesman in an age of reason . . . self-made, made, that is, neither in war nor in art, but in peaceful business . . . a harmonious human multitude'.

Apart from the greater volume of his writing now made available, thanks primarily to the skill and diligence of Franklin's recent editors (notably L. W. Labaree, William Willcox and Barbara Oberg and their teams), this printing of the *Autobiography* is different in structure from its predecessors. Van Doren, in his edition of Franklin's *Autobiographical Writings*, printed each Part of the *Autobiography* according to the date of its writing, even though the events Franklin records in each Part all take place before 1757. By contrast, other editions print the *Autobiogaphy* as if it were an organic unity, a single connected piece of composition, when in fact it was written at four distinct points. *This* book tells the Franklin story as a continuous chronological narrative, drawing on all the varied material as it becomes appropriate. I attach to each extract its source and date, and where necessary a headnote. The appendix contains explanatory biographical notes on each individual mentioned.

Even so, I cannot pretend that even this—more coherently-structured—volume gives the whole truth about Franklin. What is printed here can give but a taste of the man. It is *his* story. The journalist from his early days was always at Franklin's elbow. Thus the description of his entry into Philadelphia, aged seventeen, of the landing at Market Street Wharf, or his following the crowd to the Meeting House and falling asleep there, or of his future wife's first sight of him with his 'three great puffy rolls', is almost certainly half-fiction, or fact embroidered; but it is now one of Philadelphia's and America's great, accepted, tall tales. Like so much in Franklin's writing, as in the best fiction, an essential truth is contained. And, anyway, it makes a good yarn. To meet him is to meet one of the shrewdest, wisest and most versatile of men, a great storyteller, with an infinite curiosity, and an infinite capacity for laughing at himself as well as others. Why say more as prelude? Did not Poor Richard say, in January 1735:

> *Bad commentators spoil the best of books,*
> *So God sends meat (they say),*
> *The Devil cooks.*

ESMOND WRIGHT

CHRONOLOGY

CHAPTER ONE

1706 Born in Boston.

1714 Enters the Grammar School.

1716 His father's assistant in the tallow-chandlery business.

1718 Printer's apprentice to brother James.

1722 'Silence Dogood' essays published anonymously in *New England Courant*.

1723 Runs away to Philadelphia.

1724–26 In England; works as a printer.

1725 Writes and prints *A Dissertation on Liberty and Necessity, Pleasure and Pain*.

1726 Returns to Philadelphia.

CHAPTER TWO

1727 Forms the Junto, or 'Leather Apron' Club.

1728 Opens his own printing office.

1729 Becomes sole owner of the *Pennsylvania Gazette*.

1730 Marries Deborah Read.

1731 Founds first circulating library in America.

1732 Begins publishing *Poor Richard: An Almanack* (continued annually until 1758).

1736 Founds Union Fire Company of Philadelphia.

CHAPTER THREE

1737 Appointed postmaster of Philadelphia.

1742–44 Proposes the University of Pennsylvania; establishes the American Philosophical Society; organizes defence on frontier.

1747 First writes of his electrical experiments. Writes *Plain Truth*. Organizes first militia in Pennsylvania.

1748 Retires from active business by selling his printing firm. Elected to the Philadelphia Common Council.

1749 Appointed a Commissioner to trade with the Indians.

1751 *Experiments and Observations on Electricity* published in London. Elected to Pennsylvania Assembly; re-elected annually until 1764. Writes *Observations Concerning the Increase of Mankind*.

1752 Founds the first American fire insurance company.

1753 Receives honorary MAs from Harvard and Yale, and Copley Medal of the Royal Society. Appointed joint Deputy Postmaster General for the Colonies.

1755 Aids General Braddock in defending Pennsylvania against French and Indian attacks.

1756 Elected Fellow of the Royal Society.

CHAPTER FOUR

1757 Goes to London as agent for Pennsylvania Assembly, to plead the cause against the proprietors. Writes *The Way to Wealth*.

1759 Receives honorary LL D degree from University of St Andrews. Meets David Hume and Lord Kames.

1760 Writes *Interest of Great Britain Considered*. Secures Privy Council approval of taxation of proprietary estates in Pennsylvania.

1762 Receives honorary DCL degree from Oxford. Returns to Philadelphia.

1763 Tours northern colonies to inspect post offices.

1764 Defeated in Assembly elections. Returns to London as agent for Pennsylvania.

CHAPTER FIVE

1765 Works for repeal of Stamp Act; writes many anonymous pieces for the London press.

1766 Examined on the Stamp Act before the House of Commons.

1767 Travels in France and is presented at court.

1768 Writes *Causes of the American Discontents before 1768.*

1769 Elected president of the American Philosophical Society (reelected annually all his life).

1770 Newspaper propaganda campaign against Townshend duties; duties repealed, except on tea. Petitions for grant of land in the West. Becomes agent for Massachusetts.

1771 Begins *Autobiography.*

1772 Elected to French Academy of Sciences.

CHAPTER SIX

1774 Hutchinson letters affair. Attacked before Privy Council; dismissed as Deputy Postmaster General. Coercive acts passed; begins final negotiations to preserve the British Empire. Deborah, his wife, dies.

1775 Returns to America. Elected to Continental Congress and Pennsylvania Committee of Safety; active in support of war measures. Submits Articles of Confederation of United Colonies.

1776 Helps draft and signs Declaration of Independence. Presides at Pennsylvania Constitutional Convention. Sails for France as an American commissioner.

CHAPTER SEVEN

1778 Negotiates and signs treaty of alliance with France.

1779 Appointed Minister Plenipotentiary to France.

1781 Appointed a commissioner to negotiate peace.

CHAPTER EIGHT

1782 With John Adams and John Jay, negotiates treaty of peace with Great Britain.

1784 Negotiates treaties of commerce with Prussia and other European nations. Resumes *Autobiography* (Part II). Writes *Information to Those Who Would Remove to America.*

1785 Returns to Philadelphia.

1787 Elected president of Pennsylvania Society for Promoting the Abolition of Slavery. Delegate to the Constitutional Convention.

1789 Finishes last sections of *Autobiography.*

1790 Dies in Philadelphia.

ONE

A LIKELY LAD FOR AN APPRENTICE

From the
AUTOBIOGRAPHY

DEAR SON,

Twyford, at the Bishop of St Asaph's, 1771

I have ever had a pleasure in obtaining any little anecdotes of my ancestors. You may remember the enquiries I made among the remains of my relations when you were with me in England; and the journey I undertook for that purpose. Now imagining it may be equally agreable to you to know the circumstances of *my* life, many of which you are yet unacquainted with; and expecting a week's uninterrupted leisure in my present country retirement, I sit down to write them for you. To which I have besides some other inducements. Having emergcd from the poverty and obscurity in which I was born and bred, to a state of affluence and some degree of reputation in the world, and having gone so far through life with a considerable share of felicity, the conducing means I made use of, which, with the blessing of God, so well succeeded, my posterity may like to know, as they may find some of them suitable to their own situations, and therefore fit to be imitated. That felicity, when I reflected on it, has induced me sometimes to say, that were it offered to my choice, I should have no objection to a repetition of the same life from its beginning, only asking the advantages authors have in a second edition to correct some faults of the first. So would I if I might, besides correcting the faults, change some sinister accidents and events of it for others more favourable, but though this were denied, I should still accept the offer. However, since such a repetition is not to be expected, the next thing most like living one's life over again, seems to be a *recollection* of that life; and to make that recollection as durable as possible, the putting it down in writing. Hereby, too, I shall indulge the inclination so natural in old men, to be talking of themselves and their own past actions, and I shall indulge it, without being troublesome to others who through respect to age might think themselves obliged to give me a hearing, since this may be read or not as any one pleases. And lastly (I may as well confess it, since my denial of it will be believed by nobody) perhaps I shall a good deal gratify my own *vanity*. Indeed I scarce ever heard or saw the introductory words, *Without vanity I may say,* etc. but some vain thing immediately followed. Most people dislike vanity in others whatever share they have of it themselves, but I give it fair quarter wherever I meet with it, being persuaded that it is often productive of good to the possessor and to others that are within his sphere of action: And therefore in many cases it would not be quite absurd if a man were to thank God for his vanity among the other comforts of life . . .

The notes one of my uncles (who had the same kind of curiosity in collecting family anecdotes) once put into my hands, furnished me with several particulars relating to our ancestors. From these notes I learnt that the family had lived in the same village, Ecton in Northamptonshire, for 300 years, and how much longer he knew not (perhaps from the time when the name *Franklin* that before was the name of an order of people, was assumed by them for a surname, when others took surnames all over the kingdom), on a freehold of about thirty acres, aided by the smith's business, which had continued in the family till his time, the eldest son being always bred to that business. A custom which he and my father both followed as to their eldest sons . . .

Josiah, my father, married young, and carried his wife with three children into New England, about 1682. The Conventicles having been forbidden by law, and frequently disturbed, induced some considerable men of his acquaintance to remove to that country, and he was prevailed with to accompany them thither, where they expected to enjoy their mode of religion with freedom. By the same wife he had four children more

Franklin's birthplace, in Milk Street, Boston,
opposite Old South Church

born there, and by a second wife ten more, in all seventeen, of which I remember thirteen sitting at one time at his table, who all grew up to be men and women, and married. I was the youngest son, and the youngest child but two, and was born in Boston, New England. My mother, the second wife was Abiah Folger, a daughter of Peter Folger, one of the first settlers of New England, of whom honourable mention is made by Cotton Mather, in his Church History of that country, (entitled *Magnalia Christi Americana*) as *a godly learned Englishman*, if I remember the words rightly . . .

My elder brothers were all put apprentices to different trades. I was put to the grammar school at eight years of age, my father intending to devote me as the tithe of his sons to the service of the Church. My early readiness in learning to read (which must have been very early, as I do not remember when I could not read) and the opinion of all his friends that I should certainly make a good scholar, encouraged him in this purpose of his. My Uncle Benjamin too approved of it, and proposed to give me all his shorthand volumes of sermons I suppose as a stock to set up with, if I would learn his character. I continued however at the grammar school not quite one year, though in that time I had risen gradually from the middle of the class of that year to be the head of it, and farther was removed into the next class above it, in order to go with that into the third at the end of the year. But my father in the meantime, from a view of the expence of a college education which, having so large a family, he could not well afford, and the mean living many so educated were afterwards able to obtain, reasons that he gave to his friends in my hearing, altered his first intention, took me from the grammar school, and sent me to a school for writing and arithmetic kept by a then famous man, Mr George Brownell, very successful in his profession generally, and that by mild encouraging methods. Under him I acquired fair writing pretty soon, but I failed in the arithmetic, and made no progress in it. At ten years old, I was taken home to assist my father in his business, which was that of a tallow-chandler and sope-boiler. A business he was not bred to, but had assumed on his arrival in New England and on finding his dying trade would not maintain his family, being in little request. Accordingly I was employed in cutting wick for the candles, filling the dipping mold, and the molds for cast candles, attending the shop, going of errands, etc. I disliked the trade and had a strong inclination for the sea; but my father declared against it; however, living near the water, I was much in and about it, learnt early to swim well, and to manage boats, and when in a boat or canoe with other boys I was commonly allowed to govern, especially in any case of difficulty; and upon other occasions I was generally a leader among the boys, and sometimes led them into scrapes, of which I will mention one instance, as it shows an early projecting public spirit, though not then justly conducted. There was a salt marsh that bounded part of the mill pond, on the edge of which, at high water, we used to stand to fish for minnows. By much trampling, we had made it a mere quagmire. My proposal was to build a wharf there fit for us to stand upon, and I showed my comrades a large heap of stones which were intended for a new house near the marsh, and which would very well suit our purpose. Accordingly in the evening when the workmen were gone, I assembled a number of my playfellows; and working with them diligently like so many emmets, sometimes two or three to a stone, we brought them all away and built our little wharf. The next morning the workmen were surprized at missing the stones; which were found in our wharf; enquiry was made after the removers; we were discovered and complained of; several of us were corrected by our fathers; and though I pleaded the usefulness of the work, mine convinced me that nothing was useful which was not honest.

I think you may like to know something of his person and character. He had an excellent constitution of body, was of middle stature, but well set and very strong. He was ingenious, could draw prettily, was skilled a little in music and had a clear pleasing voice, so that when he played Psalm tunes on his violin and sung withal as he sometimes did in an evening after the business of the day was over, it was extreamly agreable to hear. He had a mechanical genius too, and on occasion was very handy in the use of other tradesmen's tools. But his great excellence lay in a sound understanding, and solid judgment in prudential matters, both in private and publick affairs. In the latter indeed he was never employed, the numerous family he had to educate and the straitness of his circumstances, keeping him close to his trade, but I remember well his being frequently visited by leading people, who consulted him for his opinion in affairs of the town or the Church he belonged to and showed a good deal of respect for his judgment and advice. He was also much consulted by private persons about their affairs when any difficulty occurred, and frequently chosen an arbitrator between contending parties. At his table he liked to have as often as he could, some sensible friend or neighbour to converse with, and always took care to start some ingenious or useful topic for discourse, which might tend to improve the minds of his children. By this means he turned our attention to what was good, just, and prudent in the conduct of life; and little or no notice was ever taken of what related to the victuals on the table, whether it was well or ill drest, in or out of season, of good or bad flavour, preferable or inferior to this or that other thing of the kind; so that I was brought up in such a perfect inattention to those matters as to be quite indifferent what kind of food was set before me, and so unobservant of it, that to this day, if I am asked I can scarce tell a few hours after dinner, what I dined upon. This has been a convenience to me in travelling, where my companions have been sometimes very unhappy for want of a suitable gratification of their more delicate, because better instructed, tastes and appetites.

My mother had likewise an excellent constitution. She suckled all her ten children. I never knew either my father or mother to have any sickness but that of which they died he at eighty-nine, and she at eighty-five years of age. They lie buried together at Boston, where I some years since placed a marble stone over their grave with this inscription:

JOSIAH FRANKLIN
And ABIAH his Wife
Lie here interred.
They lived lovingly together in Wedlock
Fifty-five Years.
Without an Estate or any gainful Employment,
By constant labour and Industry,

With God's blessing,
They maintained a large Family
Comfortably;
And brought up thirteen Children,
And seven Grandchildren
Reputably.
From this Instance, Reader,
Be encouraged to Diligence in thy Calling,
And Distrust not Providence,
He was a pious and prudent Man,
She a discreet and virtuous Woman.
Their youngest Son,
In filial Regard to their Memory,
Places this Stone.
J. F. born 1655 – Died 1744 – Ætat 89.
A. F. Born 1667 – Died 1752——85.

Franklin could, much later in life, recall episodes in his childhood, from which he drew reflections. He recounts one, in the more famous of his Bagatelles, *to his friend and confidante in Passy, Madame Brillon, on 10 November 1779:*

. . . When I was a child of seven years old, my friends, on a holiday, filled my pocket with coppers. I went directly to a shop where they sold toys for children; and, being charmed with the sound of a *whistle*, that I met by the way in the hands of another boy, I voluntarily offered and gave all my money for one. I then came home, and went whistling all over the house, much pleased with my *whistle*, but disturbing all the family. My brothers, and sisters, and cousins, understanding the bargain I had made, told me I had given four times as much for it as it was worth; put me in mind what good things I might have bought with the rest of the money; and laughed at me so much for my folly, that I cried with vexation; and the reflection gave me more chagrin than the *whistle* gave me pleasure.

This however was afterwards of use to me, the impression continuing on my mind; so that often, when I was tempted to buy some unnecessary thing, I said to myself, *Don't give too much for the whistle;* and I saved my money.

He also recalled, in a letter dated February 1773 to his French scientist friend (and later political agent) Barbeu-Dubourg, one of his earliest inventions:

When I was a boy, I made two oval pallets, each about ten inches long, and six broad, with a hole for the thumb, in order to retain it fast in the palm of my hand. They much resembled a painter's pallets. In swimming I pushed the edges of these forward, and I struck the water with their flat surfaces as I drew them back. I remember I swam faster by means of these pallets, but they fatigued my wrists. I also fitted to the soles of my feet a kind of sandals; but I was not satisfied with them, because I observed that the stroke is partly given by the inside of the feet and the ancles and not entirely with the soles of the feet.

To return: I continued thus employed in my father's business for two years, that is till I was twelve years old; and my brother John, who was bred to that business having left my father, married and set up for himself at Rhode Island, there was all appearance that I was destined to supply his place and be a tallow-chandler. But my dislike to the trade continuing, my father was under apprehensions that if he did not find one for me more agreable, I should break away and get to sea, as his son Josiah had done to his great vexation. He therefore sometimes took me to walk with him, and see joiners, bricklayers, turners, braziers, etc. at their work, that he might observe my inclination, and endeavour to fix on some trade or other on land. It has ever since been a pleasure to me to see good workmen handle their tools; and it has been useful to me, having learnt so much by it, as to be able to do little jobs myself in my house, when a workman could not readily be got; and to construct little machines for my experiments while the intention of making the experiment was fresh and warm in my mind. My father at last fixed upon the cutler's trade, and my Uncle Benjamin's son Samuel who was bred to that business in London, being about that time established in Boston, I was sent to be with him some time on liking. But his expectations of a fee with me displeasing my father, I was taken home again.

From a child I was fond of reading, and all the little money that came into my hands was ever laid out in books. Pleased with *The Pilgrim's Progress,* my first collection was of John Bunyan's works, in separate little volumes. I afterwards sold them to enable me to buy R. Burton's Historical Collections; they were small chapmen's books and cheap, forty or fifty in all. My father's little library consisted chiefly of books in polemic divinity, most of which I read, and have since often regretted, that at a time when I had such a thirst for knowledge, more proper books had not fallen in my way, since it was now resolved I should not be a clergyman. Plutarch's *Lives* there was, in which I read abundantly, and I still think that time spent to great advantage. There was also a book of Defoe's, called *An Essay on Projects,* and another of Dr Mather's, called *Essays to do Good* which perhaps gave me a turn of thinking that had an influence on some of the principal future events of my life.

This bookish inclination at length determined my father to make me a printer, though he had already one son (James) of that profession. In 1717 my brother James returned from England with a press and letters to set up his business in Boston. I liked it much better than that of my father, but still had a hankering for the sea. To prevent the apprehended effect of such an inclination, my father was impatient to have me bound to my brother. I stood out some time, but at last was persuaded and signed the indentures, when I was yet but twelve years old. I was to serve as an apprentice till I was twenty-one years of age, only I was to be allowed journeyman's wages during the last year. In a little time I made great proficiency in the business, and became a useful hand to my brother. I now had access to better books. An acquaintance with the apprentices of booksellers, enabled me sometimes to borrow a small one, which I was careful to return soon and clean. Often I sat up in my room reading the greatest part of the night, when the book was borrowed in the evening and to be returned early in the morning, lest it should be missed or wanted. And after some time an ingenious tradesman Mr Matthew Adams who had a pretty collection of books, and who frequented our printing house, took notice of me, invited me to his library, and very kindly lent me such books as I chose to read. I now took a fancy to poetry, and made some little pieces. My brother, thinking it might turn to account encouraged me, and put me on composing two occasional ballads. One was called *The Lighthouse Tragedy,* and contained an account of the drowning of Captain Worthilake with his two daughters; the other was a sailor song on the taking of *Teach* or Blackbeard the Pirate. They were wretched stuff, in the Grub Street ballad stile, and when they were printed he sent me about the town to sell them. The first sold wonderfully, the event being recent, having made a great noise. This flattered my vanity. But my father discouraged me, by ridiculing my performances, and telling me versemakers were generally beggars; so I escaped being a poet, most probably a very bad one. But as prose writing has been of great use to me in the course of my life, and was a principal means of my advancement, I shall tell you how in such a situation I acquired what little ability I have in that way.

There was another bookish lad in the town, John Collins by name, with whom I was intimately acquainted. We sometimes disputed, and very fond we were of argument, and very desirous of confuting one another. Which disputacious turn, by the way, is apt to become a very bad habit, making people often extreamly disagreeable in company, by the contradiction that is necessary to bring it into practice, and thence, besides souring and spoiling the conversation, is productive of disgusts and perhaps enmities where you may have occasion for friendship. I had caught it by reading my father's books of dispute about religion. Persons of good sense, I have since observed, seldom fall into it, except lawyers, university men, and men of all sorts that have been bred at Edinborough. A question was once somehow or other started between Collins and me, of the propriety of educating the female sex in learning, and their abilities for study. He was of opinion that it was improper, and that they were naturally unequal to it. I took the contrary side, perhaps a little for dispute's sake. He was naturally more eloquent, had a ready plenty of words, and sometimes as I thought bore me down more by his fluency than by the strength of his reasons. As we parted without settling the point, and were not to see one another again for some time, I sat down to put my arguments in writing, which I copied fair and sent to him. He answered and I replied. Three or four letters of a side had passed, when my father happened to find my papers, and read them. Without entering into the discussion, he took occasion to talk to me about the manner of my writing, observed that though I had the advantage of my antagonist in correct spelling and pointing (which I owed to the printing house) I fell far short in elegance of expression, in method and in perspicuity, of which he convinced me by several instances. I saw the justice of his remarks, and thence grew more attentive to the *manner* in writing, and determined to endeavour at improvement.

About this time I met with an odd volume of the *Spectator*. It was the third. I had never before seen any of them. I bought it, read it over and over, and was much delighted with it. I thought the writing excellent, and wished if possible to imitate it. With that view, I took some of the papers, and making short hints of the sentiment in each sentence, laid them by a few days, and then without looking at the book, tried to compleat the papers again, by expressing each hinted sentiment at length, and as fully as it had been expressed before, in any suitable words, that should come to hand.

Then I compared my *Spectator* with the original, discovered some of my faults and corrected them. But I found I wanted a stock of words or a readiness in recollecting and using them, which I thought I should have acquired before that time, if I had gone on making verses, since the continual occasion for words of the same import but of different length, to suit the measure, or of different sound for the rhyme, would have laid me under a constant necessity of searching for variety, and also have tended to fix that variety in my mind, and make me master of it. Therefore I took some of the tales and turned them into verse: And after a time, when I had pretty well forgotten the prose, turned them back again. I also sometimes jumbled my collections of hints into confusion, and after some weeks, endeavoured to reduce them into the best order, before I began to form the full sentences, and compleat the paper. This was to teach me method in the arrangement of thoughts. By comparing my work afterwards with the original, I discovered many faults and amended them; but I sometimes had the pleasure of fancying that in certain particulars of small import, I had been lucky enough to improve the method or the language and this encouraged me to think I might possibly in time come to be a tolerable English writer, of which I was extreamly ambitious.

My time for these exercises and for reading, was at night, after work or before it began in the morning; or on Sundays, when I contrived to be in the printing house alone, evading as much as I could the common attendance on publick worship, which my father used to exact of me when I was under his care: And which indeed I still thought a duty; though I could not, as it seemed to me, afford the time to practise it.

When about sixteen years of age, I happened to meet with a book, written by one Tryon, recommending a vegetable diet. I determined to go into it. My brother being yet unmarried, did not keep house, but boarded himself and his apprentices in another family. My refusing to eat flesh occasioned an inconveniency, and I was frequently chid for my singularity. I made myself acquainted with Tryon's manner of preparing some of his dishes, such as boiling potatoes or rice, making hasty pudding, and a few others, and then proposed to my brother, that if he would give me weekly half the money he paid for my board I would board myself. He instantly agreed to it, and I presently found that I could save half what he paid me. This was an additional fund for buying books. But I had another advantage in it. My brother and the rest going from the printing house to their meals, I remained there alone, and dispatching presently my light repast, (which often was no more than a bisket or a slice of bread, a handful of raisins or a tart from the pastry cook's, and a glass of water) had the rest of the time till their return, for study, in which I made the greater progress from that greater clearness of head and quicker apprehension which usually attend temperance in eating and drinking. And now it was that being on some occasion made ashamed of my ignorance in figures, which I had twice failed in learning when at school, I took Cocker's book of arithmetick, and went through the whole by myself with great ease. I also read Seller's and Sturmy's books of navigation, and became acquainted with the little geometry they contain, but never proceeded far in that science. And I read about this time Locke on Human Understanding, and the *Art of Thinking* by Messrs du Port Royal.

While I was intent on improving my language, I met with an English Grammar (I think it was Greenwood's) at the end of which there were two little sketches of the arts of rhetoric and logic, the latter finishing with a specimen of a dispute in the Socratic Method. And soon after I procured Xenophon's *Memorable Things of Socrates,* wherein there are many instances of the same method. I was charmed with it, adopted it, dropt my abrupt contradiction, and positive argumentation, and put on the humble enquirer and doubter. And being then, from reading Shaftsbury and Collins, become a real doubter in many points of our religious doctrine, I found this method safest for myself and very embarrassing to those against whom I used it, therefore I took a delight in it, practised it continually and grew very artful and expert in drawing people even of superior knowledge into concessions the consequences of which they did not foresee, entangling them in difficulties out of which they could not extricate themselves, and so obtaining victories that neither myself nor my cause always deserved. I continued this method some few years, but gradually left it, retaining only the habit of expressing myself in terms of modest diffidence, never using when I advance anything that may possibly be disputed, the words, *Certainly, undoubtedly;* or any others that give the air of positiveness to an opinion; but rather say, I conceive, or I apprehend a thing to be so or so, it appears to me, or I should think it so or so for such and such reasons, or I imagine it to be so, or it is so if I am not mistaken. This habit I believe has been of great advantage to me, when I have had occasion to inculcate my opinions and persuade men into measures that I have been from time to time engaged in promoting. And as the chief ends of conversation are to *inform,* or to be *informed,* to *please* or to *persuade,* I wish well-meaning sensible men would not lessen their power of doing good by a positive assuming manner that seldom fails to disgust, tends to create opposition, and to defeat every one of those purposes for which speech was given us, to wit, giving or receiving information, or pleasure. . . .

My brother had in 1720 or '21, begun to print a newspaper. It was the second that appeared in America, and was called *The New England Courant.* The only one before it, was *The Boston*

News Letter. I remember his being dissuaded by some of his friends from the undertaking, as not likely to succeed, one newspaper being in their judgment enough for America. At this time 1771 there are not less than five and twenty. He went on however with the undertaking, and after having worked in composing the types and printing off the sheets, I was employed to carry the papers through the streets to the customers. He had some ingenious men among his friends who amused themselves by writing little pieces for this paper, which gained it credit, and made it more in demand; and these gentlemen often visited us. Hearing their conversations, and their accounts of the approbation their papers were received with, I was excited to try my hand among them. But being still a boy, and suspecting that my brother would object to printing anything of mine in his paper if he knew it to be mine, I contrived to disguise my hand, and writing an anonymous paper I put it in at night under the door of the printing house. It was found in the morning and communicated to his writing friends when they called in as usual. They read it, commented on it in my hearing, and I had the exquisite pleasure, of finding it met with their approbation, and that in their different guesses at the author none were named but men of some character among us for learning and ingenuity. I suppose now that I was rather lucky in my judges: And that perhaps they were not really so very good ones as I then esteemed them. Encouraged however by this, I wrote and conveyed in the same way to the press several more papers, which were equally approved, and I kept my secret till my small fund of sense for such performances was pretty well exhausted, and then I discovered it; when I began to be considered a little more by my brother's acquaintance, and in a manner that did not quite please him, as he thought, probably with reason, that it tended to make me too vain.

The best of the young apprentice's anonymous contributions are the Dogood Papers. *They reveal assiduous reading and imitation of Addison and the* Spectator, *and have a distinctive Bunyanesque flavour. Stimulated by the cynical comment he heard in his brother's print shop, Franklin painted a picture of contemporary Boston as seen through the eyes of a strong-willed and forthright widow. His brother's companions*

*called themselves 'the Honest Wags' (to Increase Mather they were
Boston's 'Hell-Fire Club'), and they were in the habit of publishing their
opinions under various* noms-de-plume—*Tabitha Talkative, Icha-
bod Henroost, Fanny Mournful—to protect themselves from Harvard
and the Puritan Establishment. Both were apt to suppress any sustained
or savage criticism, which, as they saw it, would be destructive of good
order and regular church-going. In fact, James Franklin was jailed for
three weeks in 1722; and in January 1723 he was banned from publishing, and replaced at the* Courant *by Benjamin. In 1726 the* Courant *folded altogether.*

DOGOOD PAPERS, NO. I

From Monday 26 March to Monday 2 April 1722
To the Author of the *New-England Courant*

SIR,

It may not be improper in the first place to inform your
readers, that I intend once a fortnight to present them, by the
help of this paper, with a short epistle, which I presume will
add somewhat to their entertainment.

And since it is observed, that the generality of people, nowadays, are unwilling either to commend or dispraise what they
read, until they are in some measure informed who or what the
author of it is, whether he be *poor* or *rich, old* or *young,* a *scollar*
or a *leather apron man,* etc. and give their opinion of the performance, according to the knowledge which they have of the
author's circumstances, it may not be amiss to begin with a short
account of my past life and present condition, that the reader
may not be at a loss to judge whether or no my lucubrations are
worth his reading.

At the time of my birth, my parents were on ship-board in
their way from *London* to *New England.* My entrance into this
troublesome world was attended with the death of my father, a
misfortune, which though I was not then capable of knowing, I
shall never be able to forget; for as he, poor man, stood upon
the deck rejoycing at my birth, a merciless wave entred the ship,
and in one moment carried him beyond reprieve. Thus was the
first day which I saw, the *last* that was seen by my father; and
thus was my disconsolate mother at once made both a *parent*
and a *widow.*

When we arrived at *Boston* (which was not long after) I was put to nurse in a country place, at a small distance from the town, where I went to school, and past my infancy and childhood in vanity and idleness, until I was bound out apprentice, that I might no longer be a charge to my indigent mother, who was put to hard shifts for a living.

My master was a country minister, a pious good-natured young man, and a batchelor: He laboured with all his might to instil vertuous and godly principles into my tender soul, well knowing that it was the most suitable time to make deep and lasting impressions on the mind, while it was yet untainted with vice, free and unbiassed. He endeavoured that I might be instructed in all that knowledge and learning which is necessary for our sex, and denied me no accomplishment that could possibly be attained in a country place, such as all sorts of needlework, writing, arithmetick, etc. and observing that I took a more than ordinary delight in reading ingenious books, he gave me the free use of his library, which though it was but small, yet it was well chose, to inform the understanding rightly and enable the mind to frame great and noble ideas.

Before I had lived quite two years with this reverend gentleman, my indulgent mother departed this life, leaving me as it were by myself, having no relation on earth within my knowledge.

I will not abuse your patience with a tedious recital of all the frivolous accidents of my life, that happened from this time until I arrived to years of discretion, only inform you that I lived a chearful country life, spending my leisure time either in some innocent diversion with the neighbouring females, or in some shady retirement, with the best of company, *Books.* Thus I past away the time with a mixture of profit and pleasure, having no affliction but what was imaginary and created in my own fancy; as nothing is more common with us women, than to be grieving for nothing, when we have nothing else to grieve for.

As I would not engross too much of your paper at once, I will defer the remainder of my story until my next letter; in the meantime desiring your readers to exercise their patience, and bear with my humours now and then, because I shall trouble them but seldom. I am not insensible of the impossibility of pleasing all, but I would not willingly displease any; and for those who will take offence where none is intended, they are beneath the Notice of

Your Humble Servant,
SILENCE DOGOOD

[As the favour of Mrs Dogood's correspondence is acknowledged by the publisher of this paper, lest any of her letters should miscarry, he desires they may for the future be delivered at his printing house, or at the Blue Ball in Union Street, and no questions shall be asked of the bearer.]

NO. II

From Monday 9 April to Monday 16 April 1722
To the Author of the *New-England Courant*

SIR,

Histories of lives are seldom entertaining, unless they contain something either admirable or exemplar: And since there is little or nothing of this nature in my own adventures, I will not tire your readers with tedious particulars of no consequence, but will briefly, and in as few words as possible relate, the most material occurrences of my life, and according to my promise, confine all to this letter.

My reverend master who had hitherto remained a batchelor, (after much meditation on the eighteenth verse of the second chapter of *Genesis*,) took up a resolution to marry; and having made several unsuccessful fruitless attempts on the more topping sort of our sex, and being tired with making troublesome journeys and visits to no purpose, he began unexpectedly to cast a loving eye upon me, whom he had brought up cleverly to his hand.

There is certainly scarce any part of a man's life in which he appears more silly and ridiculous, than when he makes his first onset in courtship. The aukward manner in which my master first discovered his intentions, made me, in spite of my reverence to his person, burst out into an unmannerly laughter: However, having asked his pardon, and with much ado composed my countenance, I promised him I would take his proposal into serious consideration, and speedily give him an answer.

As he had been a great benefactor (and in a manner a father to me) I could not well deny his request, when I once perceived he was in earnest. Whether it was love, or gratitude, or pride, or all three that made me consent, I know not; but it is certain, he found it no hard matter, by the help of his rhetorick to conquer my heart, and perswade me to marry him.

This unexpected match was very astonishing to all the country round about and served to furnish them with discourse for a long time after; some approving it, others disliking it, as they were led by their various fancies and inclinations.

We lived happily together in the heighth of conjugal love and mutual endearments, for near seven years in which time we added two likely girls and a boy to the family of the *Dogoods*: But alas! When my sun was in its meridian altitude, inexorable unrelenting death, as if he had envied my happiness and tranquility, and resolved to make me entirely miserable by the loss of so good an husband, hastened his flight to the heavenly world, by a sudden unexpected departure from this.

I have now remained in a state of widowhood for several years, but it is a state I never much admired, and I am apt to fancy that I could be easily perswaded to marry again, provided I was sure of a good-humoured, sober, agreeable companion: But one, even with these few good qualities, being hard to find, I have lately relinquished all thoughts of that nature.

At present I pass away my leisure hours in conversation, either with my honest neighbour *Rusticus* and his family, or with the ingenious minister of our town, who now lodges at my house, and by whose assistance I intend now and then to beautify my writings with a sentence or two in the learned languages, which will not only be fashionable, and pleasing to those who do not understand it, but will likewise be very ornamental.

I shall conclude this with my own character, which (one would think) I should be best able to give. *Know then*, that I am an enemy to vice, and a friend to vertue. I am one of an extensive charity, and a great forgiver of *private* injuries: A hearty lover of the clergy and all good men, and a mortal enemy to arbitrary government and unlimited power. I am naturally very jealous for the rights and liberties of my country: and the least appearance of an incroachment on those invaluable priviledges, is apt to make my blood boil exceedingly. I have likewise a natural inclination to observe and reprove the faults of others, at which I have an excellent faculty. I speak this by way of warning to all such whose offences shall come under my cognizance, for I never intend to wrap my talent in a napkin. To be brief; I am courteous and affable, good-humoured (unless I am first provoked), and handsome, and sometimes witty, but always,

SIR, *Your Friend, and Humble Servant,*
SILENCE DOGOOD

The story of the 'apprentice' who marries her master is not far-fetched. Franklin's maternal grandmother, Mary Morrils, was, at the time of her marriage, an indentured servant (essentially a slave for a term of years, like many early immigrants) who married her employer, Peter Folger.

The views on Harvard expressed in the Dogood Papers, No. IV *reflect Benjamin's father's scorn of the college, and his incapacity to finance his son's education there.*

DOGOOD PAPERS, NO. IV

From Monday 7 May to Monday 14 May 1722
An sum etiam nunc vel Græcè loqui vel Latinè docendus? CICERO
To the Author of the *New-England Courant*

SIR,

Discoursing the other day at dinner with my reverend boarder, formerly mentioned, (whom for distinction sake we will call by the name of *Clericus,*) concerning the education of children, I asked his advice about my young son *William,* whether or no I had best bestow upon him academical learning, or (as our phrase is) *bring him up at our College:* He perswaded me to do it by all means, using many weighty arguments with me, and answering all the objections that I could form against it; telling me withal, that he did not doubt but that the lad would take his learning very well, and not idle away his time as too many there nowadays do. These words of *Clericus* gave me a curiosity to inquire a little more strictly into the present circumstances of that famous seminary of learning; but the information which he gave me, was neither pleasant, nor such as I expected.

As soon as dinner was over, I took a solitary walk into my orchard, still ruminating on *Clericus*'s discourse with much consideration, until I came to my usual place of retirement under the *great apple-tree;* where having seated myself, and carelessly laid my head on a verdant bank, I fell by degrees into a soft and undisturbed slumber. My waking thoughts remained with me in my sleep, and before I awaked again, I dreamt the following DREAM.

I fancied I was traveling over pleasant and delightful fields and meadows, and through many small country towns and villages; and as I passed along, all places resounded with the fame of the temple of LEARNING: Every peasant, who had wherewithal, was preparing to send one of his children at least to this famous place; and in this case most of them consulted their own purses instead of their children's capacities: So that I observed, a great many, yea, the most part of those who were travelling thither, were little better than dunces and blockheads. Alas! Alas!

At length I entred upon a spacious plain, in the midst of which was erected a large and stately edifice: It was to this that a great company of youths from all parts of the country were going; so stepping in among the crowd, I passed on with them, and presently arrived at the gate.

The passage was kept by two sturdy porters named *Riches* and *Poverty,* and the latter obstinately refused to give entrance to any who had not first gained the favour of the former; so that I observed, many who came even to the very gate, were obliged to travel back again as ignorant as they came, for want of this necessary qualification. However, as a spectator I gained admittance, and with the rest entred directly into the temple.

In the middle of the great hall stood a stately and magnificent throne, which was ascended to by two high and difficult steps. On the top of it sat LEARNING in awful state; she was apparelled wholly in black, and surrounded almost on every side with innumerable volumes in all languages. She seemed very busily employed in writing something on half a sheet of paper, and upon enquiry, I understood she was preparing a paper, called, *The New-England Courant.* On her right hand sat *English,* with a pleasant smiling countenance, and handsomely attired; and on her left were seated several *antique figures* with their faces vailed. I was considerably puzzled to guess who they were, until one informed me, (who stood beside me,) that those figures on her left hand were *Latin, Greek, Hebrew,* etc. and that they were very much reserved, and seldom or never unvailed their faces here, and then to few or none, though most of those who have in this place acquired so much learning as to distinguish them from *English,* pretended to an intimate acquaintance with them. I then enquired of him, what could be the reason why they continued vailed, in this place especially: He pointed to the foot of the throne, where I saw *Idleness,* attended with *Ignorance,* and these (he informed me) were they, who first vailed them, and still kept them so.

Now I observed, that the whole tribe who entred into the temple with me, began to climb the throne: but the work proving troublesome and difficult to most of them, they withdrew their hands from the plow, and contented themselves to sit at the foot, with Madam *Idleness* and her maid *Ignorance,* until those who were assisted by diligence and a docible temper, had well nigh got up the first step: But the time drawing nigh in which they could no way avoid ascending, they were fain to crave the assistance of those who had got up before them, and who, for the reward perhaps of a *pint of milk,* or a *piece of plumb-cake,* lent the lubbers a helping hand, and sat them in the eye of the world, upon a level with themselves.

The other step being in the same manner ascended, and the usual ceremonies at an end, every beetle-scull seemed well satisfied with his own portion of learning, though perhaps he was *e'en just* as ignorant as ever. And now the time of their departure being come, they marched out of doors to make room for another company, who waited for entrance: And I, having seen all that was to be seen, quitted the hall likewise, and went to make my observations on those who were just gone out before me.

Some I perceived took to merchandizing, others to travelling, some to one thing, some to another, and some to nothing; and many of them from henceforth, for want of patrimony, lived as poor as church mice, being unable to dig, and ashamed to beg, and to live by their wits it was impossible. But the most part of the crowd went along a large beaten path, which led to a temple at the further end of the plain, called, *The Temple of Theology.* The business of those who were employed in this temple being laborious and painful, I wondered exceedingly to see so many go towards it; but while I was pondering this matter in my mind, I spied its *Pecunia* behind a curtain, beckoning to them with her hand, which sight immediately satisfied me for whose sake it was, that a great part of them (I will not say all) travelled that road. In this temple I saw nothing worth mentioning, except the ambitious and fraudulent contrivances of *Plagius,* who (notwithstanding he had been severely reprehended for such practices before) was diligently transcribing some eloquent paragraphs out of *Tillotson's* works, etc. to embellish his own.

Now I bethought myself in my sleep, that it was time to be at home, and as I fancied I was travelling back thither, I reflected in my mind on the extream folly of those parents, who, blind to their children's dulness, and insensible of the solidity of their skulls, because they think their purses can afford it, will needs send them to the temple of learning, where, for want of a suitable genius, they learn little more than how to carry themselves handsomely, and enter a room genteely, (which might as well be acquired at a dancing school,) and from whence they return, after abundance of trouble and charge, as great blockheads as ever, only more proud and self-conceited.

While I was in the midst of these unpleasant reflections, *Clericus* (who with a book in his hand was walking under the trees) accidentally awaked me; to him I related my dream with all its particulars, and he, without much study, presently interpreted it, assuring me, *That it was a lively representation of* HARVARD COLLEGE, *etcetera.*

> *I remain, Sir, Your Humble Servant,*
> SILENCE DOGOOD

DOGOOD PAPERS, NO. V

From Monday 21 May to Monday 28 May 1722
Mulier Muliere magis congruet. TERENCE
To the Author of the *New-England Courant*

SIR,

I shall here present your readers with a letter from one, who
informs me that I have begun at the wrong end of my business,
and that I ought to begin at home, and censure the vices and
follies of my own sex, before I venture to meddle with yours:
Nevertheless, I am resolved to dedicate this speculation to the
fair tribe, and endeavour to show, that Mr *Ephraim* charges
women with being particularly guilty of pride, idleness, etc.
wrongfully, inasmuch as the men have not only as great a share
in those vices as the women, but are likewise in a great measure
the cause of that which the women are guilty of. I think it will
be best to produce my antagonist, before I encounter him.

To Mrs DOGOOD

MADAM,

My design in troubling you with this letter is, to desire you
would begin with your own sex first: Let the first volley of your
resentments be directed against *female* vice; let female idleness,
ignorance and folly, (which are vices more peculiar to your sex
than to ours,) be the subject of your satyrs, but more especially
female pride, which I think is intollerable. Here is a large field
that wants cultivation, and which I believe you are able (if willing) to improve with advantage; and when you have once re-
formed the women, you will find it a much easier task to reform
the men, because women are the prime causes of a great many
male enormities. This is all at present from
Your Friendly Wellwisher,
EPHRAIM CENSORIOUS

After thanks to my correspondent for his kindness in cutting
out work for me, I must assure him, that I find it a very difficult
matter to reprove women separate from the men; for what vice
is there in which the men have not as great a share as the

women? and in some have they not a far greater, as in drunkenness, swearing, etc? And if they have, then it follows, that when a vice is to be reproved, men, who are most culpable, deserve the most reprehension, and certainly therefore, ought to have it. But we will wave this point at present, and proceed to a particular consideration of what my correspondent calls *Female Vice*.

As for idleness, if I should *quære*, where are the greatest number of its votaries to be found, with us or the men? it might I believe be easily and truly answered, *With the latter*. For, notwithstanding the men are commonly complaining how hard they are forced to labour, only to maintain their wives in pomp and idleness, yet if you go among the women, you will learn, that *they have always more work upon their hands than they are able to do*, and that a *woman's work is never done*, etc. But however, suppose we should grant for once, that we are generally more idle than the men, (without making any allowance for the *weakness of the sex*,) I desire to know whose fault it is? Are not the men to blame for their folly in maintaining us in idleness? Who is there that can be handsomely supported in affluence, ease· and pleasure by another, that will chuse rather to earn his bread by the sweat of his own brows? And if a man will be so fond and so foolish, as to labour hard himself for a livelihood, and suffer his wife in the meantime to sit in ease and idleness, let him not blame her if she does so, for it is in a great measure his own fault.

And now for the ignorance and folly which he reproaches us with, let us see (if we are fools and ignoramuses) whose is the fault, the men's or ours. An ingenious writer, having this subject in hand, has the following words, wherein he lays the fault wholly on the men, for not allowing women the advantages of education.

'I have (says he) often thought of it as one of the most barbarous customs in the world, considering us as a civilized and Christian country, that we deny the advantages of learning to women. We reproach the sex every day with folly and impertinence, while I am confident, had they the advantages of education equal to us, they would be guilty of less than ourselves. One would wonder indeed how it should happen that women are conversible at all, since they are only beholding to natural parts for all their knowledge. Their youth is spent to teach them to stitch and sow, or make baubles. They are taught to read indeed, and perhaps to write their names, or so; and that is the height of a woman's education. And I would but ask any who slight the sex for their understanding, What is a man (a gentleman, I mean) good for that is taught no more? If knowledge and understanding had been useless additions to the sex, God Almighty would never have given them capacities, for he made nothing needless. What has the woman done to forfeit the priviledge of being taught? Does she plague us with her pride and impertinence? Why did we not let her learn, that she might have had more wit? Shall we upbraid women with folly, when 'tis only the error of this inhumane custom that hindred them being made wiser.'

So much for female ignorance and folly; and now let us a little consider the pride which my correspondent thinks is *intolerable*. By this expression of his, one would think he is some dejected swain, tyrannized over by some cruel haughty nymph, who (perhaps he thinks) has no more reason to be proud than himself. *Alas-a-day!* What shall we say in this case! Why truly, if women are proud, it is certainly owing to the men still; for if they will be such *simpletons* as to humble themselves at their feet, and fill their credulous ears with extravagant praises of their wit, beauty, and accomplishments (perhaps where there are none too,) and when women are by this means perswaded that they are something more than human, what wonder is it, if they carry themselves haughtily, and live extravagantly. Notwithstanding, I believe there are more instances of extravagant pride to be found among men than among women, and this fault is certainly more hainous in the former than in the latter.

Upon the whole, I conclude, that it will be impossible to lash any vice, of which the men, are not equally guilty with the women, and consequently deserve an equal (if not a greater) share in the censure. However, I exhort both to amend, where both are culpable, otherwise they may expect to be severely handled by

Sir, Your Humble Servant,
SILENCE DOGOOD

[N.B. Mrs Dogood has lately left her seat in the country, and come to Boston, where she intends to tarry for the summer season, in order to compleat her observations of the present reigning vices of the town.]

DOGOOD PAPERS, NO. XII

From Monday 3 September to Monday 10 September 1722
Quod est in corde sobrii, est in ore ebrii.
To the Author of the *New-England Courant*

SIR,

It is no unprofitable though unpleasant pursuit, diligently to inspect and consider the manners and conversation of men, who, insensible of the greatest enjoyments of human life, abandon themselves to vice from a false notion of *pleasure* and *good fellowship*. A true and natural representation of any enormity, is often the best argument against it and means of removing it, when the most severe reprehensions alone, are found ineffectual.

I would in this letter improve the little observation I have made on the vice of *drunkeness*, the better to reclaim the *good fellows* who usually pay the devotions of the evening to *Bacchus*.

I doubt not but *moderate drinking* has been improved for the diffusion of knowledge among the ingenious part of mankind, who want the talent of a ready utterance, in order to discover the conceptions of their minds in an entertaining and intelligible manner. 'Tis true, drinking does not *improve* our faculties, but it enables us to use them; and therefore I conclude, that much study and experience, and a little liquor, are of absolute necessity for some tempers, in order to make them accomplished orators. Dic. Ponder discovers an excellent judgment when he is inspired with a glass or two of *Claret*, but he passes for a fool among those of small observation, who never saw him the better for drink. And here it will not be improper to observe, that the moderate use of liquor, and a well placed and well regulated anger, often produce this same effect; and some who cannot ordinarily talk but in broken sentences and false grammar, do in the heat of passion express themselves with as much eloquence as warmth. Hence it is that my own sex are generally the most eloquent, because the most passionate. 'It has been said in the praise of some men' (says an ingenious author), 'that they could talk whole hours together upon anything; but it must be owned to the honour of the other sex, that there are many among them who can talk whole hours together upon nothing. I have known a woman branch out into a long extempore dissertation on the edging of a petticoat, and chide her servant for breaking a china cup, in all the figures of rhetorick.'

But after all it must be considered, that no pleasure can give satisfaction or prove advantageous to a *reasonable mind,* which is not attended with the *restraints of reason.* Enjoyment is not to be found by excess in any sensual gratification; but on the contrary, the immoderate cravings of the voluptuary are always succeeded with loathing and a palled apetite. What pleasure can the drunkard have in the reflection, that, while in his cups, he retained only the shape of a man, and acted the part of a beast; or that from reasonable discourse a few minutes before, he descended to impertinence and nonsense?

I cannot pretend to account for the different effects of liquor on persons of different dispositions, who are guilty of excess in the use of it. 'Tis strange to see men of a regular conversation become rakish and profane when intoxicated with drink, and yet more surprizing to observe, that some who appear to be the most profligate wretches when sober, become mighty religious in their cups, and will then, and at no other time address their Maker, but when they are destitute of reason, and actually affronting him. Some shrink in the wetting, and others swell to such an unusual bulk in their imaginations, that they can in an instant understand all arts and sciences, by the liberal education of a little vivyfying *punch,* or a sufficient quantity of other exhilerating liquor.

And as the effects of liquor are various, so are the characters given to its devourers. It argues some shame in the drunkards themselves, in that they have invented numberless words and phrases to cover their folly, whose proper significations are harmless, or have no signification at all. They are seldom known to be *drunk,* though they are very often *boozey, cogey, tipsey, foxed, merry, mellow, fuddled, groatable, confoundedly cut, see two moons,* are *among the Philistines, in a very good humour, see the sun,* or, *the sun has shone upon them;* they *clip the King's English,* are *almost froze, feavourish, in their altitudes, pretty well entered,* etc. In short, every day produces some new word or phrase which might be added to the vocabulary of the *tiplers:* But I have chose to mention these few, because if at any time a man of sobriety and temperance happens to *cut himself confoundedly,* or is *almost froze,* or *feavourish,* or accidentally *sees the sun,* etc. he may escape the imputation of being *drunk,* when his misfortune comes to be related.

I am SIR, *Your Humble Servant,*
SILENCE DOGOOD

In 1723 Benjamin began to quarrel with his brother, recalling his reasons in the Autobiography:

Though a brother, he considered himself as my master, and me as his apprentice; and accordingly expected the same services from me as he would from another; while I thought he demeaned me too much in some he required of me, who from a brother expected more indulgence. Our disputes were often brought before our father, and I fancy I was either generally in the right, or else a better pleader, because the judgment was generally in my favour: But my brother was passionate and had often beaten me, which I took extreamly amiss; and thinking my apprenticeship very tedious, I was continually wishing for some opportunity of shortening it, which at length offered in a manner unexpected.

One of the pieces in our newspaper, on some political point which I have now forgotten, gave offence to the Assembly. He was taken up, censured and imprisoned for a month by the Speaker's Warrant, I suppose because he would not discover his author. I too was taken up and examined before the Council; but though I did not give them any satisfaction, they contented themselves with admonishing me, and dismissed me; considering me perhaps as an apprentice who was bound to keep his master's secrets. During my brother's confinement, which I resented a good deal, notwithstanding our private differences, I had the management of the paper, and I made bold to give our rulers some rubs in it, which my brother took very kindly, while others began to consider me in an unfavourable light, as a young genius that had a turn for libelling and satyr. My brother's discharge was accompanied with an Order of the House, (a very odd one) *that James Franklin should no longer print the paper called the* New England Courant. There was a consultation held in our printing house among his friends what he should do in this case. Some proposed to evade the order by changing the name of the paper; but my brother seeing inconveniences in that, it was finally concluded on as a better way, to let it be printed for the future under the name of *Benjamin Franklin.* And to avoid the censure of the Assembly that might fall on him, as still printing it by his apprentice, the contrivance was, that my old indenture should be returned to me with a full discharge on the back of it, to be shown on occasion; but to secure to him the benefit of my service I was to sign new indentures for the remainder of the term, which were to be kept private. A very flimsy scheme it was, but however it was immediately executed, and the paper went on accordingly under my name for several months. At length a fresh difference arising between my brother and me, I took upon me to assert my freedom, presuming that he would not venture to produce the new indentures. It was not fair in me to take this advantage, and this I therefore reckon one of the first *errata* of my life: But the unfairness of it weighed little with me, when under the impressions of resentment, for the blows his passion too often urged him to bestow upon me. Though he was otherwise not an ill-natured man: Perhaps I was too saucy and provoking.

When he found I would leave him, he took care to prevent my getting employment in any other printing house of the town, by going round and speaking to every master, who accordingly refused to give me work. I then thought of going to New York as the nearest place where there was a printer: and I was the rather inclined to leave Boston, when I reflected that I had already made myself a little obnoxious to the governing party; and from the arbitrary proceedings of the Assembly in my brother's case it was likely I might if I stayed soon bring myself into scrapes; and farther that my indiscrete disputations about religion began to make me pointed at with horror by good people, as an infidel or atheist? I determined on the point: but my father now siding with my brother, I was sensible that if I attempted to go openly, means would be used to prevent me. My friend Collins therefore undertook to manage a little for me. He agreed with the captain of a New York sloop for my passage, under the notion of my being a young acquaintance of his that had got a naughty girl with child, whose friends would compel me to marry her, and therefore I could not appear or come away publickly. So I sold some of my books to raise a little money, was taken on board privately, and as we had a fair wind, in three days I found myself in New York near 300 miles from home, a boy of but seventeen, without the least recommendation to or knowledge of any person in the place, and with very little money in my pocket.

My inclinations for the sea, were by this time worne out, or I might now have gratified them. But having a trade, and supposing myself a pretty good workman, I offered my service to the printer in the place, old Mr William Bradford, who had been the first printer in Pensilvania, but removed from thence upon the quarrel of George Keith. He could give me no employment, having little to do, and help enough already: But, says he, my son at Philadelphia has lately lost his principal hand, Aquila Rose, by death. If you go thither I believe he may employ you. Philadelphia was a hundred miles farther. I set out, however, in a boat for Amboy, leaving my chest and things to follow me round by sea . . .

When we drew near the island we found it was at a place where there could be no landing, there being a great surff on the stony beach. So we dropt anchor and swung round towards the shore . . . and in the morning crossing the ferry, I proceeded on my journey, on foot, having fifty miles to Burlington, where I was told I should find boats that would carry me the rest of the way to Philadelphia.

It rained very hard all the day, I was thoroughly soaked, and by noon a good deal tired, so I stopt at a poor inn, where I staid all night, beginning now to wish I had never left home. I cut so miserable a figure too, that I found by the questions asked me I was suspected to be some runaway servant, and in danger of being taken up on that suspicion. However I proceeded the

South-east prospect of the city of New York

next day, and got in the evening to an inn within eight or ten miles of Burlington, kept by one Dr Brown.

He entered into conversation with me while I took some refreshment, and finding I had read a little, became very sociable and friendly. Our acquaintance continued as long as he lived. He had been, I imagine, an itinerant doctor, for there was no town in England, or country in Europe, of which he could not give a very particular account. He had some letters, and was ingenious, but much of an unbeliever, and wickedly undertook, some years after to travesty the Bible in doggrel verse as Cotton had done Virgil. By this means he set many of the facts in a very ridiculous light, and might have hurt weak minds if his work had been published: but it never was. At his house I lay that night, and the next morning reached Burlington. But had the mortification to find that the regular boats were gone, a little before my coming, and no other expected to go till Tuesday, this being Saturday. Wherefore I returned to an old woman in the town of whom I had bought gingerbread to eat on the water, and asked her advice; she invited me to lodge at her house till a passage by water should offer: and being tired with my foot travelling, I accepted the invitation. She understanding I was a printer, would have had me stay at that town and follow my business, being ignorant of the stock necessary to begin with. She was very hospitable, gave me a dinner of ox cheek with great goodwill, accepting only of a pot of ale in return. And I thought myself fixed till Tuesday should come. However walking in the evening by the side of the river, a boat came by, which I found was going towards Philadelphia, with several people in her. They took me in, and as there was no wind, we rowed all the way; and about midnight not having yet seen the city, some of the company were confident we must have passed it, and would row no farther, the others knew not where we were, so we put towards the shore, got into a creek, landed near an old fence, with the rails of which we made a fire, the night being cold, in October, and there we remained till daylight. Then one of the company knew the place to be Cooper's Creek a little above Philadelphia, which we saw as soon as we got out of the Creek, and arrived there about eight or nine o'clock, on the Sunday morning, and landed at the Market Street Wharff.

I have been the more particular in this description of my
journey, and shall be so of my first entry into that city, that you
may in your mind compare such unlikely beginnings with the
figure I have since made there. I was in my working dress, my
best cloaths being to come round by sea. I was dirty from my
journey; my pockets were stuffed out with shirts and stockings;
I knew no soul, nor where to look for lodging. I was fatigued
with travelling, rowing and want of rest. I was very hungry, and
my whole stock of cash consisted of a Dutch dollar and about a
shilling in copper. The latter I gave the people of the boat for
my passage, who at first refused it on account of my rowing; but
I insisted on their taking it, a man being sometimes more generous when he has but a little money than when he has plenty,
perhaps through fear of being thought to have but little. Then
I walked up the street, gazing about, till near the Market House
I met a boy with bread. I had made many a meal on bread, and
inquiring where he got it, I went immediately to the baker's he
directed me to in Second Street; and asked for bisket, intending
such as we had in Boston, but they it seems were not made in
Philadelphia, then I asked for a threepenny loaf, and was told
they had none such: so not considering or knowing the difference of money and the greater cheapness nor the names of his
bread, I bade him give me threepenny worth of any sort. He
gave me accordingly three great puffy rolls. I was surprized at
the quantity, but took it, and having no room in my pockets,
walked off, with a roll under each arm, and eating the other.
Thus I went up Market Street as far as Fourth Street, passing
by the door of Mr Read, my future wife's father, when she
standing at the door saw me, and thought I made as I certainly
did a most awkward ridiculous appearance. Then I turned and
went down Chestnut Street and part of Walnut Street, eating
my roll all the way, and coming round found myself again at
Market Street Wharff, near the boat I came in, to which I went
for a draught of the river water, and being filled with one of my
rolls, gave the other two to a woman and her child that came
down the river in the boat with us and were waiting to go
farther. Thus refreshed I walked again up the street, which by
this time had many clean dressed people in it who were all
walking the same way; I joined them, and thereby was led into

the great Meeting House of the Quakers near the market. I sat
down among them, and after looking round awhile and hearing nothing said; being very drowsy through labour and want
of rest the preceding night, I fell fast asleep, and continued so
till the meeting broke up, when one was kind enough to rouse
me. This was therefore the first house I was in or slept in, in
Philadelphia . . .

Then I made myself as tidy as I could, and went to Andrew
Bradford the printer's. I found in the shop the old man his
father, whom I had seen at New York, and who travelling on
horseback had got to Philadelphia before me. He introduced
me to his son, who received me civilly, gave me a breakfast, but
told me he did not at present want a hand, being lately supplied
with one. But there was another printer in town lately set up,
one Keimer, who perhaps might employ me; if not, I should be
welcome to lodge at his house, and he would give me a little
work to do now and then till fuller business should offer.

The old gentleman said, he would go with me to the new
printer: And when we found him, Neighbour, says Bradford, I
have brought to see you a young man of your business, perhaps
you may want such a one. He asked me a few questions, put a
composing stick in my hand to see how I worked, and then said
he would employ me soon, though he had just then nothing for
me to do. And taking old Bradford whom he had never seen
before, to be one of the townspeople that had a goodwill for
him, entered into a conversation on his present undertaking
and prospects; while Bradford not discovering that he was the
other printer's father, on Keimer's saying he expected soon to
get the greatest part of the business into his own hands, drew
him on by artful questions and starting little doubts, to explain
all his views, what interest he relied on, and in what manner he
intended to proceed. I who stood by and heard all, saw immediately that one of them was a crafty old sophister, and the
other a mere novice. Bradford left me with Keimer, who was
greatly surprized when I told him who the old man was.

Keimer's printing house I found, consisted of an old shat-
tered press, and one small worn-out fount of English, which he
was then using himself, composing in it an elegy on Aquila Rose
beforementioned, an ingenious young man of excellent charac-

ter much respected in the town, clerk of the Assembly, and a pretty poet. Keimer made verses, too, but very indifferently. He could not be said to write them, for his manner was to compose them in the types directly out of his head; so there being no copy, but one pair of cases, and the elegy likely to require all the letters, no one could help him. I endeavoured to put his press (which he had not yet used, and of which he understood nothing) into order fit to be worked with; and promising to come and print off his elegy as soon as he should have got it ready, I returned to Bradford's who gave me a little job to do for the present, and there I lodged and dieted. A few days after, Keimer sent for me to print off the elegy. And now he had got another pair of cases, and a pamphlet to reprint, on which he set me to work.

These two printers I found poorly qualified for their business. Bradford had not been bred to it, and was very illiterate; and Keimer though something of a scholar, was a mere compositor, knowing nothing of press-work. He had been one of the French prophets and could act their enthusiastic agitations. At this time he did not profess any particular religion, but something of all on occasion; was very ignorant of the world, and had, as I afterward found, a good deal of the knave in his composition. He did not like my lodging at Bradford's while I worked with him. He had a house indeed, but without furniture, so he could not lodge me: But he got me a lodging at Mr Read's before mentioned, who was the owner of his house. And my chest and clothes being come by this time, I made rather a more respectable appearance in the eyes of Miss Read than I had done when she first happened to see me eating my roll in the street.

I began now to have some acquaintance among the young people of the town, that were lovers of reading with whom I spent my evenings very pleasantly and gaining money by my industry and frugality, I lived very agreably, forgetting Boston as much as I could, and not desiring that any there should know where I resided, except my friend Collins who was in my secret, and kept it when I wrote to him. At length an incident happened that sent me back again much sooner than I had intended.

I had a brother-in-law, Robert Holmes, master of a sloop, that traded between Boston and Delaware. He being at Newcastle forty miles below Philadelphia, heard there of me, and wrote me a letter, mentioning the concern of my friends in Boston at my abrupt departure, assuring me of their goodwill to me, and that everything would be accommodated to my mind if I would return, to which he exhorted me very earnestly. I wrote an answer to his letter, thanked him for his advice, but stated my reasons for quitting Boston fully, and in such a light as to convince him I was not so wrong as he had apprehended. Sir William Keith governor of the province, was then at Newcastle, and Captain Holmes happening to be in company with him when my letter came to hand, spoke to him of me, and showed him the letter. The governor read it, and seemed surprized when he was told my age. He said I appeared a young man of promising parts, and therefore should be encouraged: The printers at Philadelphia were wretched ones, and if I would set up there, he made no doubt I should succeed; for his part, he would procure me the publick business, and do me every other service in his power. This my brother-in-law afterwards told me in Boston. But I knew as yet nothing of it; when one day Keimer and I being at work together near the window, we saw the governor and another gentleman (which proved to be Colonel French, of Newcastle) finely dressed, come directly across the street to our house, and heard them at the door. Keimer ran down immediately, thinking it a visit to him. But the governor enquired for me, came up, and with a condescension and politeness I had been quite unused to, made me many compliments, desired to be acquainted with me, blamed me kindly for not having made myself known to him when I first came to the place, and would have me away with him to the tavern where he was going with Colonel French to taste as he said some excellent Madeira. I was not a little surprized, and Keimer stared like a pig poisoned. I went however with the governor and Colonel French, to a tavern at the corner of Third Street, and over the Madeira he proposed my setting up my business, laid before me the probabilities of success, and both he and Colonel French, assured me I should have their interest and influence in procuring the publick business of both governments. On my doubting whether my father would assist me in it, Sir William said he would give me a letter to him, in which he would state the advantages, and he did not doubt of prevailing with him. So it was concluded I should return to Boston in the first vessel with the governor's letter recommending me to my father. In the meantime the intention was to be kept secret, and I went on working with Keimer as usual, the governor sending for me now and then to dine with him, a very great honour I thought it, and conversing with me in the most affable, familiar, and friendly manner imaginable. About the end of April 1724 a little vessel offered for Boston. I took leave of Keimer as going to see my friends. The governor gave me an ample letter, saying many flattering things of me to my father, and strongly recommending the project of my setting up at Philadelphia, as a thing that must make my fortune. We struck on a shoal in going down the bay and sprung a leak, we had a blustering time at sea, and were obliged to pump almost continually, at which I took my turn. We arrived safe however at Boston in about a fortnight. I had been absent seven months and my friends had heard nothing of me; for my brother Holmes was not yet returned; and had not written about me. My unexpected appearance surprized the family; all were however very glad to see me and made me welcome, except my brother. I went to see him at his printing house: I was better dressed than ever while in his service, having a genteel new suit from head to foot, a watch, and my pockets lined with near 5 pounds sterling in silver. He received me not very frankly, looked me all over, and turned to his work again. The journeymen were inquisitive where I had been, what sort of a country it was, and how I liked it? I praised it much, and the happy life I led in it; expressing strongly my intention of returning to it; and one of them asking what kind of money we had there, I produced a handful of silver and spread it before them, which was a kind of rare show they had not been used to, paper being the money of Boston. Then I took an opportunity of letting them see my watch: and lastly, (my brother still grim and sullen) I gave them a piece of eight to drink, and took my leave. This visit of mine offended him extreamly. For when my mother some time after spoke to him of a reconciliation, and of her wishes to see us on good terms together, and that we might live for the future as brothers, he said, I had insulted him in such a manner before his people that he could never forget or forgive it. In this however he was mistaken.

My father received the governor's letter with some apparent surprize; but said little of it to me for some days; when Captain Holmes returning, he showed it to him, asked if he knew Keith, and what kind of a man he was: Adding his opinion that he must be of small discretion, to think of setting a boy up in business who wanted yet three years of being at man's estate. Holmes said what he could in favour of the project; but my father was clear in the impropriety of it; and at last gave a flat denial to it. Then he wrote a civil letter to Sir William thanking him for the patronage he had so kindly offered me, but declining to assist me as yet in setting up, I being in his opinion too young to be trusted with the management of a business so important, and for which the preparation must be so expensive.

My friend and companion Collins, who was a clerk at the post office, pleased with the account I gave him of my new country, determined to go thither also: And while I waited for my father's determination, he set out before me by land to Rhode Island, leaving his books which were a pretty collection of mathematicks and natural philosophy, to come with mine and me to New York where he proposed to wait for me. My father, though he did not approve Sir William's proposition was yet pleased that I had been able to obtain so advantageous a character from a person of such note where I had resided, and that I had been so industrious and careful as to equip myself so handsomely in so short a time: therefore seeing no prospect of an accommodation between my brother and me, he gave his consent to my returning again to Philadelphia, advised me to behave respectfully to the people there, endeavour to obtain the general esteem, and avoid lampooning and libelling to which he thought I had too much inclination; telling me, that by steady industry and a prudent parsimony, I might save enough by the time I was one-and-twenty to set me up, and that if I came near the matter he would help me out with the rest. This was all I could obtain, except some small gifts as tokens of his and my mother's

love, when I embarked again for New York, now with their
approbation and their blessing.

*During this return visit to Boston, Franklin visited the old Puritan
minister, Cotton Mather. Much later—on 12 May 1784—he wrote to
Samuel Mather, Cotton's son, recalling an incident which exemplified
the Puritan habit of finding moral instruction in every experience.*

Mather showed me a shorter way out of the house, through a
narrow passage, which was crossed by a beam overhead. We
were talking as I withdrew, he accompanying me behind, and I
turning partly towards him when he said hastily, 'STOOP,
STOOP!' I did not understand him till I felt my head against the
beam. He was a man that never missed any occasion of giving
instruction, and upon this he said to me: 'You are young, and
have the world before you; STOOP as you go through it, you will
miss many hard bumps.' This advice, thus beat into my head,
has frequently been of use to me, and I often think of it when
I see pride mortified and misfortunes brought upon people by
carrying their heads too high.

From the Autobiography:

The sloop putting in at Newport, Rhode Island, I visited my
brother John, who had been married and settled there some
years. He received me very affectionately, for he always loved
me. A friend of his, one Vernon, having some money due to
him in Pensilvania, about 35 pounds currency, desired I would
receive it for him, and keep it till I had his directions what to
remit it in. Accordingly he gave me an order. This afterwards
occasioned me a good deal of uneasiness.

At New York I found my friend Collins, who had arrived
there some time before me. We had been intimate from children, and had read the same books together: But he had the
advantage of more time for reading, and studying and a wonderful genius for mathematical learning in which he far out-
stript me. While I lived in Boston most of my hours of leisure
for conversation were spent with him, and he continued a sober
as well as an industrious lad; was much respected for his learning

by several of the clergy and other gentlemen, and seemed to promise making a good figure in life: but during my absence he had acquired a habit of sotting with brandy; and I found by his own account and what I heard from others, that he had been drunk every day since his arrival at New York, and behaved very oddly. He had gamed too and lost his money, so that I was obliged to discharge his lodgings, and defray his expenses to and at Philadelphia: Which proved extreamly inconvenient to me. The then governor of New York, Burnet, son of Bishop Burnet, hearing from the captain that a young man, one of his passengers, had a great many books, desired he would bring me to see him. I waited upon him accordingly, and should have taken Collins with me but that he was not sober. The governor treated me with great civility, showed me his library, which was a very large one, and we had a good deal of conversation about books and authors. This was the second governor who had done me the honour to take notice of me, which to a poor boy like me was very pleasing. We proceeded to Philadelphia. I received on the way Vernon's money, without which we could hardly have finished our journey. Collins wished to be employed in some counting house; but whether they discovered his dramming by his breath, or by his behaviour, though he had some recommendations, he met with no success in any application, and continued lodging and boarding at the same house with me and at my expense. Knowing I had that money of Vernon's he was continually borrowing of me, still promising repayment as soon as he should be in business. At length he had got so much of it, that I was distressed to think what I should do, in case of being called on to remit it. His drinking continued, about which we sometimes quarrelled, for when a little intoxicated he was very fractious . . .

[Finally] a West India captain who had a commission to procure a tutor for the sons of a gentleman at Barbadoes, happening to meet with him, agreed to carry him thither. He left me then, promising to remit me the first money he should receive in order to discharge the debt. But I never heard of him after. The breaking into this money of Vernon's was one of the first great *Errata* of my life. And this affair showed that my father was not much out in his judgment when he supposed me too young to manage business of importance. But Sir William, on reading his letter, said he was too prudent. There was great difference in persons, and discretion did not always accompany years, nor was youth always without it. And since he will not set you up, says he, I will do it myself. Give me an inventory of the things necessary to be had from England, and I will send for them. You shall repay me when you are able; I am resolved to have a good printer here, and I am sure you must succeed. This was spoken with such an appearance of cordiality, that I had not the least doubt of his meaning what he said. I had hitherto kept the proposition of my setting up, a secret in Philadelphia, and I still kept it. Had it been known that I depended on the governor, probably some friend that knew him better would have advised me not to rely on him, as I afterwards heard it as his known character to be liberal of promises which he never meant to keep. Yet unsolicited as he was by me, how could I think his generous offers insincere? I believed him one of the best men in the world.

I presented him an inventory of a little printing house, amounting by my computation to about 100 pounds sterling. He liked it, but asked me if my being on the spot in England to chuse the types and see that everything was good of the kind, might not be of some advantage. Then, says he, when there, you may make acquaintances and establish correspondencies in the bookselling and stationary way. I agreed that this might be advantageous. Then, says he, get yourself ready to go with *Annis;* which was the annual ship, and the only one at that time usually passing between London and Philadelphia. But it would be some months before *Annis* sailed, so I continued working with Keimer, fretting about the money Collins had got from me; and in daily apprehensions of being called upon by Vernon, which however did not happen for some years after.

I believe I have omitted mentioning that in my first voyage from Boston, being becalmed off Block Island, our people set about catching cod and hauled up a great many. Hitherto I had stuck to my resolution of not eating animal food; and on this occasion, I considered with my master Tryon, the taking every fish as a kind of unprovoked murder, since none of them had or ever could do us any injury that might justify the slaughter.

All this seemed very reasonable. But I had formerly been a great lover of fish, and when this came hot out of the frying pan, it smelt admirably well. I balanced some time between principle and inclination: till I recollected, that when the fish were opened, I saw smaller fish taken out of their stomachs: Then thought I, if you eat one another, I don't see why we mayn't eat you. So I dined upon cod very heartily and continued to eat with other people, returning only now and then occasionally to a vegetable diet. So convenient a thing it is to be a *reasonable creature,* since it enables one to find or make a reason for everything one has a mind to do.

Keimer and I lived on a pretty good familiar footing and agreed tolerably well: for he suspected nothing of my setting up. He retained a great deal of his old enthusiasms, and loved argumentation. We therefore had many disputations. I used to work him so with my Socratic Method, and had trepanned him so often by questions apparently so distant from any point we had in hand, and yet by degrees led to the point, and brought him into difficulties and contradictions that at last he grew ridiculously cautious, and would hardly answer me the most common question, without asking first, *What do you intend to infer from that?* However it gave him so high an opinion of my abilities in the confuting way, that he seriously proposed my being his colleague in a project he had of setting up a new sect. He was to preach the doctrines, and I was to confound all opponents. When he came to explain with me upon the doctrines, I found several conundrums which I objected to, unless I might have my way a little too, and introduce some of mine. Keimer wore his beard at full length, because somewhere in the Mosaic Law it is said, *thou shalt not mar the corners of thy beard.* He likewise kept the seventh day Sabbath; and these two points were essentials with him. I disliked both, but agreed to admit them upon condition of his adopting the doctrine of using no animal food. I doubt, says he, my constitution will not bear that. I assured him it would, and that he would be the better for it. He was usually a great glutton, and I promised myself some diversion in half-starving him. He agreed to try the practice if I would keep him company. I did so and we held it for three months. We had our victuals dressed and brought to us regularly by a woman in the neighbourhood, who had from me a list of forty dishes to be prepared for us at different times, in all which there was neither fish flesh nor fowl, and the whim suited me the better at this time from the cheapness of it, not costing us above 18 pence sterling each, per week. I have since kept several Lents most strictly, leaving the common diet for that, and that for the common, abruptly, without the least inconvenience: So that I think there is little in the advice of making those changes by easy gradations. I went on pleasantly, but poor Keimer suffered grievously, tired of the project, longed for the flesh-pots of Egypt, and ordered a roast pig. He invited me and two women friends to dine with him, but it being brought too soon upon the table, he could not resist the temptation, and ate it all up before we came.

I had made some courtship during this time to Miss Read. I had a great respect and affection for her, and had some reason to believe she had the same for me: but as I was about to take a long voyage, and we were both very young, only a little above eighteen, it was thought most prudent by her mother to prevent our going too far at present, as a marriage if it was to take place would be more convenient after my return, when I should be as I expected set up in my business. Perhaps too she thought my expectations not so well founded as I imagined them to be.

My chief acquaintances at this time were, Charles Osborne, Joseph Watson, and James Ralph; all lovers of reading. The two first were clerks to an eminent scrivener or conveyancer in the town, Charles Brockden; the other was clerk to a merchant. Watson was a pious sensible young man, of great integrity. The others rather more lax in their principles of religion, particularly Ralph, who as well as Collins had been unsettled by me, for which they both made me suffer. Osborne was sensible, candid, frank, sincere and affectionate to his friends; but in literary matters too fond of criticizing. Ralph, was ingenious, genteel in his manners, and extreamly eloquent; I think I never knew a prettier talker. Both of them great admirers of poetry, and began to try their hands in little pieces. Many pleasant walks we four had together on Sundays into the woods near Schuylkill, where we read to one another and conferred on what we read . . .

The governor, seeming to like my company, had me frequently to his house; and his setting me up was always mentioned as a fixed thing. I was to take with me letters recommendatory to a number of his friends, besides the letter of credit to furnish me with the necessary money for purchasing the press and types, paper, etc. For these letters I was appointed to call at different times, when they were to be ready, but a future time was still named. Thus we went on till the ship whose departure too had been several times postponed was on the point of sailing. Then when I called to take my leave and receive the letters, his secretary, Dr Bard, came out to me and said the governor was extreamly busy, in writing, but would be down at Newcastle before the ship, and there the letters would be delivered to me.

Ralph, though married and having one child, had determined to accompany me in this voyage. It was thought he intended to establish a correspondence, and obtain goods to sell on commission. But I found afterwards, that through some discontent with his wife's relations, he purposed to leave her on their hands, and never return again. Having taken leave of my friends, and interchanged some promises with Miss Read, I left Philadelphia in the ship, which anchored at Newcastle. The governor was there. But when I went to his lodging, the secretary came to me from him with the civillest message in the world, that he could not then see me being engaged in business of the utmost importance, but should send the letters to me on board, wished me heartily a good voyage and a speedy return, etc. I returned on board, a little puzzled, but still not doubting.

Mr Andrew Hamilton, a famous lawyer of Philadelphia, had taken passage in the same ship for himself and son: and with Mr Denham a Quaker merchant, and Messrs Onion and Russel, masters of an iron work in Maryland, had engaged the Great Cabin; so that Ralph and I were forced to take up with a birth [sic] in the steerage: And none on board knowing us, were considered as ordinary persons. But Mr Hamilton and his son (it was James, since governor) returned from Newcastle to Philadelphia, the father being recalled by a great fee to plead for a seized ship. And just before we sailed Colonel French coming on board, and showing me great respect, I was more taken

notice of, and with my friend Ralph invited by the other gentlemen to come into the cabin, there being now room. Accordingly we removed thither.

Understanding that Colonel French had brought on board
the governor's dispatches, I asked the captain for those letters
that were to be under my care. He said all were put into the bag
together; and he could not then come at them; but before we
landed in England, I should have an opportunity of picking
them out. So I was satisfied for the present, and we proceeded
on our voyage. We had a sociable company in the cabin, and
lived uncommonly well, having the addition of all Mr Hamilton's stores, who had laid in plentifully. In this passage Mr
Denham contracted a friendship for me that continued during
his life. The voyage was otherwise not a pleasant one, as we had
a great deal of bad weather.

When we came into the Channel, the captain kept his word
with me, and gave me an opportunity of examining the bag for
the governor's letters. I found none upon which my name was
put, as under my care; I picked out six or seven that by the
handwriting I thought might be the promised letters, especially
as one of them was directed to Basket the king's printer, and
another to some stationer. We arrived in London the 24th of
December, 1724. I waited upon the stationer who came first in
my way, delivering the letter as from Governor Keith. I don't
know such a person, says he: but opening the letter, O, this is
from Riddlesden; I have lately found him to be a compleat
rascal, and I will have nothing to do with him, nor receive any
letters from him. So putting the letter into my hand, he turned
on his heel and left me to serve some customer. I was surprized
to find these were not the governor's letters. And after recollecting and comparing circumstances, I began to doubt his sincerity. I found my friend Denham, and opened the whole affair
to him. He let me into Keith's character, told me there was not
the least probability that he had written any letters for me, that
no one who knew him had the smallest dependence on him,
and he laught at the notion of the governor's giving me a Letter
of Credit, having as he said no credit to give. On my expressing
some concern about what I should do: He advised me to endeavour getting some employment in the way of my business.

Among the printers here, says he, you will improve yourself; and when you return to America, you will set up to greater advantage.

We both of us happened to know, as well as the stationer, that Riddlesden the attorney was a very knave. He had half ruined Miss Read's father by acquiring his note he bound for him. By his letter it appeared, there was a secret scheme on foot to the prejudice of Hamilton, (supposed to be then coming over with us,) and that Keith was concerned in it with Riddlesden. Denham, who was a friend of Hamilton's, thought he ought to be acquainted with it. So when he arrived in England, which was soon after, partly from resentment and ill-will to Keith and Riddlesden, and partly from goodwill to him: I waited on him, and gave him the letter. He thanked me cordially, the information being of importance to him. And from that time he became my friend, greatly to my advantage afterwards on many occasions.

But what shall we think of a governor's playing such pitiful tricks, and imposing so grossly on a poor ignorant boy! It was a habit he had acquired. He wished to please everybody; and, having little to give, he gave expectations. He was otherwise an ingenious sensible man, a pretty good writer, and a good governor for the people, though not for his constituents the proprietaries, whose instructions he sometimes disregarded. Several of our best laws were of his planning, and passed during his administration . . .

I immediately got into work at Palmer's, then a famous printing house in Bartholomew Close; and here I continued near a year. I was pretty diligent; but spent with Ralph a good deal of my earnings in going to plays and other places of amusement. We had together consumed all my pistoles, and now just rubbed on from hand to mouth. He seemed quite to forget his wife and child, and I by degrees my engagements with Miss Read, to whom I never wrote more than one letter, and that was to let her know I was not likely soon to return. This was another of the great *Errata* of my life, which I should wish to correct if I were to live it over again. In fact, by our expences, I was constantly kept unable to pay my passage.

At Palmer's I was employed in composing for the second

edition of Woollaston's [*sic*] *Religion of Nature*. Some of his reasonings not appearing to me well-founded, I wrote a little meta-
physical piece, in which I made remarks on them. It was
entitled, *A Dissertation on Liberty and Necessity, Pleasure and Pain*.
I inscribed it to my friend Ralph. I printed a small number. It
occasioned my being more considered by Mr Palmer, as a young
man of some ingenuity, though he seriously expostulated with
me upon the principles of my pamphlet which to him appeared
abominable. My printing this pamphlet was another *Erratum*.

*The essay, which he later regretted having published, took a young
man's contentious and anarchic line: if God is infinitely good and wise,
then everyone created by him must be so also. Using the God-
as-Clockmaker image which was made popular by Robert Boyle in the
seventeenth century, and which was to be even more popular in the
eighteenth, he declared that the universe was an intricate but harmonious whole—one in which chance and even choice played no part at all.
Since people behave according to God's will, how can there be any
distinction between virtue and vice? Later Franklin totally disowned
such views.*
    *In due course, he moved from Palmer's printing house, in St Bar-
tholomew's Lady Chapel, to Watts's, near Lincoln's Inn Fields:*

At my first admission into this printing house, I took to working
at press, imagining I felt a want of the bodily exercise I had
been used to in America, where presswork is mixed with composing, I drank only water; the other workmen, near fifty in
number, were great guzzlers of beer. On occasion I carried up
and downstairs a large form of types in each hand, when others
carried but one in both hands. They wondered to see from this
and several instances that the water-American as they called me
was *stronger* than themselves who drank *strong* beer. We had an
alehouse boy who attended always in the house to supply the
workmen. My companion at the press, drank every day a pint
before breakfast, a pint at breakfast with his bread and cheese;
a pint between breakfast and dinner; a pint at dinner; a pint in
the afternoon about six o'clock, and another when he had done
his day's work. I thought it a detestable custom. But it was
necessary, he supposed, to drink *strong* beer that he might be

strong to labour. I endeavoured to convince him that the bodily strength afforded by beer could only be in proportion to the grain or flour of the barley dissolved in the water of which it was made; that there was more flour in a pennyworth of bread, and therefore if he would eat that with a pint of water, it would give him more strength than a quart of beer. He drank on however, and had 4 or 5 shillings to pay out of his wages every Saturday night for that muddling liquor; an expence I was free from. And thus these poor devils keep themselves always under.

Watts after some weeks desiring to have me in the composing room, I left the pressmen. A new *Bienvenu* or sum for drink; being 5 shillings, was demanded of me by the compositors. I thought it an imposition, as I had paid below. The master thought so too, and forbade my paying it. I stood out two or three weeks, was accordingly considered as an excommunicate, and had so many little pieces of private mischief done me, by mixing my sorts, transposing my pages, breaking my matter, etc. etc. and if I were ever so little out of the room, and all ascribed to the Chapel ghost, which they said ever haunted those not regularly admitted, that notwithstanding the master's protection, I found myself obliged to comply and pay the money; convinced of the folly of being on ill terms with those one is to live with continually. I was now on a fair footing with them, and soon acquired considerable influence. I proposed some reasonable alterations in their Chapel Laws, and carried them against all opposition. From my example a great part of them, left their muddling breakfast of beer and bread and cheese, finding they could with me be supplied from a neighbouring house with a large porringer of hot water-gruel, sprinkled with pepper, crumbed with bread, and a bit of butter in it, for the price of a pint of beer, viz., 3 halfpence. This was a more comfortable as well as cheaper breakfast, and kept their heads clearer. Those who continued sotting with beer all day, were often, by not paying, out of credit at the alehouse, and used to make interest with me to get beer, *their light,* as they phrased it, *being out.* I watched the pay table on Saturday night, and collected what I stood engaged for them, having to pay sometimes near 30 shillings a week on their accounts. This, and my being esteemed a pretty good Riggite, that is a jocular verbal satyrist, supported my consequence in the society. My constant attendance, (I never making a St Monday), recommended me to the master; and my uncommon quickness at composing, occasioned my being put upon all work of dispatch which was generally better paid. So I went on now very agreably.

My lodging in Little Britain being too remote, I found another in Duke Street opposite to the Romish Chapel. It was two pair of stairs backwards at an Italian warehouse. A widow lady kept the house; she had a daughter and a maid-servant, and a journey-man who attended the warehouse, but lodged abroad. After sending to enquire my character at the house where I last lodged, she agreed to take me in at the same rate 3/6 per week, cheaper as she said from the protection she expected in having a man lodge in the house. She was a widow, an elderly woman, had been bred a Protestant, being a clergyman's daughter, but was converted to the Catholic religion by her husband, whose memory she much revered; had lived much among people of distinction, and knew a thousand anecdotes of them as far back as the times of Charles the Second. She was lame in her knees with the gout, and therefore seldom stirred out of her room, so sometimes wanted company; and hers was so highly amusing to me; that I was sure to spend an evening with her whenever she desired it. Our supper was only half an anchovy each, on a very little strip of bread and butter, and half a pint of ale between us. But the entertainment was in her conversation. My always keeping good hours, and giving little trouble in the family, made her unwilling to part with me; so that when I talked of a lodging I had heard of, nearer my business, for 2 shillings a week, which, intent as I now was on saving money, made some difference; she bid me not think of it, for she would abate me 2 shillings a week for the future, so I remained with her at 1/6 as long as I staid in London . . .

At Watts's printing house I contracted an acquaintance with an ingenious young man, one Wygate, who having wealthy relations, had been better educated than most printers, was a tolerable Latinist, spoke French, and loved reading. I taught him and a friend of his, to swim, at twice going into the river, and they soon became good swimmers. They introduced me to some gentlemen from the country who went to Chelsea by water to see the College and Don Saltero's Curiosities. In our return, at the request of the company, whose curiosity Wygate had excited, I stript and leapt into the river, and swam from near Chelsea to Blackfryars, performing on the way many feats of activity both upon and under water, that surprized and pleased those to whom they were novelties. I had from a child been ever delighted with the exercise, had studied and practised all Thevenot's motions and positions, added some of my own, aiming at the graceful and easy, as well as the useful. All these I took this occasion of exhibiting to the company, and was much flattered by their admiration. And Wygate, who was desirous of becoming a master, grew more and more attached to me, on that account, as well as from the similarity of our studies. He at length proposed to me travelling all over Europe together, supporting ourselves everywhere by working at our business. I was once inclined to it. But mentioning it to my good friend Mr Denham, with whom I often spend an hour, when I had leisure, he dissuaded me from it, advising me to think only of returning to Pensilvania, which he was now about to do.

I must record one trait of this good man's character. He had formerly been in business at Bristol, but failed in debt to a number of people, compounded and went to America. There, by a close application to business as a merchant, he acquired a plentiful fortune in a few years. Returning to England in the ship with me, he invited his old creditors to an entertainment, at which he thanked them for the easy composition they had favoured him with, and when they expected nothing but the treat, every man at the first remove, found under his plate an order on a banker for the full amount of the unpaid remainder with interest.

He now told me he was about to return to Philadelphia, and should carry over a great quantity of goods in order to open a store there: He proposed to take me over as his clerk, to keep his books (in which he would instruct me) copy his letters, and attend the store. He added, that as soon as I should be acquainted with mercantile business he would promote me by sending me with a cargo of flour and bread etc. to the West Indies, and procure me commissions from others; which would be profitable, and if I managed well, would establish me handsomely. The thing pleased me, for I was grown tired of London, remembered with pleasure the happy months I had spent in Pennsylvania, and wished again to see it. Therefore I immediately agreed, on the terms of 50 pounds a year, Pennsylvania money less indeed than my then present gettings as a compositor, but affording a better prospect.

I now took leave of printing; as I thought for ever, and was daily employed in my new business; going about with Mr Denham among the tradesmen, to purchase various articles, and seeing them packed up, doing errands, calling upon workmen to dispatch, etc. and when all was on board, I had a few days leisure . . .

Thus I spent about eighteen months in London. Most part of the time, I worked hard at my business, and spent but little upon myself except in seeing plays, and in books. My friend Ralph had kept me poor. He owed me about 27 pounds; which I was now never likely to receive; a great sum out of my small earnings. I loved him notwithstanding, for he had many amiable qualities. Though I had by no means improved my fortune. But I had picked up some very ingenious acquaintance whose conversation was of great advantage to me, and I had read considerably. We sailed from Gravesend on the 23rd of July 1726.

TWO

THE LEATHER-APRON MAN

The Autobiography *makes but brief mention of Franklin's return trip to Philadelphia in 1726 on the* Berkshire, *since he had kept a separate account of it, 'minutely related', in* Journal of a Voyage, *extracts from which follow, displaying not only Franklin's lively curiosity and interest in things new to his experience, but (at the age of twenty) his acute perceptions of the ways of man.*

Friday, 22 July, 1726. Yesterday in the afternoon we left London, and came to an anchor off Gravesend about eleven at night. I lay ashore all night, and this morning took a walk up to the Windmill Hill, from whence I had an agreeable prospect of the country for above twenty miles round, and two or three reaches of the river, with ships and boats sailing both up and down, and Tilbury Fort on the other side, which commands the river and passage to London. This Gravesend is a *cursed biting* place; the chief dependence of the people being the advantage they make of imposing upon strangers. If you buy anything of them, and give half what they ask, you pay twice as much as the thing is worth. Thank God, we shall leave it tomorrow . . .

Sunday, 24 July. This morning we weighed anchor, and coming to the Downs, we set our pilot ashore at Deal, and passed through. And now, whilst I write this, sitting upon the quarterdeck, I have methinks one of the pleasantest scenes in the world before me. 'Tis a fine, clear day, and we are going away before the wind with an easy, pleasant gale. We have near fifteen sail of ships in sight, and I may say in company. On the left hand appears the coast of France at a distance, and on the right is the town and castle of Dover, with the green hills and chalky cliffs of England, to which we must now bid farewell. Albion, farewell! . . .

Friday, 29 July. All this afternoon I spent agreeably enough at the draft-board. It is a game I much delight in; but it requires a clear head, and undisturbed; and the persons playing, if they would play well, ought not much to regard the *consequence* of the game, for that diverts and withdraws the attention of the mind from the game itself, and makes the player liable to make many false open moves; and I will venture to lay it down for an infallible rule, that, if two persons *equal* in judgment play for a considerable sum, he that loves money most shall lose; his anxiety for the success of the game confounds him. Courage is almost as requisite for the good conduct of this game as in a real battle; for, if the player imagines himself opposed by one that is much his superior in skill, his mind is so intent on the defensive part, that an advantage passes unobserved . . .

Sunday, 31 July. This morning the wind being moderated, our pilot designed to weigh, and, taking advantage of the tide, get a little further to windward. Upon which the boat came ashore, to hasten us on board. We had no sooner returned and hoisted in our boat, but the wind began again to blow very hard at west, insomuch that, instead of going any further, we were obliged to weigh and run down again to Cowes for the sake of more secure riding, where we came to an anchor again in a very little time; and the pudding, which our mess made and put into the pot at Yarmouth, we dined upon at Cowes . . .

Friday, 5 August. Called up this morning and hurried aboard, the wind being north-west. About noon we weighed and left Cowes a third time, and, sailing by Yarmouth, we came into the channel through the Needles; which passage is guarded by Hurst Castle, standing on a spit of land which runs out from the main land of England within a mile of the Isle of Wight. Towards night the wind veered to the westward, which put us under apprehensions of being forced into port again: but presently after it fell a flat calm, and then we had a small breeze that was fair for half an hour, when it was succeeded by a calm again.

Saturday, 6 August. This morning we had a fair breeze for some hours, and then a calm that lasted all day. In the afternoon I leaped overboard and swam round the ship to wash myself. Saw several porpoises this day. About eight o'clock we came to an anchor in forty fathom water against the tide of flood, somewhere below Portland, and weighed again about eleven, having a small breeze . . .

Friday, 19 August. This day we have had a pleasant breeze at east. In the morning we spied a sail upon our larboard bow, about two leagues' distance. About noon she put out English colours, and we answered with our ensign, and in the afternoon we spoke with her. She was a ship, of New York, Walter Kippen, master, bound from Rochelle, in France, to Boston, with salt. Our captain and Mr D—— went on board, and stayed till evening, it being fine weather. Yesterday, complaints being made that Mr G——n, one of the passengers, had, with a fraudulent design, marked the cards, a court of justice was called immediately, and he was brought to his trial in form. A Dutchman, who could speak no English, deposed by his interpreter that, when our mess was on shore at Cowes, the prisoner at the bar marked all the Court cards on the back with a pen.

I have sometimes observed, that we are apt to fancy the person that cannot speak intelligibly to us, proportionably stupid in understanding, and, when we speak two or three words of English to a foreigner, it is louder than ordinary, as if we thought him deaf, and that he had lost the use of his ears as well as his tongue. Something like this I imagine might be the case of Mr G——n; he fancied the Dutchman could not see what he was about, because he could not understand English, and therefore boldly did it before his face . . . In fine the jury brought him in guilty, and he was condemned to be carried up to the round-top, and made fast there, in view of all the ship's company, during the space of three hours, that being the place where the act was committed, and to pay a fine of two bottles of brandy. But the prisoner resisting authority and refusing to submit to punishment, one of the sailors stepped up aloft and let down a rope to us, which we, with much struggling, made fast about his middle, and hoisted him up into the air, sprawling, by main force. We let him hang, cursing and swearing, for near a quarter of an hour; but at length, he crying out Murder! and looking black in the face, the rope being overtort about his middle, we thought proper to let him down again; and our mess have excommunicated him till he pays his fine, refusing either to play, eat, drink, or converse with him . . .

Sunday, 21 August. This morning we lost sight of the *Yorker,* having a brisk gale of wind at east. Towards night a poor little bird came on board us, being almost tired to death, and suffered itself to be taken by the hand. We reckon ourselves near two hundred leagues from land, so that no doubt a little rest was very acceptable to the unfortunate wanderer, who 'tis like, was blown off the coast in thick weather, and could not find its way back again. We receive it hospitably, and tender it victuals and drink; but he refuses both, and I suppose will not live long. There was one came on board some days ago, in the same circumstances with this, which I think the cat destroyed . . .

Thursday, 25 August. Our excommunicated shipmate thinking proper to comply with the sentence the court passed upon him, and expressing himself willing to pay the fine, we have this morning received him into unity again. Man is a sociable being, and it is, for aught I know, one of the worst of punishments to be excluded from society. I have read abundance of fine things on the subject of solitude, and I know 'tis a common boast in the mouths of those that affect to be thought wise, *that they are never less alone than when alone.* I acknowledge solitude an agreeable refreshment to a busy mind; but were these thinking people obliged to be always alone, I am apt to think they would quickly find their very being insupportable to them. I have heard of a gentleman, who underwent seven years' close confinement, in the Bastile, at Paris. He was a man of sense, he was a thinking man, but being deprived of all conversation, to what purpose should he think; for he was denied even the instruments of expressing his thoughts in writing. There is no burden so grievous to man as time that he knows not how to dispose of. He was forced at last to have recourse to this invention; he daily scattered pieces of paper about the floor of his little room, and then employed himself in picking them up again and sticking them in rows and figures on the arm of his elbow-chair; and he used to tell his friends, after his release, that he verily believed, if he had not taken this method he should have lost his senses. One of the philosophers, I think it was Plato, used to say, that he had

rather be the veriest stupid block in nature, than the possessor
of all knowledge without some intelligent being to communicate it to ...

Tuesday, 30 August. Contrary wind still. This evening, the
moon being near full, as she rose after eight o'clock, there
appeared a rainbow in a western cloud, to windward of us. The
first time I ever saw a rainbow in the night, caused by the moon.

Friday, 2 September. This morning the wind changed; a little
fair. We caught a couple of dolphins, and fried them for dinner. They eat indifferent well. These fish make a glorious appearance in the water; their bodies are of a bright green, mixed
with a silver colour, and their tails of a shining golden yellow;
but all this vanishes presently after they are taken out of their
element, and they change all over to a light gray. I observed
that cutting off pieces of a just-caught, living dolphin for baits,
those pieces did not lose their lustre and fine colours when the
dolphin died, but retained them perfectly. Everyone takes notice of that vulgar error of the painters, who always represent
this fish monstrously crooked and deformed, when it is, in reality, as beautiful and well-shaped a fish as any that swims. I
cannot think what could be the original of this chimera of theirs,
(since there is not a creature in nature that in the least resem-
bles their dolphin) unless it proceeded at first from a false
imitation of a fish in the posture of leaping, which they have
since improved into a crooked monster, with a head and eyes
like a bull, a hog's snout, and a tail like a blown tulip. But the
sailors give me another reason though a whimsical one, viz. that
as this most beautiful fish is only to be caught at sea, and that
very far to the southward, they say the painters wilfully deform
it in their representations, lest pregnant women should long for
what it is impossible to procure for them.

Tuesday, 6 September. This afternoon the wind still continuing
in the same quarter, increased till it blew a storm, and raised the
sea to a greater height than I had ever seen it before ...

Sunday, 11 September. We have had a hard gale of wind all this
day, accompanied with showers of rain. 'Tis uncomfortable being upon deck; and, though we have been all together all day
below, yet the long continuance of these contrary winds has made
us so dull, that scarce three words have passed between us.

Wednesday, 14 September. This afternoon, about two o'clock, it being fair weather and almost calm, as we sat playing drafts upon deck, we were surprized with a sudden and unusual darkness of the sun, which, as we could perceive, was only covered with a small, thin cloud; when that was passed by, we discovered that that glorious luminary laboured under a very great eclipse. At least ten parts out of twelve of him were hid from our eyes, and we were apprehensive he would have been totally darkened . . .

Wednesday, 21 September. This morning our steward was brought to the geers and whipped, for making an extravagant use of flour in the puddings, and for several other misdemeanours. It has been perfectly calm all this day, and very hot. I was determined to wash myself in the sea today, and should have done so, had not the appearance of a shark, that mortal enemy to swimmers, deterred me; he seemed to be about five foot long, moves round the ship at some distance, in a slow, majestic manner, attended by near a dozen of those they call pilot-fish, of different sizes; the largest of them is not so big as a small mackerell, and the smallest not bigger than my little finger. Two of these diminutive pilots keep just before his nose, and he seems to govern himself in his motions by their direction; while the rest surround him on every side indifferently. A shark is never seen without a retinue of these, who are his purveyors, discovering and distinguishing his prey for him; while he in turn gratefully protects them from the ravenous, hungry dolphin. They are commonly counted a very greedy fish; yet this refuses to meddle with the bait thrown out for him. 'Tis likely he has already made a full meal.

Friday, 23 September. This morning we spied a sail to windward of us about two leagues. We showed our jack upon the ensign-staff, and shortened sail for them till about noon, when she came up with us. She was a snow, from Dublin, bound for New York, having upwards of fifty servants on board of both sexes; they all appeared upon deck, and seemed very much pleased at the sight of us. There is really something strangely chearing to the spirits in the meeting of a ship at sea, containing a society of creatures of the same species and in the same circumstances with ourselves, after we had been long separated and excommunicated as it were from the rest of mankind. My heart fluttered in my breast with joy, when I saw so many human countenances, and I could scarce refrain from that kind of laughter, which proceeds from some degree of inward pleasure. When we have been for a considerable time tossing on the vast waters, far from the sight of any land or ships, or any mortal creature but ourselves (except a few fish and sea-birds), the whole world, for aught we know, may be under a second deluge, and we, like Noah and his company in the ark, the only surviving remnant of the human race . . .

Tuesday, 27 September. The fair wind continues still. I have laid a bowl of punch, that we are in Philadelphia next Saturday se'nnight; for we reckon ourselves not above 150 leagues from land . . .

Saturday, 1 October. Last night our consort, who goes incomparably better upon a wind than our vessel, got so far to windward and ahead of us, that this morning we could see nothing of him, and it is like shall see him no more. These south-wests are hot, damp winds, and bring abundance of rain and dirty weather with them . . .

Monday, 3 October. The water is now very visibly changed to the eyes of all except the captain and mate, and they will by no means allow it; I suppose because they did not see it first. Abundance of dolphins are about us, but they are very shy, and keep at a distance. Wind north-west . . .

Tuesday Night. Since eleven o'clock we have struck three fine dolphins, which are a great refreshment to us. This afternoon we have seen abundance of grampuses, which are seldom far from land; but towards evening we had a more evident token, to wit, a little tired bird, something like a lark, came on board us, who certainly is an American, and 'tis likely was ashore this day. It is now calm. We hope for a fair wind next . . .

Friday, 7 October. Last night, about nine o'clock, sprung up a fine gale at north-east, which run us in our course at the rate of seven miles an hour all night. We were in hopes of seeing land this morning, but cannot. The water, which we thought was changed, is now as blue as the sky; so that, unless at that time we were running over some unknown shoal, our eyes strangely deceived us. All the reckonings have been out these several days; though the captain says 'tis his opinion we are yet a hundred leagues from land; for my part I know not what to think of it; we have run all this day at a great rate, and now night is come on we have no soundings. Sure the American continent is not all sunk under water since we left it . . .

Sunday, 9 October. We have had the wind fair all the morning; at twelve o'clock we sounded, perceiving the water visibly changed, and struck ground at twenty-five fathoms, to our universal joy. After dinner one of our mess went up aloft to look out, and presently pronounced the long wished-for sound, LAND! LAND! In less than an hour we could descry it from the deck, appearing like tufts of trees. I could not discern it so soon as the rest; my eyes were dimmed with the suffusion of two small drops of joy . . .

Monday, 10 October. This morning we stood in again for land; and we that had been here before all agreed that it was Cape Henlopen; about noon we were come very near, and to our great joy saw the pilot-boat come off to us, which was exceeding welcome. He brought on board about a peck of apples with him; they seemed the most delicious I ever tasted in my life; the salt provisions we had been used to gave them a relish. We had extraordinary fair wind all the afternoon, and ran above a hundred miles up the Delaware before ten at night. The country appears very pleasant to the eye, being covered with woods, except here and there a house and plantation. We cast anchor when the tide turned, about two miles below Newcastle, and there lay till the morning tide.

Tuesday, 11 October. This morning we weighed anchor with a gentle breeze, and passed by Newcastle, whence they hailed us and bade us welcome. It is extreme fine weather. The sun enlivens our stiff limbs with his glorious rays of warmth and brightness. The sky looks gay, with here and there a silver cloud. The fresh breezes from the woods refresh us; the immediate prospect of liberty, after so long and irksome confinement, ravishes us. In short, all things conspire to make this the most joyful day I ever knew. As we passed by Chester, some of the company went on shore, impatient once more to tread on *terra firma,* and designing for Philadelphia by land. Four of us remained on board, not caring for the fatigue of travel when we knew the voyage had much weakened us. About eight at night, the wind failing us, we cast anchor at Redbank, six miles from Philadelphia, and thought we must be obliged to lie on board that night; but, some young Philadelphians happening to be out upon their pleasure in a boat, they came on board, and offered to take us up with them; we accepted of their kind proposal, and about ten o'clock landed at Philadelphia, heartily congratulating each upon our having happily completed so tedious and dangerous a voyage. Thank God!

The young Franklin found many changes in Philadelphia when he finally stepped ashore. In his Autobiography *he wrote:*

Keith was no longer governor, being superceded by Major Gordon: I met him walking the streets as a common citizen. He seemed a little ashamed at seeing me, but passed without saying anything. I should have been as much ashamed at seeing Miss Read, had not her friends, despairing with reason of my return, after the receipt of my letter, persuaded her to marry another, one Rogers, a potter, which was done in my absence. With him however she was never happy, and soon parted from him, refusing to cohabit with him, or bear his name, it being now said that he had another wife. Keimer had got a better house, a shop well supplied with stationary, plenty of new types, a number of hands though none good, and seemed to have a great deal of business.

Mr Denham took a store in Water Street, where we opened our goods. I attended the business diligently, studied accounts, and grew in a little time expert at selling. We lodged and boarded together, he counselled me as a father, having a sincere regard for me: I respected and loved him: and we might have gone on together very happily: But in the beginning of February 1726[7?], when I had just passed my twenty-first year, we both were taken ill. My distemper was a pleurisy, which very nearly carried me off: I suffered a good deal, gave up the point in my own mind, and was rather disappointed when I found myself recovering; regretting in some degree that I must now some time or other have all that disagreeable work to do over again. I forget what his distemper was. It held him a long time, and at length

A north-west view of the State House in Philadelphia

*A view of Second Street north from Market Street, Philadelphia,
showing Christ Church*

carried him off. He left me a small legacy in a nuncupative will, as a token of his kindness for me, and he left me once more to the wide world. For the store was taken into the care of his executors, and my employment under him ended: My brother-in-law Holmes, being now at Philadelphia, advised my return to my business. And Keimer tempted me with an offer of large wages by the year to come and take the management of his printing house, that he might better attend his stationer's shop. I had heard a bad character of him in London, from his wife and her friends, and was not fond of having any more to do with him. I tried for farther employment as a merchant's clerk; but not readily meeting with any, I closed again with Keimer.

I found in *his* house these hands; Hugh Meredith a Welsh-Pensilvanian, thirty years of age, bred to country work: honest, sensible, had a great deal of solid observation, was something of a reader, but given to drink: Stephen Potts, a young country man of full age, bred to the same: of uncommon natural parts, and great wit and humour, but a little idle. These he had agreed with at extream low wages, per week, to be raised a shilling every three months, as they would deserve by improving in their business, and the expectation of these high wages to come on hereafter was what he had drawn them in with. Meredith was to work at press, Potts at bookbinding, which he by agreement, was to teach them, though he knew neither one nor t'other. John——a wild Irishman brought up to no business, whose service for four years Keimer had purchased from the captain of a ship. He too was to be made a pressman. George Webb, an Oxford scholar, whose time for four years he had likewise bought, intending him for a compositor: of whom more presently. And David Harry, a country boy, whom he had taken apprentice. I soon perceived that the intention of engaging me at wages so much higher than he had been used to give, was to have these raw cheap hands formed through me, and as soon as I had instructed them, then, they being all articled to him, he should be able to do without me. I went on however, very chearfully; put his printing house in order, which had been in great confusion, and brought his hands by degrees to mind their business and to do it better . . .

John the Irishman soon ran away. With the rest I began to live very agreably; for they all respected me, the more as they found Keimer incapable of instructing them, and that from me they learnt something daily. We never worked on a Saturday, that being Keimer's Sabbath. So I had two days for reading. My acquaintance with ingenious people in the town, increased. Keimer himself treated me with great civility, and apparent regard; and nothing now made me uneasy but my debt to Vernon, which I was yet unable to pay being hitherto but a poor economist. He however kindly made no demand of it.

Our printing house often wanted sorts, and there was no letter founder in America. I had seen types cast at James's in London, but without much attention to the manner: However I now contrived a mould, made use of the letters we had, as puncheons, struck the matrices in lead, and thus supplied in a pretty tolerable way all deficiencies. I also engraved several things on occasion. I made the ink, I was warehouseman and everything, in short quite a factotum.

But however serviceable I might be, I found that my services became every day of less importance, as the other hands improved in the business. And when Keimer paid my second quarter's wages, he let me know that he felt them too heavy, and thought I should make an abatement. He grew by degrees less civil, put on more of the master, frequently found fault, was captious and seemed ready for an out-breaking. I went on nevertheless with a good deal of patience, thinking that his incumbered circumstances were partly the cause. At length a trifle snapt our connexion. For a great noise happening near the courthouse, I put my head out of the window to see what was the matter. Keimer being in the street looked up and saw me, called out to me in a loud voice and angry tone to mind my business, adding some reproachful words, that nettled me the more for their publicity, all the neighbours who were looking out on the same occasion being witnesses how I was treated. He came up immediately into the printing house, continued the quarrel, high words passed on both sides, he gave me the quarter's warning we had stipulated, expressing a wish that he had not been obliged to so long a warning: I told him his wish was unnecessary for I would leave him that instant; and so taking my hat walked out of doors; desiring Meredith whom I saw below to take care of some things I left, and bring them to my lodging.

Meredith came accordingly in the evening, when we talked my affair over. He had conceived a great regard for me, and was very unwilling that I should leave the house while he remained in it. He dissuaded me from returning to my native country which I began to think of. He reminded me that Keimer was in debt for all he possessed, that his creditors began to be uneasy, that he kept his shop miserably, sold often without profit for ready money, and often trusted without keeping accounts. That he must therefore fail; which would make a vacancy I might profit of. I objected my want of money. He then let me know, that his father had a high opinion of me, and from some discourse that had passed between them, he was sure would advance money to set us up, if I would enter into partnership with him. My time, says he, will be out with Keimer in the spring. By that time we may have our press and types in from London: I am sensible I am no workman. If you like it, your skill in the business shall be set against the stock I furnish; and we will share the profits equally. The proposal was agreable, and I consented. His father was in town, and approved of it, the more as he saw I had great influence with his son, had prevailed on him to abstain long from dram-drinking, and he hoped might break him of that wretched habit entirely, when we came to be so closely connected. I gave an inventory to the father, who carried it to a merchant; the things were sent for; the secret was to be kept till they should arrive, and in the meantime I was to get work if I could at the other printing house. But I found no vacancy there, and so remained idle a few days, when Keimer, on a prospect of being employed to print some paper money, in New Jersey, which would require cuts and various types that I only could supply, and apprehending Bradford might engage me and get the jobb from him, sent me a very civil message, that old friends should not part for a few words the effect of sudden passion, and wishing me to return. Meredith persuaded me to comply, as it would give more opportunity for his improvement under my daily instructions. So I returned, and we went on more smoothly than for some time before. The New Jersey jobb was obtained. I contrived a copper-plate press for it, the first that had been seen in the country. I cut several ornaments and checks for the bills. We went together to Burlington, where I executed the whole to satisfaction, and he received so

large a sum for the work, as to be enabled thereby to keep his head
much longer above water . . .

Before I enter upon my public appearance in business it may
be well to let you know the then state of my mind, with regard
to my principles and morals, that you may see how far those influenced the future events of my life. My parent's [*sic*] had early
given me religious impressions, and brought me through my
childhood piously in the Dissenting way. But I was scarce fifteen
when, after doubting by turns of several points as I found them
disputed in the different books I read, I began to doubt of Rev-
elation itself. Some books against Deism fell into my hands; they
were said to be the substance of sermons preached at Boyle's lectures. It happened that they wrought an effect on me quite contrary to what was intended by them: For the arguments of the
Deists which were quoted to be refuted, appeared to me much
stronger than the refutations. In short I soon became a thorough
Deist. . . . I never doubted, for instance, the existence of the Deity;
that he made the world, and governed it by his providence; that
the most acceptable service of God was the doing good to man;
that our souls are immortal; and that all crime will be punished,
and virtue rewarded, either here or hereafter. These I esteemed
the essentials of every religion; and, being to be found in all the
religions we had in our country, I respected them all, though with
different degrees of respect, as I found them more or less mixed
with other articles, which, without any tendency to inspire, promote or confirm morality, served principally to divide us, and
make us unfriendly to one another . . . Though I seldom attended any public worship, I had still an opinion of its propriety,
and of its utility when rightly conducted, and I paid my annual
subscription for the support of the only Presbyterian minister or
meeting we had in Philadelphia . . .

It was about this time I conceived the bold and arduous project
of arriving at moral perfection. I wished to live without committing any fault at any time; I would conquer all that either natural
inclination, custom, or company might lead me into. As I knew,
or thought I knew, what was right and wrong, I did not see why
I might not always do the one and avoid the other. But I soon
found I had undertaken a task of more difficulty than I had imagined. While my care was employed in guarding against one fault,

X

I was often surprized by another; habit took the advantage of inattention; inclination was sometimes too strong for reason. I concluded, at length, that the mere speculative conviction that it was our interest to be completely virtuous, was not sufficient to prevent our slipping; and that the contrary habits must be broken, and good ones acquired and established, before we can have any dependence on a steady, uniform rectitude of conduct. For this purpose I therefore contrived the following method.

In the various enumerations of the moral virtues I had met with in my reading, I found the catalogue more or less numerous, as different writers included more or fewer ideas under the same name. Temperance, for example, was by some confined to eating and drinking, while by others it was extended to mean the moderating every other pleasure, appetite, inclination, or passion, bodily or mental, even to our avarice and ambition. I proposed to myself, for the sake of clearness, to use rather more names, with fewer ideas annexed to each, than a few names with more ideas; and I included under thirteen names of virtues all that at that time occurred to me as necessary or desirable, and annexed to each a short precept, which fully expressed the extent I gave to its meaning.

These names of virtues, with their precepts, were:

1. *Temperance*
Eat not to dullness; drink not to elevation.

2. *Silence*
Speak not but what may benefit others or yourself; avoid trifling conversation.

3. *Order*
Let all your things have their places; let each part of your business have its time.

4. *Resolution*
Resolve to perform what you ought; perform without fail what you resolve.

5. *Frugality*
Make no expense but to do good to others or yourself; *i.e.*, waste nothing.

6. *Industry*
Lose no time; be always employed in something useful; cut off all unnecessary actions.

7. *Sincerity*
Use no hurtful deceit; think innocently and justly, and, if you speak, speak accordingly.

8. *Justice*
Wrong none by doing injuries, or omitting the benefits that are your duty.

9. *Moderation*
Avoid extreams; forbear resenting injuries so much as you think they deserve.

10. *Cleanliness*
Tolerate no uncleanliness in body, cloaths, or habitation.

11. *Tranquillity*
Be not disturbed at trifles, or at accidents common or unavoidable.

12. *Chastity*
Rarely use venery but for health or offspring, never to dullness, weakness, or the injury of your own or another's peace or reputation.

13. *Humility*
Imitate Jesus and Socrates.

My intention being to acquire the *habitude* of all these virtues, I judged it would be well not to distract my attention by attempting the whole at once, but to fix it on one of them at a time; and, when I should be master of that, then to proceed to another, and so on, till I should have gone through the thirteen; and, as the previous acquisition of some might facilitate the acquisition of certain others, I arranged them with that view, as they stand above. Temperance first, as it tends to procure that coolness and clearness of head, which is so necessary where constant vigilance was to be kept up, and guard maintained against the unremitting attraction of ancient habits, and the force of perpetual temptations. This being acquired and established, Silence would be more easy; and my desire being to gain knowledge at the same time that I improved in virtue, and considering that in conversation it was obtained rather by the use of the ears than of the tongue, and therefore wishing to break a habit I was getting into of prattling, punning, and joking, which only made me acceptable to trifling company, I gave *Silence* the second place. This and the next, *Order,* I expected would allow me more time for attending to my project and my studies. *Resolution,* once become habitual, would keep me firm in my endeavours to obtain all the subsequent virtues; *Frugality* and Industry freeing me from my remaining debt, and producing affluence and independence, would make more easy the practice of Sincerity and Justice, etc., etc. Conceiving then, that, agreeably to the advice of Pythagoras in his *Golden Verses,* daily examination would be necessary, I contrived the following method for conducting that examination.

I made a little book, in which I allotted a page for each of the virtues. I ruled each page with red ink, so as to have seven columns, one for each day of the week, marking each column with a letter for the day. I crossed these columns with thirteen red lines, marking the beginning of each line with the first letter of one of the virtues, on which line, and in its proper column, I might mark, by a little black spot, every fault I found upon examination to have been committed respecting that virtue upon that day . . .

I entered upon the execution of this plan for self-examination, and continued it with occasional intermissions for some time. I was surprized to find myself so much fuller of faults than I had imagined; but I had the satisfaction of seeing them diminish . . .

My scheme of ORDER gave me the most trouble; and I found that, though it might be practicable where a man's business was such as to leave him the disposition of his time, that of a journeyman printer, for instance, it was not possible to be exactly observed by a master, who must mix with the world, and often receive people of business at their own hours. Order, too, with regard to places for things, papers, etc., I found extreamly difficult to acquire. I had not been early accustomed to it, and, having an exceeding good memory, I was not so sensible of the inconvenience attending want of method. This article, therefore, cost me so much painful attention, and my faults in it vexed me so much, and I made so little progress in amendment, and had such frequent relapses, that I was almost ready to give up the attempt, and content myself with a faulty character in that respect, like the man who, in buying an ax of a smith, my neighbour, desired to have the whole of its surface as bright as the edge. The smith consented to grind it bright for him if he would turn the wheel; he turned, while the smith pressed the broad face of the ax hard and heavily on the stone, which made the turning of it very fatiguing. The man came every now and then from the wheel to see how the work went on, and at length would take his ax as it was, without farther grinding. 'No,' said the smith, 'turn on, turn on; we shall have it bright by-and-by; as yet, it is only speckled.' 'Yes,' says the man, *'but I think I like a speckled ax best.'* And I believe this may have been the case with many, who, having, for want of some such means as I employed, found the difficulty of obtaining good and breaking bad habits in other points of vice and virtue, have given up the struggle, and concluded that *'a speckled ax was best';* for something, that pretended to be reason, was every now and then suggesting to me that such extream nicety as I exacted of myself might be a kind of foppery in morals, which, if it were known, would make me ridiculous; that a perfect character might be attended with the inconvenience of being envied and hated; and that a benevolent man should allow a few faults in himself, to keep his friends in countenance . . .

❨ In reality, there is, perhaps, no one of our natural passions so hard to subdue as *Pride*. Disguise it, struggle with it, beat it down, stifle it, mortify it as much as one pleases, it is still alive, and will every now and then peep out and show itself; you will see it, perhaps, often in this history; for, even if I could conceive that I had compleatly overcome it, I should probably be proud of my humility . . . ❩

I should have mentioned before, that in the autumn of the preceeding year I had formed most of my ingenious acquaintance into a club of mutual improvement, which we called the

Junto. We met on Friday evenings. The rules I drew up required that every member in his turn should produce one or more queries on any point of morals, politics or natural philosophy, to be discussed by the company, and once in three months produce and read an essay of his own writing on any subject he pleased. Our debates were to be under the direction of a president and to be conducted in the sincere spirit of enquiry after truth, without fondness for dispute, or desire of victory; and to prevent warmth all expressions of positiveness in opinions or direct contradiction, were after some time made contraband and prohibited under small pecuniary penalties.

The Junto, modelled on Cotton Mather's neighbourhood Benefit Societies, thus consisted of a group of friends with many interests but linked by a hunger for self-improvement. In it were silver-smiths and glaziers, printers and surveyors, shoemakers and iron-masters, all working people and thus, as they also called themselves, a Club of Leather Aprons. One Junto spawned others. From it emerged the first subscription library in America, the American Philosophical Society (founded in 1744 and still active) and Franklin's civic projects, such as the Union Fire Company, the city hospital and, eventually, the University of Pennsylvania.

The first members were Joseph Breintnal, a copyer of deeds for the scriveners; a good-natured friendly middle-aged man, a great lover of poetry, reading all he could meet with, and writing some that was tolerable; very ingenious in many little nick-nackeries, and of sensible conversation. Thomas Godfrey, a self-taught mathematician, great in his way, and afterwards inventor of what is now called Hadley's Quadrant. But he knew little out of his way, and was not a pleasing companion, as like most great mathematicians I have met with, he expected universal precision in everything said, or was forever denying or distinguishing upon trifles, to the disturbance of all conversation. He soon left us. Nicholas Scull, a surveyor, afterwards Surveyor-General, who loved books, and sometimes made a few verses. William Parsons, bred a shoemaker, but loving reading, had acquired a considerable share of mathematics, which he first studied with a view to astrology that he afterwards laught at. He also became Surveyor-General. William Maugridge, a joiner, a most exquisite mechanic and a solid sensible man. Hugh Meredith, Stephen Potts, and George Webb, I have characterized before. Robert Grace, a young gentleman of some fortune, generous, lively and witty, a lover of punning and of his friends. And William Coleman, then a merchant's clerk, about my age, who had the coolest clearest head, the best heart, and the exactest morals, of almost any man I ever met with. He became afterwards a merchant of great note, and one of our provincial judges. Our friendship continued without interruption to his death upwards of forty years. And the club continued almost as long, and was the best school of philosophy, and politics that then existed in the province; for our queries which were read the week preceding their discussion, put us on reading with attention upon the several subjects, that we might speak more to the purpose: and here too we acquired better habits of conversation, everything being studied in our Rules which might prevent our disgusting each other . . .

George Webb, who had found a friend that lent him wherewith to purchase his time of Keimer, now came to offer himself as a journeyman to us. We could not then imploy him, but I foolishly let him know, as a secret, that I soon intended to begin a newspaper, and might then have work for him. My hopes of success as I told him were founded on this, that the then only newspaper [the *American Weekly Mercury*], printed by Bradford was a paltry thing, wretchedly managed, no way entertaining; and yet was profitable to him. I therefore thought a good paper could scarcely fail of good encouragement. I requested Webb not to mention it, but he told it to Keimer, who immediately, to be beforehand with me, published proposals for printing one himself, on which Webb was to be employed. I resented this, and to counteract them, as I could not yet begin our paper, I wrote several pieces of entertainment for Bradford's paper, under the title of The Busy-body which Breintnal continued some months. By this means the attention of the publick was fixed on that paper, and Keimer's proposals which we burlesqued and ridiculed, were disregarded. He began his paper however, and after carrying it on three-quarters of a year, with at most only ninety subscribers, he offered it to me for a trifle, and I having been ready some time to go on with it, took it in hand directly, and it proved in a few years extreamely profit-able to me.

I perceive that I am apt to speak in the singular number, though our partnership still continued. The reason may be, that in fact the whole management of the business lay upon me. Meredith was no compositor, a poor pressman, and seldom sober. My friends lamented my connection with him, but I was to make the best of it.

But now another difficulty came upon me, which I had never the least reason to expect. Mr Meredith's father, who was to have paid for our printing house according to the expectations given me, was able to advance only one hundred pounds, cur-rency, which had been paid, and a hundred more was due to the merchant; who grew impatient and sued us all. We gave bail, but saw that if the money could not be raised in time, the suit must come to a judgment and execution, and our hopeful prospects must with us be ruined, as the press and letters must be sold for payment, perhaps at half price. In this distress two true friends whose kindness I have never forgotten nor ever shall forget while I can remember anything, came to me sepa-rately, unknown to each other, and without any application from me, offering each of them to advance me all the money that should be necessary to enable me to take the whole busi-ness upon myself if that should be practicable, but they did not like my continuing the partnership with Meredith, who as they said was often seen drunk in the streets, and playing at low games in alehouses, much to our discredit. These two friends were *William Coleman* and *Robert Grace*. I told them I could not propose a separation while any prospect remained of the Merediths fulfilling their part of our agreement. Because I thought myself under great obligations to them for what they had done and would do if they could. But if they finally failed in their performance, and our partnership must be dissolved, I should then think myself at liberty to accept the assistance of my friends. Thus the matter rested for some time. When I said to my partner, perhaps your father is dissatisfied at the part you have undertaken in this affair of ours, and is unwilling to ad-vance for you and me what he would for you alone: If that is the case, tell me, and I will resign the whole to you and go about

my business. No, says he, my father has really been disappointed and is really unable; and I am unwilling to distress him
farther. I see this is a business I am not fit for. I was bred a
farmer, and it was a folly in me to come to town and put myself
at thirty years of age an apprentice to learn a new trade. Many
of our Welsh people are going to settle in North Carolina where
land is cheap: I am inclined to go with them, and following my
old employment. You may find friends to assist you. If you will
take the debts of the company upon you, return to my father
the hundred pound he has advanced, pay my little personal
debts, and give me 30 pounds and a new saddle, I will relinquish the partnership and leave the whole in your hands. I
agreed to this proposal. It was drawn up in writing, signed and
sealed immediately. I gave him what he demanded and he went
soon after to Carolina; from whence he sent me next year two
long letters, containing the best account that had been given of
that country, the climate, soil, husbandry, etc. for in those matters he was very judicious. I printed them in the papers, and
they gave grate satisfaction to the publick.

As soon as he was gone, I recurred to my two friends; and
because I would not give an unkind preference to either, I took
half what each had offered and I wanted, of one, and half of the
other; paid off the company debts, and went on with the business in my own name, advertising that the partnership was
dissolved. I think this was in or about the year 1729 [14 July
1730] . . .

I now opened a little stationer's shop. I had in it blanks of all
sorts, the correctest that ever appeared among us, being assisted in that by my friend Breintnal; I had also paper, parchment, chapmen's books, etc. One Whitemarsh, a compositor I
had known in London, an excellent workman now came to me
and worked with me constantly and diligently, and I took an
apprentice the son of Aquila Rose. I began now gradually to
pay off the debt I was under for the printing house. In order to
secure my credit and character as a tradesman, I took care not
only to be in *reality* industrious and frugal, but to avoid all
appearances of the contrary. I drest plainly; I was seen at no
places of idle diversion; I never went out a fishing or shooting;

a book, indeed, sometimes debauched me from my work; but that was seldom, snug, and gave no scandal: and to show that I was not above my business, I sometimes brought home the paper I purchased at the stores, through the streets on a wheel-barrow. Thus being esteemed an industrious thriving young man, and paying duly for what I bought, the merchants who imported stationary solicited my custom, others proposed sup-plying me with books, I went on swimmingly. In the meantime Keimer's credit and business declining daily, he was at last forced to sell his printing house to satisfy his creditors. He went to Barbadoes, there lived some years, in very poor circum-stances . . .

In the meantime, that hard-to-be-governed passion of youth, had hurried me frequently into intrigues with low women that fell in my way, which were attended with some expence and great inconvenience, besides a continual risque to my health by a distemper which of all things I dreaded, though by great good luck I escaped it.

A friendly correspondence as neighbours and old acquain-tances, had continued between me and Mrs Read's family, who all had a regard for me from the time of my first lodging in their house. I was often invited there and consulted in their affairs, wherein I sometimes was of service. I pitied poor Miss Read's unfortunate situation, who was generally dejected, sel-dom chearful, and avoided company. I considered my giddi-ness and inconstancy when in London as in a great degree the cause of her unhappiness; though the mother was good enough to think the fault more her own than mine, as she had pre-vented our marrying before I went thither, and persuaded the other match in my absence. Our mutual affection was revived, but there were now great objections to our union. That match was indeed looked upon as invalid, a preceeding wife being said to be living in England; but this could not easily be proved, because of the distance. And though there was a report of his death, it was not certain. Then though it should be true, he had left many debts which his successor might be called on to pay. We ventured however, over all these difficulties, and I took her to wife 1 September 1730. None of the inconveniencies hap-pened that we had apprehended, she proved a good and faith-

Deborah Franklin

ful helpmate, assisted me much by attending the shop, we throve together, and have ever mutually endeavoured to make each other happy. Thus I corrected that great *Erratum* as well as I could.

There was no grand passion between Franklin and Deborah. She did not share her husband's intellectual tastes nor join in his social activities. But Debby was long-suffering as well as industrious, frugal and kind-hearted. She also brought William, Benjamin's illegitimate son by an unknown mother, into their home to live with them. William may, of course, have been her own son, unacknowledged lest Rogers return? We shall never know.

The Franklins had two children of their own: Francis Folger Franklin (Franky), born in 1732, who died of smallpox when he was four; and Sarah (Sally), born in 1743. When Debby died in 1774, she had not seen her husband since he left for London in 1764.

At the time I established myself in Pennsylvania, there was not a good bookseller's shop in any of the colonies to the southward of Boston. In New York and Philadelphia the printers were indeed stationers; they sold only paper, etc., almanacs, ballads, and a few common school-books. Those who loved reading were obliged to send for their books from England; the members of the Junto had each a few. We had left the alehouse, where we first met, and hired a room to hold our club in. I proposed that we should all of us bring our books to that room, where they would not only be ready to consult in our conferences, but become a common benefit, each of us being at liberty to borrow such as he wished to read at home. This was accordingly done, and for some time contented us.

Finding the advantage of this little collection, I proposed to render the benefit from books more common, by commencing a public subscription library. I drew a sketch of the plan and rules that would be necessary, and got a skilful conveyancer, Mr Charles Brockden, to put the whole in form of articles of agreement to be subscribed, by which each subscriber engaged to pay a certain sum down for the first purchase of books, and an annual contribution for increasing them. So few were the readers at that time in Philadelphia, and the majority of us so poor, that I was not able, with great industry, to find more than fifty persons, mostly young tradesmen, willing to pay down for this purpose 40 shillings each, and 10 shillings per annum. On this little fund we began. The books were imported; the library was opened one day in the week for lending to the subscribers, on their promissory notes to pay double the value if not duly returned. The institution soon manifested its utility, was imitated by other towns, and in other provinces. The libraries were augmented by donations; reading became fashionable; and our people, having no publick amusements to divert their attention from study, became better acquainted with books, and in a few years were observed by strangers to be better instructed and more intelligent than people of the same rank generally are in other countries.

When we were about to sign the above-mentioned articles, which were to be binding on us, our heirs, etc., for fifty years, Mr Brockden, the scrivener, said to us, 'You are young men, but it is scarcely probable that any of you will live to see the expiration of the term fixed in the instrument.' A number of us, however, are yet living; but the instrument was after a few years rendered null by a charter that incorporated and gave perpetuity to the company.

The objections and reluctances I met with in soliciting the subscriptions, made me soon feel the impropriety of presenting one's self as the proposer of any useful project, that might be supposed to raise one's reputation in the smallest degree above that of one's neighbours, when one has need of their assistance to accomplish that project. I therefore put myself as much as I could out of sight and stated it as a scheme of a *number of friends*, who had requested me to go about and propose it to such as they thought lovers of reading. In this way my affair went on more smoothly, and I ever after practised it on such occasions; and, from my frequent successes, can heartily recommend it. The present little sacrifice of your vanity will afterwards be amply repaid. If it remains a while uncertain to whom the merit belongs, someone more vain than yourself will be encouraged to claim it, and then even envy will be disposed to do you justice by plucking those assumed feathers, and restoring them to their right owner.

When Franklin next resumed his Autobiography *in retirement in Philadelphia in 1788, at the age of eighty-two, he recollected his enthusiasm, at the age of twenty-four, for a project more ambitious than his own model for perfect behaviour, more far-reaching in membership than the Junto: 'A United Party for Virtue, by forming the virtuous and good men of all nations into a regular body, to be governed by suitable good and wise rules.' Among the notes that survived the war, he found one that had 'the substance of an intended creed, containing . . . the essentials of every known religion':*

'That there is one God, who made all things.

'That he governs the world by his providence.

'That he ought to be worshiped by adoration, prayer, and thanksgiving.

'But that the most acceptable service of God is doing good to man.

'That the soul is immortal.

'And that God will certainly reward virtue and punish vice, either here or hereafter.'

My ideas at that time were, that the sect should be begun and spread at first among young and single men only; that each person to be initiated should not only declare his assent to such creed, but should have exercised himself with the thirteen weeks' examination and practice of the virtues, as in the before-mentioned model; that the existence of such a society should be kept a secret, till it was become considerable, to prevent solicitations for the admission of improper persons, but that the members should each of them search among his acquaintance for ingenuous, well-disposed youths, to whom, with prudent caution, the scheme should be gradually communicated; that the members should engage to afford their advice, assistance, and support to each other in promoting one another's interests, business, and advancement in life; that, for distinction, we should be called *The Society of the Free and Easy:* free, as being, by the general practice and habit of the virtues, free from the dominion of vice; and particularly by the practice of industry and frugality, free from debt, which exposes a man to confinement, and a species of slavery to his creditors.

This is as much as I can now recollect of the project, except that I communicated it in part to two young men, who adopted it with some enthusiasm; but my then narrow circumstances, and the necessity I was under of sticking close to my business, occasioned my postponing the further prosecution of it at that time; and my multifarious occupations, public and private, induced me to continue postponing, so that it has been omitted till I have no longer strength or activity left sufficient for such an enterprise; though I am still of opinion that it was a practicable scheme, and might have been very useful, by forming a great number of good citizens; and I was not discouraged by the seeming magnitude of the undertaking, as I have always thought that one man of tolerable abilities may work great changes, and accomplish great affairs among mankind, if he first forms a good plan, and, cutting off all amusements or other employments that would divert his attention, makes the execution of that same plan his sole study and business.

In 1729 Benjamin Franklin became the sole owner of the Pennsylvania Gazette, *the newspaper which, under Keimer, had failed to prosper. Two years later, as its editor (having bought out Meredith), he wrote 'an apology for printers'—as relevant now as it was then:*

I request all who are angry with me on the account of printing things they don't like, calmly to consider these following particulars.

1. That the opinions of men are almost as various as their faces; an observation general enough to become a common proverb, *So many men so many minds.*

2. That the business of printing has chiefly to do with men's opinions; most things that are printed tending to promote some, or oppose others.

3. That hence arises the peculiar unhappiness of that business, which other callings are no way liable to; they who follow printing being scarce able to do anything in their way of getting a living, which shall not probably give offence to some, and perhaps to many; whereas the smith, the shoemaker, the carpenter, or the man of any other trade, may work indifferently for people of all persuasions, without offending any of them: and the merchant may buy and sell with Jews, Turks, Hereticks

and Infidels of all sorts, and get money by every one of them, without giving offence to the most orthodox, of any sort; or suffering the least censure or ill-will on the account from any man whatever.

4. That it is as unreasonable in any one man or set of men to expect to be pleased with everything that is printed, as to think that nobody ought to be pleased but themselves.

5. Printers are educated in the belief, that when men differ in opinion, both sides ought equally to have the advantage of being heard by the publick; and that when truth and error have fair play, the former is always an overmatch for the latter: Hence they chearfully serve all contending writers that pay them well, without regarding on which side they are of the question in dispute.

6. Being thus continually employed in serving both parties, printers naturally acquire a vast unconcernedness as to the right or wrong opinions contained in what they print; regarding it only as the matter of their daily labour: They print things full of spleen and animosity, with the utmost calmness and indifference, and without the least ill-will to the persons reflected on; who nevertheless unjustly think the printer as much their enemy as the author, and join both together in their resentment.

7. That it is unreasonable to imagine printers approve of everything they print, and to censure them on any particular thing accordingly; since in the way of their business they print such great variety of things opposite and contradictory. It is likewise as unreasonable what some assert, 'That printers ought not to print anything but what they approve;' since if all of that business should make such a resolution, and abide by it, an end would thereby be put to free writing, and the world would afterwards have nothing to read but what happened to be the opinions of printers.

8. That if all printers were determined not to print anything till they were sure it would offend nobody, there would be very little printed.

9. That if they sometimes print vicious or silly things not worth reading, it may not be because they approve such things themselves, but because the people are so viciously and cor-

ruptly educated that good things are not encouraged. I have
known a very numerous impression of Robin Hood's Songs go
off in this province at 2 shillings per book, in less than a twelve-
month; when a small quantity of David's Psalms (an excellent
version) have lain upon my hands above twice the time.

10. That notwithstanding what might be urged in behalf of
a man's being allowed to do in the way of his business whatever
he is paid for, yet printers do continually discourage the printing of great numbers of bad things, and stifle them in the birth.
I myself have constantly refused to print anything that might
countenance vice, or promote immorality; though by complying in such cases with the corrupt taste of the majority I might
have got much money. I have also always refused to print such
things as might do real injury to any person, how much soever
I have been solicited, and tempted with offers of great pay; and
how much soever I have by refusing got the ill-will of those who
would have employed me. I have hitherto fallen under the
resentment of large bodies of men, for refusing absolutely to
print any of their party or personal reflections. In this manner
I have made myself many enemies, and the constant fatigue of
denying is almost insupportable. But the publick being unacquainted with all this, whenever the poor printer happens either through ignorance or much perusasion, to do anything
that is generally thought worthy of blame, he meets with no
more friendship or favour on the above account, than if there
were no merit in't at all. Thus, as Waller says,

> Poets lose half the praise they would have got
> Were it but known what they discreetly blot;

Yet are censured for every bad line found in their works with
the utmost severity.

*The 'Apology' was a remarkably brave statement to be made by a young
editor with no resources and no standing other than his own talents. As
a declaration of intent, it recalled his brother's readiness to confront
authority, although Philadelphia was more tolerant than Boston. But,
given the frequent paucity of hard news, Franklin had often to invent,
to embroider, to tell a tale, to use many pseudonyms. He never quite
broke himself of the habit. However, he certainly produced a readable,*

*varied and fascinating journal, as the following example shows. He
also rapidly became the most active master printer and publisher in the
most thriving city in North America:*

A WITCH TRIAL AT MOUNT HOLLY

From the *Pennsylvania Gazette,* 22 October 1730

Saturday last, at Mount Holly, about eight miles from this place
[Burlington, N.J.] near 300 people were gathered together to
see an experiment or two tried on some persons accused of
witchcraft. It seems the accused had been charged with making
their neighbours' sheep dance in an uncommon manner, and
with causing hogs to speak and sing psalms, etc., to the great
terror and amazement of the king's good and peaceable subjects in this province; and the accusers, being very positive that
if the accused were weighed in scales against a Bible, the Bible
would prove too heavy for them; or that, if they were bound
and put into the river they would swim; the said accused, desirous to make innocence appear, voluntarily offered to undergo the said trials if two of the most violent of their accusers
would be tried with them. Accordingly the time and place was
agreed on and advertised about the country; the accusers were
one man and one woman: and the accused the same. The parties being met and the people got together, a grand consultation was held, before they proceeded to trial; in which it was
agreed to use the scales first; and a committee of men were
appointed to search the men, and a committee of women to
search the women, to see if they had anything of weight about
them, particularly pins. After the scrutiny was over a huge
great Bible belonging to the justice of the place was provided,
and a lane through the populace was made from the justice's
house to the scales, which were fixed on a gallows erected for
that purpose opposite to the house, that the justice's wife and
the rest of the ladies might see the trial without coming amongst
the mob, and after the manner of moorfields a large ring was
also made. Then came out of the house a grave, tall man carrying the Holy Writ before the supposed wizard etc., (as solemnly as the sword-bearer of London before the Lord Mayor)
the wizard was first put in the scale, and over him was read a

chapter out of the books of Moses, and then the Bible was put in the other scale, (which, being kept down before) was immediately let go; but, to the great surprize of the spectators, flesh and bones came down plump, and outweighed that great good Book by abundance. After the same manner the others were served, and their lumps of mortality severally were too heavy for Moses and all the prophets and apostles. This being over, the accusers and the rest of the mob, not satisfied with this experiment, would have the trial by water. Accordingly a most solemn procession was made to the mill-pond, where both accused and accusers being stripped (saving only to the women their shifts) were bound hand and foot and severally placed in the water, lengthways, from the side of a barge or flat, having for security only a rope about the middle of each, which was held by some in the flat. The accused man being thin and spare with some difficulty began to sink at last; but the rest, every one of them, swam very light upon the water. A sailor in the flat jumped out upon the back of the man accused thinking to drive him down to the bottom; but the person bound, without any help, came up some time before the other. The woman accuser being told that she did not sink, would be ducked a second time; when she swam again as light as before. Upon which she declared, that she believed the accused had bewitched her to make her so light, and that she would be ducked again a hundred times but she would duck the Devil out of her. The accused man, being surprized at his own swimming, was not so confident of his innocence as before, but said, 'If I am a witch, it is more than I know.' The more thinking part of the spectators were of opinion that any person so bound and placed in the water (unless they were mere skin and bones) would swim, till their breath was gone, and their lungs filled with water. But it being the general belief of the populace that the women's shifts and the garters with which they were bound helped to support them, it is said they are to be tried again the next warm weather, naked.

From 1733 to 1758 Franklin also published Poor Richard's Almanack. *This was a familiar format—when Franklin's first appeared, there were already six being printed in Philadelphia. In 'Poor Richard'*

Franklin printed common-sense observations and wise saws, culled mainly from Rabelais and Swift and Sterne—and he did not pretend to originality—'gleanings', he called them, 'of all ages and nations'. 'Why should I give my readers bad lines *of my own, when* good ones *of other people's are so plenty?' He made it not only the formula for his own financial success but the first great syndicated column in American journalism. He served up a rich fare: maxims, epigrams and proverbs, welcome as much for their familiarity as for their terseness; much commonplace moralizing, much worldly shrewdness, not a little bawdiness— for 'squeamish stomachs cannot eat without pickles'. He had to be, he said in 1737, 'not only . . . a piece of a wit, but a very wag'. He wrote with unerring skill and great charm for the colonial equivalent of the man in the street, in this case the man on the farm and on the frontier. He was 'the Roger de Coverley of the masses', to use Carl Becker's phrase, the voice of the New Man in the New World. Or as William Smith said in his eulogy in 1790, Poor Richard became 'the farmer's philosopher, the rural sage, the yeoman's and peasant's oracle'.*

Franklin wrote easily on half a hundred topics. The essay he printed in 1735 (and which we now know he wrote himself) also reveals his viewpoint—'Self-denial not the essence of virtue'. He confessed with gusto that he practised the frugality he preached just as long as poverty forced him to—and not a moment longer.

If many of these proverbs were centuries old, Franklin gave them vigour, clarity and punch, transforming them in the process. The Scots proverb 'A listening damsel and a speaking castle shall never end with honour' became, in Franklin's version, 'Neither a fortress nor a maid will hold out long after they begin to parley'. The English proverb 'God restoreth health and the physician hath the thanks' was changed to 'God restoreth health and the physician takes the fee'. 'Fresh fish and new-come guests smell, but that they are three days old' became, recalling his own father's view on visits from relations, 'Fish, and guests stink after three days'. 'The maintaining of one vice costeth more than ten virtues' became 'What maintains one vice would bring up two children', and 'A muffled cat is no good mouser' changed to 'The cat in gloves catches no mice'. He aimed at balance and brevity. 'The greatest talkers are the least doers' became 'Great talkers, little doers'. He knew the value of alliteration: 'Men and melons are hard to know'; 'Sloth and silence are fool's virtues'. In other cases Franklin added a thought to give the original a new twist, as in the proverb 'The king's cheese goes half away in parings', which he changed to 'The king's cheese is half wasted in parings; but no matter, 'tis made of the people's milk'.

Poor Richard has been regarded by many as the mentor of early American capitalism. His advice is certainly keyed to the two notes struck in his sayings: 'Work hard and count your pennies'; 'The sleeping fox catches no poultry'; 'Then plough deep, while sluggards sleep, and you shall have corn to sell and to keep'; 'Lost time is never found again'; 'He that hath a trade hath an estate, and he that hath a calling hath an office of profit and honour'.

The identification of Poor Richard with these principles was due to the collection of those sayings exhorting to industry and frugality into the preface to the 1757 Almanack, *to be put in the mouth of Father Abraham, and then to be separately printed as* The Way to Wealth. *It became, as* Bonhomme Richard, *fashionable in France (with immeasurable consequences in 1776). It has gone through some 1300 editions since it was first compiled.*

Not that all Poor Richard's moralities were exhortations to business enterprise. Some were of a homelier and an earthier sort. 'Love your neighbour, but don't pull down your hedge'; 'When you are good to others, you are best to yourself'; 'Three may keep a secret if two of them are dead'; 'A single man is like the odd half of a pair of scissors'; 'He that takes a wife takes care'; 'Keep your eyes wide open before marriage, half shut afterwards'; 'You cannot pluck roses without fear of thorns, nor enjoy a fair wife without danger of horns'. Yet in nothing is Franklin more typical of his century and of his country than in his insistence that self-reliance and hard work are basic to liberty. A political creed was clear, but left, as always, implicit. He believed in free speech, free goods and free men. He opposed the efforts of all exploiters, whether merchants in England, Scots factors in America, landowners or priests, to restrain man's natural freedoms. And freedom, he argued, paid.

Here are some examples:

PREFACE TO POOR RICHARD, 1733

COURTEOUS READER,

I might in this place attempt to gain thy favour, by declaring that I write Almanacks with no other view than that of the publick good; but in this I should not be sincere; and men are nowadays too wise to be deceived by pretences how specious soever. The plain truth of the matter is, I am excessive poor, and my wife, good woman, is, I tell her, excessive proud; she cannot bear, she says, to sit spinning in her shift of tow, while I do nothing but gaze at the stars; and has threatened more than once to burn all my books and rattling-traps (as she calls my instruments) if I do not make some profitable use of them for the good of my family. The printer has offered me some considerable share of the profits, and I have thus begun to comply with my dame's desire.

PREFACE TO POOR RICHARD, 1734

COURTEOUS READERS,

Your kind and charitable assistance last year, in purchasing so large an impression of my Almanacks, has made my circumstances much more easy in the world, and requires my grateful acknowledgment. My wife has been enabled to get a pot of her own, and is no longer obliged to borrow one from a neighbour; nor have we ever since been without something of our own to put in it. She has also got a pair of shoes, two new shifts, and a new warm petticoat; and for my part, I have bought a second-hand coat, so good, that I am now not ashamed to go to town or be seen there. These things have rendered her temper so much more pacifick than it used to be, that I may say, I have slept more, and more quietly within this last year, than in the three foregoing years put together. Accept my hearty thanks therefor, and my sincere wishes for your health and prosperity.

[ADVERTISEMENT] Notice is hereby given to all persons, that there is come to town, a very wonderful and surprizing creature to all persons in these parts of the world; and it is in scripture the very same creature, which is there called a *Camel*. It is impossible to describe the creature, and therefore all persons of ingenious curiosity have an opportunity of satisfying themselves.

The creature was brought with great difficulty from the desarts of Arabia in that quarter of the world which is called Asia, to New England; a curiosity which never was in this country, and very likely never will be again.

Constant attendance will be given to all persons desirous of seeing said creature at the house of Owen Owen, Esq. at the Sign of the Indian King in Philadelphia.

[22 *May 1740*]

Friend Franklin, I have again necessity for troubling thy newspaper, about Mary my wife: It was force that made me comply with publishing the last Advertisement in thy paper. Pray insert in thy paper now, that she abuses me her husband so much that I cannot live with her: And I forwarn all persons from trusting her on my account, after the date hereof.

15 March 1742,3

RICHARD LEADAME
[*17 March*]

COURTS

A person threatning to go to law, was dissuaded from it by his friend, who desired him to *consider,* for the law was chargeable. I don't care, replied the other, I will not consider, I'll go to law. Right, said his friend, for if you go to law I am sure you don't consider.

> *A farmer once made a complaint to a judge,*
> *My bull, if it please you, sir, owing a grudge,*
> *Belike to one of your good worship's cattle,*
> *Has slain him outright in a mortal battle:*
> *I'm sorry at heart because of the action,*
> *And want to know how must be made satisfaction.*
> *Why, you must give me your bull, that's plain*
> *Says the judge, or pay me the price of the slain.*
> *But I have mistaken the case, sir, says John,*
> *The dead bull I talk of, and please you, 's my own:*
> *And yours is the beast that the mischief has done.*
> *The judge soon replies with a serious face:*
> *Say you so; then this accident alters the case.*

[*1743*]

COURTEOUS READER,

This is the fifteenth time I have entertained thee with my annual productions; I hope to thy profit as well as mine. For besides the astronomical calculations, and other things usually contained in Almanacks, which have their daily use indeed while the year continues, but then become of no value, I have constantly interspersed *moral* sentences, *prudent* maxims, and *wise* sayings, many of them containing *much good sense* in *very few* words, and therefore apt to leave *strong* and *lasting* impressions on the memory of young persons, whereby they may receive benefit as long as they live, when both Almanack and Almanack-maker have been long thrown by and forgotten. If I now and then insert a joke or two, that seem to have little in them, my apology is, that such may have their use, since perhaps for their sake light airy minds peruse the rest, and so are struck by somewhat of more weight and moment. The verses on the heads of the months are also generally designed to have the same tendency. I need not tell thee that not many of them are of my own making. If thou hast any judgment in poetry, thou wilt easily discern the workman from the bungler. I know as well as thee, that I am no *poet born;* and it is a trade I never learnt, nor indeed could learn. *If I make verses, 'tis in spight—Of Nature and my stars, I write.* Why then should I give my readers *bad lines* of my own, when *good ones* of other people's are so plenty? 'Tis methinks a poor excuse for the bad entertainment of guests, that the food we set before them, though coarse and ordinary, is *of one's own raising, off one's own plantation,* etc. when there is plenty of what is ten times better, to be had in the market. On the contrary, I assure ye, my friends, that I have procured the best I could for ye, and *much good may't do ye.*

I cannot omit this opportunity of making honourable mention of the late deceased ornament and head of our profession, Mr JACOB TAYLOR, who for upwards of forty years (with some few intermissions only) supplied the good people of this and the neighbouring colonies, with the most compleat ephemeris and most accurate calculations that have hitherto appeared in America. He was an ingenious mathematician, as well as an expert and skilful astronomer; and moreover, no mean philos-

opher, but what is more than all, He was a PIOUS and an HON-
EST man. *Requiescat in pace.*

I am thy poor friend, to serve thee,

R. SAUNDERS

[*1746*]

Monday. October hath xxxi days.

One to destroy, is murder by the law,
And gibbets keep the lifted hand in awe.
To murder thousands, takes a specious name,
War's glorious art, and gives immortal fame.
O great alliance! O divine renown!
With death and pestilence to share the crown!
When men extol a wild destroyer's name,
Earth's builder and preserver they blaspheme.

[*1747*]

In 1736, Franklin became Clerk of the Pennsylvania General As-
sembly and began to turn his thoughts to public affairs:

The city watch was one of the first things that I conceived to
want regulation. It was managed by the constables of the respective wards in turn; the constable warned a number of
housekeepers to attend him for the night. Those who chose
never to attend, paid him 6 shillings a year to be excused, which
was supposed to be for hiring substitutes, but was, in reality,
much more than was necessary for that purpose, and made the
constableship a place of profit; and the constable, for a little
drink, often got such ragamuffins about him as a watch, that
respectable housekeepers did not choose to mix with. Walking
the rounds, too, was often neglected, and most of the nights
spent in tippling. I thereupon wrote a paper to be read in
Junto, representing these irregularities, but insisting more particularly on the inequality of this 6-shilling tax of the constables,
respecting the circumstances of those who paid it, since a poor
widow housekeeper, all whose property to be guarded by the
watch did not perhaps exceed the value of 50 pounds, paid as
much as the wealthiest merchant, who had thousands of
pounds' worth of goods in his stores.

On the whole, I proposed as a more effectual watch, the hiring of proper men to serve constantly in that business; and as a more equitable way of supporting the charge, the levying a tax that should be proportioned to the property. This idea, being approved by the Junto, was communicated to the other clubs, but as arising in each of them; and though the plan was not immediately carried into execution, yet, by preparing the minds of people for the change, it paved the way for the law obtained a few years after, when the members of our clubs were grown into more influence.

About this time I wrote a paper (first to be read in Junto, but it was afterward published) on the different accidents and carelessnesses by which houses were set on fire, with cautions against them, and means proposed of avoiding them. This was much spoken of as a useful piece, and gave rise to a project, which soon followed it, of forming a company for the more ready extinguishing of fires, and mutual assistance in removing and securing of goods when in danger. Associates in this scheme were presently found, amounting to thirty. Our articles of agreement obliged every member to keep always in good order, and fit for use, a certain number of leather buckets, with strong bags and baskets (for packing and transporting of goods), which were to be brought to every fire; and we agreed to meet once a month and spend a social evening together, in discoursing and communicating such ideas as occurred to us upon the subject of fires, as might be useful in our conduct on such occasions.

The utility of this institution soon appeared, and many more desiring to be admitted than we thought convenient for one company, they were advised to form another, which was accordingly done; and this went on, one new company being formed after another, till they became so numerous as to include most of the inhabitants who were men of property; and now, at the time of my writing this, though upward of fifty years since its establishment, that which I first formed, called the Union Fire Company, still subsists and flourishes, though the first members are all deceased but myself and one, who is older by a year than I am.

Franklin reckoned that he had abundant reason to be satisfied with being established in business in Pennsylvania. He was also happily

married, as can be judged by the following verses—to which he did not
lay claim, but which were probably composed by him around 1742. By
that time he had been married for twelve years:

> *Of their Chloes and Phillisses poets may prate*
> *   I sing my plain country Joan*
> *Now twelve years my wife, still the joy of my life*
> *   Blest day that I made her my own,*
> *   My dear friends*
> *   Blest day that I made her my own.*

> *Not a word of her face, her shape, or her eyes,*
> *   Of flames or of darts shall you hear;*
> *Though I beauty admire 'tis virtue I prize,*
> *   That fades not in seventy years,*
> *   My dear friends*

> *In health a companion delightfull and dear,*
> *   Still easy, engaging, and free,*
> *In sickness no less than the faithfullest nurse*
> *   As tender as tender can be,*
> *   My dear friends*

> *In peace and good order, my household she keeps*
> *   Right careful to save what I gain*
> *Yet chearfully spends, and smiles on the friends*
> *   I've the pleasures to entertain*
> *   My dear friends*

> *She defends my good name ever where I'm to blame,*
> *   Friend firmer was ne'er to man given,*
> *Her compassionate breast, feels for all the distrest,*
> *   Which draws down the blessing from heaven,*
> *   My dear friends*

> *Am I laden with care, she takes off a large share,*
> *   That the burthen ne'er makes me to reel,*
> *Does good fortune arrive, the joy of my wife,*
> *   Quite doubles the pleasures I feel,*
> *   My dear friends*

Benjamin Franklin aged about 40

In raptures the giddy rake talks of his fair,
*   Enjoyment shall make him despise,*
I speak my cool sence, that long experience,
*   And enjoyment have changed in no wise,*
                    My dear friends

Some faults we have all, and so may my Joan,
*   But then they're exceedingly small;*
And now I'm used to 'em, they're just like my own,
*   I scarcely can see 'em at all,*
                    My dear friends,
*   I scarcely can see them at all.*

Were the fairest young princess, with million in purse
*   To be had in exchange for my Joan,*
She could not be a better wife, mought be a worse,
*   So I'd stick to my Joggy alone*
                    My dear friends
*   I'd cling to my lovely ould Joan.*

THREE

A MIDDLING AND A RISING PEOPLE

In 1748, at the age of forty-two, Franklin realized that he was financially secure: from his newspapers, from Poor Richard's Almanack, *and from his eighteen paper mills, he estimated that his business was worth £2000 per annum. Accordingly, he brought David Hall, his foreman, into partnership with him—a partnership that lasted eighteen years.*

Franklin was, by now, for a Philadelphia tradesman, a man of means. In trade, he had found his own way to wealth. 'I flattered myself that, by the sufficient though modest fortune I had acquired, I had secured leisure during the rest of my life for philosophical studies and amusement.'

He summed up his own and his family's progress in a letter to his mother:

Philadelphia, 12 April 1750

HONOURED MOTHER:

We received your kind letter of the 2nd instant, and we are glad to hear you still enjoy such a measure of health, notwithstanding your great age. We read your writing very easily. I never met with a word in your letters but what I could readily understand; for, though the hand is not always the best, the sense makes everything plain.

As to your grandchildren, Will is now nineteen years of age, a tall, proper youth, and much of a beau. He acquired a habit of idleness on the expedition to Canada in the winter of 1746–47, but begins of late to apply himself to business, and I hope will become an industrious man. He imagined his father had got enough for him, but I have assured him that I intend to spend what little I have myself, if it please God that I live long enough; and, as he by no means wants sense, he can see by my going on that I mean to be as good as my word.

Sally grows a fine girl, and is extremely industrious with her needle, and delights in her book. She is of a most affectionate temper, and perfectly dutiful and obliging to her parents and to all. Perhaps I flatter myself too much, but I have hopes that she will prove an ingenious, sensible, notable, and worthy woman, like her Aunt Jenny. She goes now to the dancing-school.

For my own part, at present, I pass my time agreeably enough. I enjoy, through mercy, a tolerable share of health. I read a great deal, ride a little, do a little business for myself, more for others, retire when I can, and go into company when I please; so the years roll round, and the last will come, when I would rather have it said 'He lived usefully' than 'He died rich.'

Franklin was now free—and financially secure—to be philosopher, scientific experimenter, and civic doer-of-good. He listed his activities in the Autobiography. *First, electricity:*

In 1746, being at Boston, I met there with a Dr Spence, who was lately arrived from Scotland, and showed me some electric experiments. They were imperfectly performed, as he was not very expert; but, being on a subject quite new to me, they equally surprized and pleased me. Soon after my return to Philadelphia, our library company received from Mr P. Collinson, Fellow of the Royal Society of London, a present of a glass tube, with some account of the use of it in making such experiments. I eagerly seized the opportunity of repeating what I had seen at Boston; and, by much practice, acquired great readiness in performing those, also, which we had an account of from England, adding a number of new ones. I say much practice, for my house was continually full, for some time, with people who came to see these new wonders.

To divide a little this incumbrance among my friends, I caused a number of similar tubes to be blown at our glass-house, with which they furnished themselves, so that we had at length several performers. Among these, the principal was Mr Kinnersley, an ingenious neighbour, who, being out of business, I encouraged to undertake showing the experiments for money, and drew up for him two lectures, in which the experiments were ranged in such order, and accompanied with such explanations in such method, as that the foregoing should assist in comprehending the following. He procured an elegant apparatus for the purpose, in which all the little machines that I had roughly made for myself were nicely formed by instrument-makers. His lectures were well attended, and gave great satisfaction; and after some time he went through the colonies, exhibiting them in every capital town, and picked up some money. In the West India Islands, indeed, it was with difficulty the experiments could be made, from the general moisture of the air.

Obliged as we were to Mr Collinson for his present of the tube, etc., I thought it right he should be informed of our success in using it, and wrote him several letters containing accounts of our experiments. He got them read in the Royal Society, where they were not at first thought worth so much notice as to be printed in their *Transactions*. One paper, which I wrote for Mr Kinnersley, on the sameness of lightning with electricity, I sent to Dr Mitchel, an acquaintance of mine, and one of the members also of that society, who wrote me word that it had been read, but was laughed at by the connoisseurs. The papers, however, being shown to Dr Fothergill, he thought them of too much value to be stifled, and advised the printing of them. Mr Collinson then gave them to *Cave* for publication in his *Gentleman's Magazine;* but he chose to print them separately in a pamphlet, and Dr Fothergill wrote the preface. Cave, it seems, judged rightly for his profit, for by the additions that arrived afterward they swelled, to a quarto volume, which has had five editions, and cost him nothing for copy-money.

It was, however, some time before those papers were much taken notice of in England. A copy of them happening to fall into the hands of the Count de Buffon, a philosopher deservedly of great reputation in France, and, indeed, all over Europe, he prevailed with M. Dalibard to translate them into French, and they were printed at Paris. The publication offended the Abbé Nollet, preceptor in Natural Philosophy to the

royal family, and an able experimenter, who had formed and
published a theory of electricity, which then had the general
vogue. He could not at first believe that such a work came from
America, and said it must have been fabricated by his enemies
at Paris, to decry his system. Afterwards, having been assured
that there really existed such a person as Franklin at Philadelphia, which he had doubted, he wrote and published a volume
of letters, chiefly addressed to me, defending his theory, and
denying the verity of my experiments, and of the positions de-
duced from them.

I once purposed answering the abbé, and actually began the
answer; but, on consideration that my writings contained a description of experiments which anyone might repeat and ver-
ify, and if not to be verified, could not be defended; or of
observations offered as conjectures, and not delivered dogmat-
ically, therefore not laying me under any obligation to defend
them; and reflecting that a dispute between two persons, writing in different languages, might be lengthened greatly by mis-
translations, and thence misconceptions of one another's
meaning, much of one of the abbé's letters being founded on an
error in the translation, I concluded to let my papers shift for
themselves, believing it was better to spend what time I could
spare from public business in making new experiments, than in
disputing about those already made. I therefore never answered M. Nollet, and the event gave me no cause to repent my
silence; for my friend M. le Roy, of the Royal Academy of
Sciences, took up my cause and refuted him; my book was
translated into the Italian, German, and Latin languages; and
the doctrine it contained was by degrees universally adopted by
the philosophers of Europe, in preference to that of the abbé;
so that he lived to see himself the last of his sect, except Mon-
sieur B——, of Paris, his *élève* and immediate disciple.

What gave my book the more sudden and general celebrity,
was the success of one of its proposed experiments, made by
Messrs Dalibard and de Lor at Marly, for drawing lightning
from the clouds. This engaged the public attention everywhere.
M. de Lor, who had an apparatus for experimental philosophy,
and lectured in that branch of science, undertook to repeat
what he called the *Philadelphia Experiments;* and, after they were

performed before the king and court, all the curious of Paris flocked to see them. I will not swell this narrative with an account of that capital experiment, nor of the infinite pleasure I received in the success of a similar one I made soon after with a kite at Philadelphia, as both are to be found in the histories of electricity.

Dr Wright, an English physician, when at Paris, wrote to a friend, who was of the Royal Society, an account of the high esteem my experiments were in among the learned abroad, and of their wonder that my writings had been so little noticed in England. The Society, on this, resumed the consideration of the letters that had been read to them; and the celebrated Dr Watson drew up a summary account of them, and of all I had afterwards sent to England on the subject, which he accompanied with some praise of the writer. This summary was then printed in their *Transactions;* and some members of the Society in London, particularly the very ingenious Mr Canton, having verified the experiment of procuring lightning from the clouds by a pointed rod, and acquainting them with the success, they soon made me more than amends for the slight with which they had before treated me. Without my having made any application for that honour, they chose me a member, and voted that I should be excused the customary payments, which would have amounted to 25 guineas; and ever since have given me their *Transactions* gratis. They also presented me with the gold medal of Sir Godfrey Copley for the year 1753, the delivery of which was accompanied by a very handsome speech of the president, Lord Macclesfield, wherein I was highly honoured.

Franklin maintained an enthusiastic correspondence with Peter Collinson but was, winningly, quick to admit feelings of doubt about some of his electrical experiments.

TO PETER COLLINSON

Philadelphia, 11 July 1747

SIR,

In my last I informed you that, in pursuing our electrical enquiries, we had observed some particular phenomena, which we looked upon to be new, and of which I promised to give you some account, though I apprehended they might possibly not be new to you, as so many hands are daily employed in electrical experiments on your side the water, some or other of which would probably hit on the same observations.

The first is the wonderful effect of pointed bodies, both in *drawing off* and *throwing off* the electrical fire.* For example,

Place an iron shot of three or four inches diameter on the mouth of a clean dry glass bottle. By a fine silken thread from the cieling, right over the mouth of the bottle, suspend a small cork ball, about the bigness of a marble; the thread of such a length, as that the cork ball may rest against the side of the shot. Electrify the shot, and the ball will be repelled to the distance of four or five inches, more or less, according to the quantity of electricity. When in this state, if you present to the shot the point of a long slender sharp bodkin, at six or eight inches distance, the repellency is instantly destroyed, and the cork flies to the shot. A blunt body must be brought within an inch, and draw a spark, to produce the same effect. To prove that the electrical fire is *drawn off* by the point, if you take the blade of the bodkin out of the wooden handle, and fix it in a stick of sealing-wax, and then present it at the distance aforesaid, or if you bring it very near, no such effect follows; but sliding one finger along the wax till you touch the blade, and the ball flies to the shot immediately. If you present the point in the dark, you will see, sometimes at a foot distance, and more, a light gather upon it, like that of a firefly, or glow-worm; the less sharp the point, the nearer you must bring it to observe the light; and, at whatever distance you see the light, you may draw off the electrical fire, and destroy the repellency. If a cork ball so suspended be repelled by the tube, and a point be presented quick to it, though at a considerable distance, 'tis surprizing to see how suddenly it flies back to the tube. Points of wood will do near as well as those of iron, provided the wood is not dry; for perfectly dry wood will no more conduct electricity than sealing-wax.

* A practical result of this observation was Franklin's invention of the lightning rod.

To shew that points will *throw off* as well as *draw off* the electrical fire; lay a long sharp needle upon the shot, and you cannot electrize the shot so as to make it repel the rock ball. Or fix a needle to the end of a suspended gun-barrel, or iron rod, so as to point beyond it like a little bayonet; and while it remains there, the gun-barrel, or rod, cannot by applying the tube to the other end be electrized so as to give a spark, the fire continually running out silently at the point. In the dark you may see it make the same appearance as it does in the case before mentioned.

The repellency between the cork ball and the shot is likewise destroyed, 1. by sifting fine sand on it; this does it gradually, 2. by breathing on it, 3. by making a smoke about it from burning wood, 4. by candlelight, even though the candle is at a foot distance: these do it suddenly. The light of a bright coal from a wood fire; and the light of red-hot iron do it likewise; but not at so great a distance. Smoke from dry rosin dropt on hot iron, does not destroy the repellency; but is attracted by both shot and cork ball, forming proportionable atmospheres round them, making them look beautifully, somewhat like some of the figures in *Burnet's* or *Whiston's Theory of the Earth.*

N.B. This experiment should be made in a closet, where the air is very still, or it will be apt to fail.

The light of the sun thrown strongly on both cork and shot by a looking-glass for a long time together, does not impair the repellency in the least. This difference between firelight and sunlight is another thing that seems new and extraordinary to us.

We had for some time been of opinion, that the electrical fire was not created by friction, but collected, being really an element diffused among, and attracted by other matter, particularly by water and metals. We had even discovered and demonstrated its afflux to the electrical sphere, as well as its efflux, by means of little light windmill-wheels made of stiff paper vanes, fixed obliquely and turning freely on fine wire axes; also by little wheels of the same matter, but formed like water-wheels. Of the disposition and application of which wheels, and the various phenomena resulting, I could, if I had time, fill you a sheet. The impossibility of electrizing one's self (though standing on wax) by rubbing the tube, and drawing the fire from it; and the manner of doing it, by passing the tube near a person or thing standing on the floor, etc. had also occurred to us some months before Mr *Watson's* ingenious *Sequel* came to hand, and these were some of the new things I intended to have communicated to you. But now I need only mention some particulars not hinted in that piece, with our reasonings thereupon; though perhaps the latter might well enough be spared.

1. A person standing on wax, and rubbing the tube, and another person on wax drawing the fire, they will both of them, (provided they do not stand so as to touch one another) appear to be electrized, to a person standing on the floor; that is, he will perceive a spark on approaching each of them with his knuckle.

2. But, if the persons on wax touch one another during the exciting of the tube, neither of them will appear to be electrized.

3. If they touch one another after exciting the tube, and drawing the fire as aforesaid, there will be a stronger spark between them, than was between either of them and the person on the floor.

4. After such strong spark, neither of them discover any electricity.

These appearances we attempt to account for thus: We suppose, as aforesaid, that electrical fire is a common element, of which every one of the three persons above mentioned has his equal share, before any operation is begun with the tube. *A,* who stands on wax and rubs the tube, collects the electrical fire from himself into the glass; and his communication with the common stock being cut off by the wax, his body is not again immediately supplied. *B,* (who stands on wax likewise) passing his knuckle along near the tube, receives the fire which was collected by the glass from *A;* and his communication with the common stock being likewise cut off, he retains the additional quantity received. To *C,* standing on the floor, both appear to be electrized: for he having only the middle quantity of electrical fire, receives a spark upon approaching *B,* who has an over quantity; but gives one to *A,* who has an under quantity. If *A* and *B* approach to touch each other, the spark is stronger, because the difference between them is greater: After such touch there is no spark between either of them and *C*, because the electrical fire in all is reduced to the original equality. If they touch while electrizing, the equality is never destroyed, the fire only circulating. Hence have arisen some new terms among us: we say, *B*, (and bodies like circumstanced) is electrized *positively; A, negatively.** Or rather, *B* is electrized *plus; A, minus.* And we daily in our experiments electrize bodies *plus or minus,* as we think proper. To electrize *plus or minus,* no more needs to be known than this, that the parts of the tube or sphere that are rubbed, do, in the instant of the friction, attract the electrical fire, and therefore take it from the thing rubbing: the same parts immediately, as the friction upon them ceases, are disposed to give the fire they have received, to any body that has less. Thus you may circulate it, as Mr *Watson* has shewn; you may also accumulate or subtract it upon, or from any body, as you connect that body with the rubber or with the receiver, the communication with the common stock being cut off. We think that ingenious gentleman was deceived when he imagined (in his *Sequel*) that the electrical fire came down the wire from the cieling to the gun-barrel, thence to the sphere, and so electrized the machine and the man turning the wheel, etc. We suppose it was *driven off*, and not brought on through that wire; and that the machine and man, etc., were electrized *minus, i.e.* had less electrical fire in them than things in common.

As the vessel is just upon sailing, I cannot give you so large an account of *American* electricity as I intended: I shall only mention a few particulars more. We find granulated lead better to fill the phial with, than water, being easily warmed, and keeping warm and dry in damp air. We fire spirits with the wire of the phial. We light candles, just blown out, by drawing a spark among the smoke, between the wire and snuffers. We represent lightning, by passing the wire in the dark, over a China plate, that has gilt flowers, or applying it to gilt frames of looking-glasses, etc. We electrize a person twenty or more times running, with a touch of the finger on the wire, thus: He stands on wax. Give him the electrized bottle in his hand. Touch the wire with your finger, and

---

* Franklin thus introduces these terms into the vocabulary of science; previously, experimenters had talked of 'vitreous' and 'resinous' electricity.

then touch his hand or face; there are sparks every time. We increase the force of the electrical kiss vastly, thus: Let *A* and *B* stand on wax; or *A* on wax, and *B* on the floor; give one of them the electrized phial in hand; let the other take hold of the wire; there will be a small spark; but when their lips approach, they will be struck and shocked. The same if another gentleman and lady, *C* and *D*, standing also on wax, and joining hands with *A* and *B*, salute or shake hands. We suspend by fine silk thread a counterfeit spider, made of a small piece of burnt cork, with legs of linnen thread, and a grain or two of lead stuck in him, to give him more weight. Upon the table, over which he hangs, we stick a wire upright, as high as the phial and wire, two or three inches from the spider: then we animate him, by setting the electrified phial at the same distance on the other side of him; he will immediately fly to the wire of the phial, bend his legs in touching it; then spring off, and fly to the wire on the table; thence again to the wire of the phial, playing with his legs against both, in a very entertaining manner, appearing perfectly alive to persons unacquainted. He will continue this motion an hour or more in dry weather. We electrify, upon wax in the dark, a book that has a double line of gold round upon the covers, and then apply a knuckle to the gilding; the fire appears everywhere upon the gold like a flash of lightning: not upon the leather, nor, if you touch the leather instead of the gold. We rub our tubes with buckskin, and observe always to keep the same side to the tube, and never to sully the tube by handling; thus they work readily and easily, without the least fatigue, especially if kept in tight pasteboard cases, lined with flannel, and sitting close to the tube. This I mention, because the *European* papers on electricity, frequently speak of rubbing the tube, as a fatiguing exercise. Our spheres are fixed on iron axes, which pass through them. At one end of the axis there is a small handle, with which you turn the sphere like a common grindstone. This we find very commodious, as the machine takes up but little room, is portable, and may be enclosed in a tight box, when not in use. 'Tis true, the sphere does not turn so swift as when the great wheel is used: but swiftness we think of little importance, since a few turns will charge the phial, etc., sufficiently.

I am, etc.

B. FRANKLIN

TO PETER COLLINSON

Philadelphia, 14 August 1747
SIR,

I have lately written two long letters to you on the subject of electricity, one by the governor's vessel, the other per Mesnard. On some further experiments since I have observed a phenomenon or two, that I cannot at present account for on the principle laid down in those letters, and am therefore become a little diffident of my hypothesis, and ashamed that I have expressed myself in so positive a manner. In going on with these experiments how many pretty systems do we build which we soon find ourselves obliged to destroy! If there is no other use discovered of electricity this however is something considerable, that it may *help to make a vain man humble.*

I must now request that you would not expose those letters; or if you communicate them to any friends you would at least conceal my name. I have not time to add but that I am, sir,

Your obliged and most humble servant
B. FRANKLIN

Franklin's best known explanation for his identification of lightning and electricity is contained in a letter to John Lining of Charleston, South Carolina, in 1755:

Your question, how I came first to think of proposing the experiment of drawing down the lightning in order to ascertain its sameness with the electric fluid, I cannot answer better than by giving you an extract from the minutes I used to keep of the experiments I made, with memorandums of such as I proposed to make, the reasons for making them, and the observations that arose upon them, from which minutes my letters were afterwards drawn. By this extract you will see that the thought was not so much 'an out-of-the-way one' but that it might have occurred to any electrician.

'*7 November 1749*. Electrical fluid agrees with lightning in these particulars:

1. Giving light.
2. Colour of the light.

3. Crooked direction.
4. Swift motion.
5. Being conducted by metals.
6. Crack or noise in exploding.
7. Subsisting in water or ice.
8. Rending bodies it passes through.
9. Destroying animals.
10. Melting metals.
11. Firing inflammable substances.
12. Sulphureous smell.

The electric fluid is attracted by points. We do not know whether this property is in lightning. But since they agree in all the particulars wherein we can already compare them, is it not probable they agree likewise in this? Let the experiment be made . . .'

The education of Pennsylvanian youth was another preoccupation:

PROPOSALS RELATING TO THE EDUCATION OF YOUTH IN PENSILVANIA

PHILADELPHIA: PRINTED IN THE YEAR, MDCCXLIX

Advertisement to the Reader

It has long been regretted as a misfortune to the youth of this province, that we have no ACADEMY, in which they might receive the accomplishments of a regular education . . . Those who incline to favour the design with their advice, either as to the parts of learning to be taught, the order of study, the method of teaching, the economy of the school, or any other matter of importance to the success of the undertaking, are desired to communicate their sentiments as soon as may be, by letter directed to B. FRANKLIN, *Printer*, in PHILADELPHIA.

PROPOSALS

The good education of youth has been esteemed by wise men in all ages, as the surest foundation of the happiness both of private families and of commonwealths. Almost all governments have therefore made it a principal object of their attention, to establish and endow with proper revenues, such seminaries of learning, as might supply the succeeding age with men qualified to serve the publick with honour to themselves, and to their country.

Many of the first settlers of these provinces were men who had received a good education in *Europe,* and to their wisdom and good management we owe much of our present prosperity. But their hands were full, and they could not do all things. The present race are not thought to be generally of equal ability: For though the *American* youth are allowed not to want capacity; yet the best capacities require cultivation, it being truly with them, as with the best ground, which unless well tilled and sowed with profitable seed, produces only ranker weeds . . .

As to their STUDIES, it would be well if they could be taught *everything* that is useful, and *everything* that is ornamental: But art is long, and their time is short. It is therefore proposed that they learn those things that are likely to be *most useful* and *most ornamental.* Regard being had to the several professions for which they are intended.

All should be taught to write a *fair hand,* and swift, as that is useful to all. And with it may be learnt something of *drawing,* by imitation of prints, and some of the first principles of perspective.

Arithmetick, accounts, and some of the first principles of *geometry* and *astronomy.*

The *English* language might be taught by grammar; in which some of our best writers, as *Tillotson, Addison, Pope, Algernoon Sidney, Cato's Letters,* etc., should be classicks: the *stiles* principally to be cultivated, being the *clear* and the *concise.* Reading should also be taught, and pronouncing properly, distinctly, emphatically; not with an even tone, which *under-does,* nor a theatrical, which *over-does* Nature.

To form their stile they should be put on writing letters to each other, making abstracts of what they read; or writing the same things in their own words; telling or writing stories lately read, in their own expressions. All to be revised and corrected by the tutor, who should give his reasons, and explain the force and import of words, etc . . .

History will show the wonderful effects of ORATORY, in governing, turning and leading great bodies of mankind, armies, cities, nations. When the minds of youth are struck with admiration at this, then is the time to give them the principles of that art, which they will study with taste and application. Then they may be made acquainted with the best models among the antients, their beauties being particularly pointed out to them. Modern political oratory being chiefly performed by the pen and press, its advantages over the antient in some respects are to be shown; as that its effects are more extensive, more lasting, etc.

History will also afford frequent opportunities of showing the necessity of a *publick religion,* from its usefulness to the publick; the advantage of a religious character among private persons; the mischiefs of superstition, etc. and the excellency of the CHRISTIAN RELIGION above all others antient or modern . . .

The history of *commerce,* of the invention of arts, rise of manufactures, progress of trade, change of its seats, with the reasons, causes, etc., may also be made entertaining to youth, and will be useful to all. And this, with the accounts in other history of the prodigious force and effect of engines and machines used in war, will naturally introduce a desire to be instructed in *mechanicks,* and to be informed of the principles of that art by which weak men perform such wonders, labour is saved, manufactures expedited, etc. This will be the time to show them prints of antient and modern machines, to explain them, to let them be copied, and to give lectures in mechanical philosophy.

With the whole should be constantly inculcated and cultivated, that *benignity of mind,* which shows itself in *searching for* and *seizing* every opportunity *to serve* and *to oblige;* and is the foundation of what is called GOOD BREEDING; highly useful to the possessor, and most agreeable to all.

The idea of what is *true merit* should also be often presented to youth, explained and impressed on their minds, as consisting in an *inclination* joined with an *ability* to serve mankind, one's country, friends and family; which *ability* is (with the blessing of God) to be acquired or greatly encreased by *true learning;* and should indeed be the great *aim* and *end* of all learning.

The Academy (now the University of Pennsylvania) was opened in 1751.

Also in 1751, Franklin quite openly (and rather out of character) sought the office of Deputy Postmaster General. He sought it by solicitation, as did Cadwallader Colden and John Mitchell. He wrote to Peter Collinson:

The occasion of my writing this, *via* Ireland, is that I have just received advice that the Deputy Postmaster General of America (Mr Elliot Benger residing in Virginia) who has for some time been in declining way is thought to be near his end. My friends advise me to apply for this post . . .

I have not heretofore made much scruple of giving you trouble when the public good was to be promoted by it, but 'tis with great reluctance that I think of asking you to interest yourself in my private concerns, as I know you have little time to spare. The place is in the disposal of the Postmasters General of Britain with some of whom or their friends you may possibly have acquaintance.

Thanks, presumably, to Collinson's aid, and the local support of William Allen, Franklin became Deputy Postmaster General of North America in 1753 (he had been postmaster at Philadelphia since 1737). He held the post until 1774.

One of Franklin's other interests was in population growth, sparked off by an observation on the increase of pigeons, then of human beings. This involved much statistical research and calculation. The fascination lay at the roots of his faith in the development of the New World, which he saw as the dynamic centre of what he then called 'The Empire on this Side'—in a sense, the tail that would wag the dog. On this was based his later conviction of America's own power and growth. His Observations Concerning the Increase of Mankind *was remarkable, and totally Anglo-American—even, in places, racist.*

OBSERVATIONS

CONCERNING THE INCREASE OF MANKIND, PEOPLING OF COUNTRIES, ETC

Written in Pensilvania, 1751

Tables of the proportion of marriages to births, of deaths to births, of marriages to the numbers of inhabitants, etc., formed on observations [*sic*] made upon the bills of mortality, christ-nings, etc., of populous cities, will not suit countries; nor will tables formed on observations made on full-settled old coun-tries, as *Europe,* suit new countries, as *America.*

For people increase in proportion to the number of mar-riages, and that is greater in proportion to the ease and conve-nience of supporting a family. When families can be easily supported, more persons marry, and earlier in life.

In cities, where all trades, occupations, and offices are full, many delay marrying till they can see how to bear the charges of a family; which charges are greater in cities, as luxury is more common: many live single during life, and continue ser-vants to families, journeymen to trades; etc., hence cities do not by natural generation supply themselves with inhabitants; the deaths are more than the births.

In countries full-settled, the case must be nearly the same; all lands being occupied and improved to the heighth; those who cannot get land, must labour for others that have it; when labourers are plenty, their wages will be low; by low wages a family is supported with difficulty; this difficulty deters many from marriage, who therefore long continue servants and sin-gle. Only as the cities take supplies of people from the country, and thereby make a little more room in the country; marriage is a little more encouraged there, and the births exceed the deaths.

Europe is generally full settled with husbandmen, manufac-turers, etc. and therefore cannot now much increase in people: *America* is chiefly occupied by Indians, who subsist mostly by hunting. But as the hunter, of all men, requires the greatest quantity of land from whence to draw his subsistence, (the hus-bandman subsisting on much less, the gardner on still less, and the manufacturer requiring least of all), the *Europeans* found *America* as fully settled as it well could be by hunters; yet these, having large tracks, were easily prevailed on to part with por-tions of territory to the newcomers, who did not much interfere with the natives in hunting, and furnished them with many things they wanted.

Land being thus plenty in *America,* and so cheap as that a labouring man, that understands husbandry, can in a short

time save money enough to purchase a piece of new land sufficient for a plantation, whereon he may subsist a family, such
are not afraid to marry; for, if they even look far enough forward to consider how their children, when grown up, are to be
provided for, they see that more land is to be had at rates
equally easy, all circumstances considered.

Hence marriages in *America* are more general, and more generally early, than in *Europe*. And if it is reckoned there, that
there is but one marriage per annum among a hundred persons, perhaps we may here reckon two; and if in *Europe* they
have but four births to a marriage (many of their marriages
being late), we may here reckon eight, of which if one half grow
up, and our marriages are made, reckoning one with another at
twenty years of age, our people must at least be doubled every
twenty years.

But notwithstanding this increase, so vast is the territory of
North America, that it will require many ages to settle it fully;
and, till it is fully settled, labour will never be cheap here, where
no man continues long a labourer for others, but gets a plantation of his own, no man continues long a journeyman to a
trade, but goes among those new settlers, and sets up for himself, etc. Hence labour is no cheaper now in *Pennsylvania,* than
it was thirty years ago, though so many thousand labouring
people have been imported.

The danger therefore of these colonies interfering with their
Mother Country in trades that depend on labour, manufactures, etc., is too remote to require the attention of *Great Britain.*

But in proportion to the increase of the colonies, a vast demand is growing for British manufactures, a glorious market
wholly in the power of *Britain,* in which foreigners cannot interfere, which will increase in a short time even beyond her
power of supplying, though her whole trade should be to her
colonies: Therefore *Britain* should not too much restrain manufactures in her colonies. A wise and good mother will not do
it. To distress, is to weaken, and weakening the children weak-
ens the whole family . . .

'Tis an ill-grounded opinion that by the labour of slaves,
America may possibly vie in cheapness of manufactures with
Britain. The labour of slaves can never be so cheap here as the

labour of working men is in *Britain*. Anyone may compute it. Interest of money is in the colonies from 6 to 10 per cent. Slaves one with another cost 30 pounds sterling per head. Reckon then the interest of the first purchase of a slave, the insurance or risque on his life, his cloathing and diet, expences in his sickness and loss of time, loss by his neglect of business (neglect is natural to the man who is not to be benefited by his own care or diligence), expence of a driver to keep him at work, and his pilfering from time to time, almost every slave being *by Nature* a thief, and compare the whole amount with the wages of a manufacturer of iron or wood in *England*, you will see that labour is much cheaper there than it ever can be by Negroes here. Why then will *Americans* purchase slaves? Because slaves may be kept as long as a *man* pleases, or has occasion for their labour; while hired men are continually leaving their masters (often in the midst of his business,) and setting up for themselves . . .

Thus there are supposed to be now upwards of one million *English* souls in *North America*, (though 'tis thought scarce 80,000 have been brought over sea,) and yet perhaps there is not one the fewer in *Britain*, but rather many more, on account of the employment the colonies afford to manufacturers at home. This million doubling, suppose but once in twenty-five years, will, in another century, be more than the people of *England*, and the greatest number of *Englishmen* will be on this side the water. What an accession of power to the *British* Empire by sea as well as land! What increase of trade and navigation! What numbers of ships and seamen! We have been here but little more than a hundred years, and yet the force of our privateers in the late war, united, was greater, both in men and guns, than that of the whole *British* Navy in Queen *Elizabeth's* time. How important an affair then to *Britain* is the present treaty for settling the bounds between her colonies and the *French*, and how careful should she be to secure room enough, since on the room depends so much the increase of her people.

Which leads me to add one remark, that the number of purely white people in the world is proportionably very small. All *Africa* is black or tawny; *Asia* chiefly tawny; *America* (exclusive of the newcomers) wholly so. And in *Europe*, the *Spaniards*,

Italians, French, Russians, and *Swedes,* are generally of what we call a swarthy complexion; as are the *Germans* also, the *Saxons* only excepted, who, with the *English,* make the principal body of white people on the face of the earth. I could wish their numbers were increased. And while we are, as I may call it, *scouring* our planet, by *clearing America* of woods, and so making this side of our globe reflect a brighter light to the eyes of inhabitants in *Mars* or *Venus,* why should we, in the sight of superior beings, darken its people? Why increase the sons of *Africa,* by planting them in *America,* where we have so fair an opportunity, by excluding all blacks and tawneys, of increasing the lovely white and red? But perhaps I am partial to the complexion of my country, for such kind of partiality is natural to mankind.

Civic reform, population growth and defence of the Pennsylvania frontier fed Franklin's interest in colonial unity. The mainland colonies were very diverse, not only in soil and products, but in racial composition and in their constitutions. Some, like Georgia, were in part defence outposts, in part welfare experiments: some, like Rhode Island, Connecticut and Massachusetts, were governed by charters: some like Pennsylvania and Maryland were proprietaries, given to individuals or their ancestors as royal largesse. Each had closer and more direct links with London, Liverpool and Glasgow (and with the Board of Trade), than with each other.

Franklin was a Pennsylvania delegate in 1754 at an Intercolonial Defence Conclave at Albany (attended only, however, by Pennsylvania and Massachusetts), and helped to devise, with Lieutenant-Colonel Hutchinson of Boston, a plan for Colonial Union. It proposed a Colonial Parliament with a President, but won the support neither of the other colonies nor of Britain. Had it been adopted, it might have averted the eventual separation. Thus thought Franklin, and said so in letters to Cadwallader Colden, fellow-scientist, Acting Governor of Massachusetts, and Commander-in-Chief of all the colonies, and later in his Autobiography.

Having been for some time employed by the Postmaster General of America as his comptroller in regulating several offices, and bringing the officers to account, I was, upon his death in

1753, appointed, jointly with Mr William Hunter, to succeed him, by a commission from the Postmaster General in England. The American office never had hitherto paid anything to that of Britain. We were to have 600 pounds a year between us, if we could make that sum out of the profits of the office. To do this, a variety of improvements were necessary; some of these were inevitably at first expensive, so that in the first four years the office became above 900 pounds in debt to us. But it soon after began to repay us; and before I was displaced by a freak of the ministers, of which I shall speak hereafter, we had brought it to yield *three times* as much clear revenue to the Crown as the post office of Ireland. Since that imprudent transaction, they have received from it—not one farthing!

The business of the post office occasioned my taking a journey this year to New England, where the College of Cambridge, of their own motion, presented me with the degree of Master of Arts. Yale College, in Connecticut, had before made me a similar compliment. Thus, without studying in any college, I came to partake of their honours. They were conferred in consideration of my improvements and discoveries in the electric branch of natural philosophy.

In 1754, war with France being again apprehended, a congress of commissioners from the different colonies was, by order of the Lord of Trade, to be assembled at Albany, there to confer with the chiefs of the Six Nations* concerning the means of defending both their country and ours. Governor Hamilton, having received this order, acquainted the House with it, requesting they would furnish proper presents for the Indians, to be given on this occasion; and naming the Speaker (Mr Norris) and myself to join Mr Thomas Penn and Mr Secretary Peters as commissioners to act for Pennsylvania. The House approved the nomination, and provided the goods for the present, though they did not much like treating out of the provinces; and we met the other commissioners at Albany about the middle of June.

In our way thither, I projected and drew a plan for the union of all the colonies under one government, so far as might be

* The Iroquois, a confederation of Indian tribes.

necessary for defence, and other important general purposes. As we passed through New York I had there shown my project to Mr James Alexander and Mr Kennedy, two gentlemen of great knowledge in public affairs, and, being fortified by their approbation, I ventured to lay it before the Congress. It then appeared that several of the commissioners had formed plans of the same kind. A previous question was first taken, whether a union should be established, which passed in the affirmative unanimously. A committee was then appointed, one member from each colony, to consider the several plans and report. Mine happened to be preferred, and, with a few amendments, was accordingly reported.

By this plan the general government was to be administered by a President-General, appointed and supported by the Crown, and a Grand Council was to be chosen by the representatives of the people of the several colonies, met in their respective assemblies. The debates upon it in Congress went on daily, hand in hand with the Indian business. Many objections and difficulties were started, but at length they were all overcome, and the plan was unanimously agreed to, and copies ordered to be transmitted to the Board of Trade and to the assemblies of the several provinces. Its fate was singular: the assemblies did not adopt it, as they all thought there was too much *prerogative* in it, and in England it was judged to have too much of the *democratic*. The Board of Trade therefore did not approve it, nor recommend it for the approbation of his Majesty; but another scheme was formed, supposed to answer the same purpose better, whereby the governors of the provinces, with some members of their respective councils, were to meet and order the raisings of troops, building of forts, etc., and to draw on the treasury of Great Britain for the expense, which was afterwards to be refunded by an Act of Parliament laying a tax on America. My plan, with my reasons in support of it, is to be found among my political papers that are printed.

Being the winter following in Boston, I had much conversation with Governor Shirley upon both the plans. Part of what passed between us on the occasion may also be seen among those papers. The different and contrary reasons of dislike to my plan makes me suspect that it was really the true medium;

*Franklin's cartoon urging the American colonies to defence
was the first American political cartoon*

*'Magna Britannia' or 'The Colonies Reduced'
another cartoon designed by Franklin*

and I am still of opinion it would have been happy for both sides the water if it had been adopted. The colonies, so united, would have been sufficiently strong to have defended themselves; there would then have been no need of troops from England; of course, the subsequent pretence for taxing America, and the bloody contest it occasioned, would have been avoided. But such mistakes are not new; history is full of the errors of states and princes.

> Look round the habitable world, how few
> Know their own good, or, knowing it, pursue!

Those who govern, having much business on their hands, do not generally like to take the trouble of considering and carrying into execution new projects. The best public measures are therefore seldom *adopted from previous wisdom, but forced by the occasion.*

The governor of Pennsylvania, in sending it down to the Assembly, expressed his approbation of the plan, 'as appearing to him to be drawn up with great clearness and strength of judgment, and therefore recommended it as well worthy of their closest and most serious attention'. The House, however, by the management of a certain member, took it up when I happened to be absent, which I thought not very fair, and reprobated it without paying any attention to it at all, to my no small mortification.

Franklin felt strongly on other colonial matters and wrote to Governor Shirley accordingly:

Tuesday morning [*17 December 1754*]

SIR,

I apprehend, that excluding the *people* of the colonies from all share in the choice of the Grand Council will give extreme dissatisfaction, as well as the taxing them by Act of Parliament, where they have no representative. It is very possible, that this general government might be as well and faithfully administered without the people, as with them; but where heavy burthens have been laid on them, it has been found useful to make it, as much as possible, their own act; for they bear better when they have, or think they have some share in the direction; and when any public measures are generally grievous, or even distasteful to the people, the wheels of government move more heavily.

Wednesday morning [*18 December 1754*]

SIR,

I mentioned it yesterday to your excellency as my opinion, that excluding the *people* of the colonies from all share in the choice of the Grand Council, would probably give extreme dissatisfaction, as well as the taxing them by Act of Parliament, where they have no representative. In matters of general concern to the people, and especially where burthens are to be laid upon them, it is of use to consider, as well what they will be apt to think and say, as what they ought to think; I shall therefore, as your excellency requires it of me, briefly mention what of either kind occurs to me on this occasion.

First they will say, and perhaps with justice, that the body of the people in the colonies are as loyal, and as firmly attached to the present constitution, and reigning family, as any subjects in the king's dominions.

That there is no reason to doubt the readiness and willingness of the representatives they may choose, to grant from time to time such supplies for the defence of the country, as shall be judged necessary, so far as their abilities will allow.

That the people in the colonies, who are to feel the immediate mischiefs of invasion and conquest by an enemy in the loss of their estates, lives and liberties, are likely to be better judges of the quantity of forces necessary to be raised and maintained, forts to be built and supported, and of their own abilities to bear the expence, than the Parliament of England at so great a distance.

That governors often come to the colonies merely to make fortunes, with which they intend to return to Britain; are not always men of the best abilities or integrity; have many of them no estates here, nor any natural connexions with us, that should make them heartily concerned for our welfare; and might possibly be fond of raising and keeping up more forces than necessary, from the profits accruing to themselves, and to make provision for their friends and dependants.

That the counsellors in most of the colonies being appointed by the Crown, on the recommendation of governors, are often of small estates, frequently dependant on the governors for offices, and therefore too much under influence.

That there is therefore great reason to be jealous of a power in such governors and councils, to raise such sums as they shall judge necessary, by draft on the lords of the treasury, to be afterwards laid on the colonies by Act of Parliament, and paid by the people here; since they might abuse it by projecting useless expeditions, harassing the people, and taking them from their labour to execute such projects, merely to create offices and employments, and gratify their dependants, and divide profits.

That the Parliament of England is at a great distance, subject to be misinformed and misled by such governors and councils, whose united interests might probably secure them against the effect of any complaint from hence.

That it is supposed an undoubted right of Englishmen, not to be taxed but by their own consent given through their representatives.

That the colonies have no representatives in Parliament.

That to propose taxing them by Parliament, and refuse them the liberty of choosing a representative council, to meet in the colonies, and consider and judge of the necessity of any general tax, and the quantum, shews suspicion of their loyalty to the Crown, or of their regard for their country, or of their common sense and understanding, which they have not deserved.

That compelling the colonies to pay money without their consent, would be rather like raising contributions in an enemy's country, than taxing of Englishmen for their own public benefit.

That it would be treating them as a conquered people, and not as true British subjects.

That a tax laid by the representatives of the colonies might easily be lessened as the occasions should lessen, but being once laid by Parliament under the influence of the representations made by governors, would probably be kept up and continued for the benefit of governors, to the grievous burthen and discouragement of the colonies, and prevention of their growth and increase.

That a power in governors to march the inhabitants from one end of the British and French colonies to the other, being a country of at least 1500 square miles, without the approbation or the consent of their representatives first obtained, such expeditions might be grievous and ruinous to the people, and would put them on footing with the subjects of France in Canada, that now groan under such oppression from their governor, who for two years past has harrassed them with long and destructive marches to Ohio.

That if the colonies in a body may be well governed by governors and councils appointed by the Crown, without representatives, particular colonies may as well or better be so governed; a tax may be laid upon them all by Act of Parliament for support of government, and their assemblies may be dismissed as an useless part of the constitution.

That the powers proposed by the Albany Plan of Union, to be vested in a Grand Council representative of the people, even with regard to military matters, are not so great as those the colonies of Rhode Island and Connecticut are entrusted with by their charters, and have never abused; for by this plan, the President-General is appointed by the Crown, and controls all by his negative; but in those governments, the people choose the governor, and yet allow him no negative.

That the British colonies bordering on the French are properly frontiers of the British Empire; and the frontiers of an empire are properly defended at the joint expence of the body of the people in such empire: It would now be thought hard by Act of Parliament to oblige the Cinque Ports or sea-coasts of Britain to maintain the whole navy, because they are more immediately defended by it, not allowing them at the same time a vote in choosing members of the Parliament; and if the frontiers in America bear the expence of their own defence, it seems hard to allow them no share in voting the money, judging of the necessity and sum, or advising the measures.

That besides the taxes necessary for the defence of the frontiers, the colonies pay yearly great sums to the Mother Country unnoticed: For taxes paid in Britain by the land-holder or artificer, must enter into and increase the price of the produce of land and of manufactures made of it; and great part of this is paid by consumers in the colonies, who thereby pay a considerable part of the British taxes.

We are restrained in our trade with foreign nations, and where we could be supplied with any manufacture cheaper from them, but must buy the same dearer from Britain; the difference of price is a clear tax to Britain.

We are obliged to carry a great part of our produce directly to Britain; and where the duties laid upon it lessen its price to the planter, or it sells for less than it would in foreign markets; the difference is a tax paid to Britain.

Some manufactures we could make, but are forbidden, and must take them of British merchants; the whole price is a tax paid to Britain.

22 December 1754

Now I look on the colonies as so many counties gained to Great Britain, and more advantageous to it than if they had been gained out of the seas around its coasts, and joined to its land: For being in different climates, they afford greater variety of produce, and being separated by the ocean, they increase much more its shipping and seamen; and since they are all included in the British Empire, which has only extended itself by their means; and the strength and wealth of the parts are the strength and wealth of the whole; what imports it to the general state, whether a merchant, a smith, or a hatter, grow rich in Old or New England? And if, through increase of people, two smiths are wanted for one employed before, why may not the *new* smith be allowed to live and thrive in the *new* country, as well as the *old* one in the *old*? In fine, why should the countenance of a state be *partially* afforded to its people, unless it be most in favour of those who have most merit? And if there be any difference, those who have most contributed to enlarge Britain's empire and commerce, increase her strength, her wealth, and the numbers of her people, at the risk of their own lives and private fortunes in new and strange countries, methinks ought rather to expect some preference. With the greatest respect and esteem, I have the honour to be

Your Excellency's most obedient and most humble servant,

B. FRANKLIN

In his Autobiography, *Franklin detailed the defences on the frontier.*

War being in a manner commenced with France, the government of Massachusetts Bay projected an attack upon Crown Point, and sent Mr Quincy to Pennsylvania, and Mr Pownall, afterward Governor Pownall, to New York, to solicit assistance. As I was in the Assembly, knew its temper, and was Mr Quincy's countryman, he applied to me for my influence and assistance. I dictated his address to them, which was well received. They voted an aid of 10,000 pounds, to be laid out in provisions. But the governor refusing his assent to their bill (which included this with other sums granted for the use of the Crown), unless a clause were inserted exempting the proprietary estate from bearing any part of the tax that would be necessary, the Assembly, though very desirous of making their grant to New England effectual, were at a loss how to accomplish it. Mr Quincy laboured hard with the governor to obtain his assent, but he was obstinate.

I then suggested a method of doing the business without the governor, by orders on the trustees of the Loan Office, which, by law, the Assembly had the right of drawing. There was, indeed, little or no money at that time in the office, and therefore I proposed that the orders should be payable in a year, and to bear an interest of five per cent. With these orders I supposed the provisions might easily be purchased. The Assembly, with very little hesitation, adopted the proposal. The orders were immediately printed, and I was one of the committee directed to sign and dispose of them. The fund for paying them was the interest of all the paper currency then extant in the province upon loan, together with the revenue arising from the excise, which being known to be more than sufficient, they obtained instant credit, and were not only received in payment for the provisions, but many moneyed people, who had cash lying by them, vested it in those orders, which they found advantageous, as they bore interest while upon hand, and might on any occasion be used as money; so that they were eagerly all bought up, and in a few weeks none of them were to be seen. Thus this important affair was by my means completed. Mr Quincy returned thanks to the Assembly in a handsome memorial, went home highly pleased with the success of his embassy, and ever after bore for me the most cordial and affectionate friendship.

The British government, not choosing to permit the union of the colonies as proposed at Albany, and to trust that union with their defence, lest they should thereby grow too military, and feel their own strength, suspicions and jealousies at this time being entertained of them, sent over General Braddock with two regiments of regular English troops for that purpose. He landed at Alexandria, in Virginia, and thence marched to Frederictown, in Maryland, where he halted for carriages. Our Assembly apprehending, from some information, that he had conceived violent prejudices against them, as averse to the service, wished me to wait upon him, not as from them, but as Postmaster General, under the guise of proposing to settle with him the mode of conducting with most celerity and certainty the despatches between him and the governors of the several provinces, with whom he must necessarily have continual correspondence, and of which they proposed to pay the expense. My son accompanied me on this journey.

We found the general at Frederictown, waiting impatiently for the return of those he had sent through the back parts of Maryland and Virginia to collect waggons. I stayed with him several days, dined with him daily, and had full opportunity of removing all his prejudices, by the information of what the Assembly had before his arrival actually done, and were still willing to do, to facilitate his operations. When I was about to depart, the returns of waggons to be obtained were brought in, by which it appeared that they amounted only to twenty-five, and not all of those were in serviceable condition. The general and all the officers were surprized, declared the expedition was then at an end, being impossible, and exclaimed against the ministers for ignorantly landing them in a country destitute of the means of conveying their stores, baggage, etc., not less than 150 waggons being necessary.

I happened to say I thought it was pity they had not been landed rather in Pennsylvania, as in that country almost every farmer had his waggon. The general eagerly laid hold of my words, and said, 'Then you, sir, who are a man of interest there, can probably procure them for us; and I beg you will undertake it.' I asked what terms were to be offered the owners of the waggons; and I was desired to put on paper the terms that appeared to me necessary. This I did, and they were agreed to, and a commission and instructions accordingly prepared immediately. What those terms were will appear in the advertisement I published as soon as I arrived at Lancaster, which being, from the great and sudden effect it produced, a piece of some curiosity, I shall insert it at length, as follows:

ADVERTISEMENT

Lancaster, 26 April 1755

Whereas, 150 waggons, with four horses to each waggon, and 1500 saddle or pack horses, are wanted for the service of his Majesty's forces now about to rendezvous at Will's Creek, and his excellency General Braddock having been pleased to empower me to contract for the hire of the same, I hereby give notice that I shall attend for that purpose at Lancaster from this day to next Wednesday evening, and at York from next Thursday morning till Friday evening, where I shall be ready to agree for waggons and teams, or single horses, on the following terms, viz:

1. That there shall be paid for each waggon, with four good horses and a driver, 15 shillings per diem; and for each able horse with a pack-saddle, or other saddle and furniture, 2 shillings per diem; and for each able horse without a saddle, 18 pence per diem.

2. That the pay commence from the time of their joining the forces at Will's Creek, which must be on or before the 20th of May ensuing, and that a reasonable allowance be paid over and above for the time necessary for their travelling to Will's Creek and home again after their discharge.

3. Each waggon and team, and every saddle or pack horse, is to be valued by indifferent persons chosen between me and the owner; and in case of the loss of any waggon, team, or other horse in the service, the price according to such valuation is to be allowed and paid.

4. Seven days' pay is to be advanced and paid in hand by me to the owner of each waggon and team, or horse, at the time of contracting, if required, and the remainder to be paid by General Braddock, or by the paymaster of the army, at the time of their discharge, or from time to time, as it shall be demanded.

5. No drivers of waggons, or persons taking care of the hired horses, are on any account to be called upon to do the duty of soldiers, or be otherwise employed than in conducting or taking care of their carriages or horses.

6. All oats, Indian corn, or other forage that waggons or horses bring to the camp, more than is necessary for the subsistence of the horses, is to be taken for the use of the army, and a reasonable price paid for the same.

Note—My son, William Franklin, is empowered to enter into like contracts with any person in Cumberland county.

B. FRANKLIN

I received of the general about 800 pounds, to be disbursed in advance-money to the waggon owners, etc.; but that sum being insufficient, I advanced upward of 200 pounds more, and in two weeks the 150 waggons, with 259 carrying horses, were on their march for the camp. The advertisement promised payment according to the valuation, in case any waggon or horse should be lost. The owners, however, alleging they did not know General Braddock, or what dependence might be had on his promise, insisted on my bond for the performance, which I accordingly gave them.

While I was at the camp, supping one evening with the officers of Colonel Dunbar's regiment, he represented to me his concern for the subalterns, who, he said, were generally not in affluence, and could ill afford, in this dear country, to lay in the stores that might be necessary in so long a march, through a wilderness, where nothing was to be purchased. I commiserated their case, and resolved to endeavour procuring them some relief. I said nothing, however, to him of my intention, but wrote the next morning to the committee of the Assembly, who had the disposition of some public money, warmly recommending the case of these officers to their consideration, and proposing that a present should be sent them of necessaries and refreshments. My son, who had some experience of a camp life, and of its wants, drew up a list for me, which I enclosed in my letter. The committee approved, and used such diligence that, conducted by my son, the stores arrived at the camp as soon as the waggons. They consisted of twenty parcels, each containing

6 lbs. loaf sugar
6 lbs. good Muscovado do.
1 lb. good green tea
1 lb. good bohea do.
6 lbs. good ground coffee
6 lbs. chocolate
½ cwt. best white biscuit
½ lb. pepper
1 quart best white wine
   vinegar

1 Gloucester cheese
1 keg containing 20 lbs.
   good butter
2 doz. old Maderia wine
2 gallons Jamaica spirits
1 bottle flour of mustard
2 well-cured hams
½ doz. dried tongues
6 lbs. rice
6 lbs. raisins

These twenty parcels, well packed, were placed on as many horses, each parcel, with the horse, being intended as a present for one officer. They were very thankfully received, and the kindness acknowledged by letters to me from the colonels of both regiments, in the most grateful terms. The general, too, was highly satisfied with my conduct in procuring him the waggons, etc., and readily paid my account of disbursements, thanking me repeatedly, and requesting my farther assistance in sending provisions after him. I undertook this also, and was busily employed in it till we heard of his defeat, advancing, for the service, of my own money, upwards of 1000 pounds sterling, of which I sent him an account. It came to his hands, luckily for me, a few days before the battle, and he returned me immediately an order on the paymaster for the round sum of 1000 pounds, leaving the remainder to the next account. I consider this payment as good luck, having never been able to obtain that remainder.

This general was, I think, a brave man, and might probably have made a figure as a good officer in some European war. But he had too much self-confidence, too high an opinion of the validity of regular troops, and too mean a one of both Americans and Indians.

Travels on post office business, and even soldiering, did, however, bring friendships. One of Franklin's most affectionate correspondents was young Catherine Ray of Block Island, off the Rhode Island coast. This was but one of Franklin's many friendships with women about which we know very little. This one, however, did raise eyebrows. They met in January 1755, when Franklin was travelling through New England on an inspection of post offices; they journeyed in each other's company for some two or three weeks, with 'loitering visits on the road'. He deposited her on the shore of Block Island Sound, from which she sailed back home. She was twenty-three, Franklin nearly fifty. Three years later she married William Greene, of Warwick, Rhode Island. In the spring of 1763, when, again, Franklin was inspecting the forty-eight post offices strung out from Falmouth (Portland), Maine to Norfolk, Virginia, he was nursed by her when he had a bad fall from his chaise. Her son, Ray, would serve as senator from Rhode Island in the U.S. Senate from 1797 to 1801.

TO MISS CATHERINE RAY

Philadelphia, 4 March 1755

DEAR KATY:

Your kind letter of January 20th is but just come to hand, and I take this first opportunity of acknowledging the favour. It gives me great pleasure to hear, that you got home safe and well that day. I thought too much was hazarded, when I saw you put off to sea in that very little skiff, tossed by every wave. But the call was strong and just, a sick parent. I stood on the shore, and looked after you, till I could no longer distinguish you, even with my glass; then returned to your sister's, praying for your safe passage. Towards evening all agreed that you must certainly be arrived before that time, the weather having been so favourable; which made me more easy and cheerful, for I had been truly concerned for you.

I left New England slowly, and with great reluctance. Short day's journeys, and loitering visits on the road, for three or four weeks, manifested my unwillingness to quit a country, in which I drew my first breath, spent my earliest and most pleasant days, and had now received so many fresh marks of the people's goodness and benevolence, in the kind and affectionate treatment I had everywhere met with. I almost forgot I had a *home*, till I was more than half way towards it; till I had, one by one, parted with all my New England friends, and was got into the western borders of Connecticut, among mere strangers. Then, like an old man, who, having buried all he loved in this

world, begins to think of Heaven, I began to think of and wish
for home; and, as I drew nearer, I found the attraction stronger
and stronger. My diligence and speed increased with my impa-
tience. I drove on violently, and made such long stretches, that
a very few days brought me to my own house, and to the arms
of my good old wife and children, where I remain, thanks to God,
at present well and happy.

Persons subject to the *hyp* complain of the north-east wind, as
increasing their malady. But since you promised to send me
kisses in that wind, and I find you as good as your word, it is to
me the gayest wind that blows, and gives me the best spirits. I
write this during a north-east storm of snow, the greatest we
have had this winter. Your favours come mixed with the snowy
fleeces, which are pure as your virgin innocence, white as your
lovely bosom, and—as cold. But let it warm towards some worthy young man, and may Heaven bless you both with every kind
of happiness.

*By June 1755 Catherine had written Franklin three letters to which he
had not replied. Then on 28 June he admitted that he had 'said a
thousand things that nothing should have tempted me to have said to
anybody else . . . Tell me you are well and forgive me and love me one
thousandth part so well as I do you and then I will be contented . . .'*

*Some of the letters between Franklin and Catherine have never
been found—strange in one who so carefully protected his vast
correspondence—but Mrs Franklin seems to have been aware of Katy's
virtues.*

TO MISS CATHERINE RAY

Philadelphia, 11 September 1755

Begone, business, for an hour, at least, and let me chat a little
with my Katy . . .

Now it is near four months since I have been favoured with a
single line from you; but I will not be angry with you, because it
is my fault. I ran in debt to you three or four letters; and as I did
not pay, you would not trust me any more, and you had some
reason. But, believe me, I am honest; and, though I should never
make equal returns, you shall see I will keep fair accounts. Equal

returns I can never make, though I should write to you by every post; for the pleasure I receive from one of yours is more than you can have from two of mine. The small news, the domestic occurrences among our friends, the natural pictures you draw of persons, the sensible observations and reflections you make, and the easy, chatty manner in which you express everything, all contribute to heighten the pleasure; and the more as they remind me of those hours and miles, that we talked away so agreeably, even in a winter journey, a wrong road, and a soaking shower.

I long to hear whether you have continued ever since in that monastery [Block Island]; or have broke into the world again, doing pretty mischief; how the lady Wards do, and how many of them are married, or about it; what is become of Mr B—— and Mr L——, and what the state of your heart is at this instant? But that, perhaps, I ought not to know; and, therefore, I will not conjure, as you sometimes say I do. If I could conjure, it should be to know what was that *oddest question about me that ever was thought of,* which you tell me a lady had just sent to ask you.

I commend your prudent resolutions, in the article of granting favours to lovers. But, if I were courting you, I could not hardly approve such conduct. I should even be malicious enough to say you were too *knowing,* and tell you the old story of the Girl and the Miller. I enclose you the songs you write for, and with them your Spanish letter with a translation. I honour that honest Spaniard for loving you. It showed the goodness of his taste and judgment. But you must forget him, and bless some worthy young Englishman.

You have spun a long thread, five thousand and twenty-two yards. It will reach almost from Rhode Island hither. I wish I had hold of one end of it, to pull you to me. But you would break it rather than come. The cords of love and friendship are longer and stronger, and in times past have drawn me farther; even back from England to Philadelphia. I guess that some of the same kind will one day draw you out of that Island . . .

Mrs Franklin was very proud, that a young lady should have so much regard for her old husband, as to send him such a present. We talk of you every time it comes to table. She is sure you are a sensible girl, and a notable housewife, and talks of bequeathing me to you as a legacy; but I ought to wish you a better, and hope she will live these hundred years; for we are grown old together, and if she has any faults, I am so used to 'em that I don't perceive 'em; as the song says,

> *Some faults we have all, and so has my Joan,*
> 　　*But then they're exceedingly small;*
> *And, now I am used, they are like my own,*
> 　　*I scarcely can see 'em at all,*
> 　　　　　　　　　*My dear friends,*
> 　　*I scarcely can see 'em at all.*

Indeed, I begin to think she has none, as I think of you. And since she is willing I should love you, as much as you are willing to be loved by me, let us join in wishing the old lady a long life and a happy.

FOUR

THE OLD ENGLAND MAN

After the frontier crisis of 1755, General Braddock's defeat in his attempt to capture Fort Dusquesne (the future Pittsburgh), and Franklin's efforts as 'General' Franklin, to strengthen Pennsylvania's western defences, the Quaker party won the election in 1756. This was a victory not only for the Quakers but for Franklin himself in his campaign to replace the role of the proprietors with that of the Crown. The Assembly therefore resolved to send Franklin to London to present its case for the defence, and to secure approval for its policy of taxing the proprietary estates.

Franklin was by then fifty. He did not return home for five years, and though he filled his letters to Debby with warm sentiments and gifts galore he was, apart from a two year period between 1762 and 1764, an absentee husband for fifteen years.

Craven Street, recommended by the agent Robert Charles, seemed like a second home to him, and London became almost as familiar as Philadelphia. He liked living among the bustle of traders and markets, the smell of print and the excitement of differing opinions.

Even before his arrival Franklin had earned himself an international reputation, as discoverer of the identification of lightning and electricity, as printer, publisher and civic planner. He had acquired a host of British friends. Besides Collinson, the Quaker merchant and botanist with whom he and his son William stayed on their arrival in London, there was the physician and botanist Dr John Fothergill, another Quaker; Dr Pemberton of the Royal Society (which had in 1753 awarded him its Copley medal and which in 1756 would elect him to a Fellowship); Dr William Strahan, the Scottish-born printer and publisher of Dr Johnson's Dictionary, Gibbon *and* The London Chronicle *(Franklin called him 'Straney'); and Richard Jackson the lawyer, who would succeed him as Pennsylvania agent in 1762, when Franklin briefly returned to Philadelphia.*

In fifteen years of London residence (from 1757 to '62, and from 1764 to '75) he reigned as uncrowned king at Mrs Stevenson's in Craven Street, where he could genially describe himself as 'Big Man', 'Great Person' and 'Dr Fatsides'. Polly, Mrs Stevenson's eighteen-year-old daughter, became as close to him as any daughter could be. The street with no embankment to shelter it as now, ran from the river—a major artery—to the busy Hungerford Market. The coffee houses of the Strand and the City were close by, and Franklin enjoyed a busy social round: Mondays at the George and Vulture, Thursdays at St Paul's (later the London) Coffee House, and erratically at the Dog Tavern or the Pennsylvania Coffee House. He mixed with the great—a visit or two to Lord Despencer's in Wycombe, another to Lord Shelburne's to meet the Abbé Morellet—but he was never of the Establishment. He felt, significantly, most at home in Scotland with Hume and Kames, 'Jupiter' Carlyle and 'Jolly Jack Phosphorus' (John Anderson). His scientific experiments continued, but with longer and longer interruptions: experiments with 'musical glasses', with heating rooms, cures for colds, the design of clocks, phonetics, the cause of lead-poisoning, and a multitude of other subjects. And always letters, to a host of friends.

He lived well: he had a coach of his own, hired for 12 guineas a month (the price went up to 15 pounds on his second trip to Scotland in 1771), and he had two black servants, King and Peter, who had made the journey with father and son—though King ran away after a year. William Franklin was a tall, handsome twenty-seven-year-old, enrolled as a student in the Middle Temple. He was often a guest at the Duke of Northumberland's town house across the way and his tastes were expensive. His tentative engagement to Elizabeth Graeme of Philadelphia lapsed, and in 1760 he fathered an illegitimate son, 'Temple'. Franklin père sent presents home, two case-loads of them: china and tableware, blankets and tablecloths, a harpsichord costing 42 guineas for Sally.

I also forgot, among the china, to mention a large fine jug for beer, to stand in the cooler. I fell in love with it at first sight; for I thought it looked like a fat jolly dame, clean and tidy, with a neat blue and white calico gown on, good-natured and lovely, and put me in mind—of somebody.

William Strahan

The honours continued: a LLD of St Andrews in 1759, a DCL of Oxford in 1762. Certainly Franklin was reluctant to leave the home country with its 'sensible, virtuous and elegant minds' when the time came in 1762.

But this is to anticipate. Father and son crossed the Atlantic in 1757, the journey from New York to Falmouth taking only thirty days. William, writing to his then fiancée, recounted high winds, being 'several times chac'd', and being almost wrecked on the Isles of Scilly. He wrote with feeling, 'let the pleasures of the country be ever so great, they are dearly earn'd by a voyage across the Atlantick.'

In the Autobiography *his father was more eloquent on the six-week delay before the packet,* London Wall, *sailed (this was due to the need to escort Commander-in-Chief Lord Loudoun's forces on their way to Cape Breton in the war with the French in Canada): but both in New York and at sea he wasted no time: an improved* Poor Richard's Almanack *was prepared, the twenty-sixth and last under his name, drawing together 'into a connected discourse' some one hundred of the aphorisms and maxims that had appeared in previous editions. This time they issued from the mouth of yet another* persona, *Father Abraham, 'a plain clean old man, with white locks', called on by the crowd at a public auction to comment on the trials of meeting heavy taxes.*

The maxims of Father Abraham all preach industry, thrift, and canniness. In Pennsylvania, Franklin thought that 'the book discouraged useless expense in foreign superfluities' and that it produced that growing plenty of money observable for several years after its publication. Separately published as The Way to Wealth, *frequently reprinted, borrowed, quoted and translated into many languages, it was largely responsible for the image of Franklin as the patron saint of savings banks, high priest of prudence and enterprise, and mentor of hard-driving young immigrants like Scotch-Irish Thomas Mellon and Scotch-American Andrew Carnegie. Translated into French as* La Science du Bonhomme Richard, ou moyen facile de payer les impôts, *the Almanack helped Franklin's standing in France, where he was already well-known as a scientist. But the collection represents only one facet—and that twinkling with humour—of a many-faceted personality.*

THE WAY TO WEALTH

Preface to *Poor Richard Improved:* 1758

COURTEOUS READER,

I have heard that nothing gives an author so great pleasure, as to find his works respectfully quoted by other learned authors. This pleasure I have seldom enjoyed; for though I have been, if I may say it without vanity, an *eminent author* of Almanacks annually now a full quarter of a century, my brother authors in the same way, for what reason I know not, have ever been very sparing in their applauses; and no other author has taken the least notice of me, so that did not my writings produce me some solid *pudding*, the great deficiency of *praise* would have quite discouraged me.

Judge then how much I must have been gratified by an incident I am going to relate to you. I stopt my horse lately where a great number of people were collected at a vendue of merchant goods. The hour of sale not being come, they were conversing on the badness of the times, and one of the company called to a plain clean old man, with white locks, *Pray, Father* Abraham, *what think you of the times? Won't these heavy taxes quite ruin the country? How shall we ever be able to pay them? What would you advise us to?*—Father *Abraham* stood up, and replied, If you'd have my advice, I'll give it you in short, for a *word to the wise is enough,* and *many words won't fill a bushel,* as *Poor Richard says.* They joined in desiring him to speak his mind, and gathering round him, he proceeded as follows . . .

If time be of all things the most precious, *wasting time* must be, as *Poor Richard* says, *the greatest prodigality,* since, as he elsewhere tells us, *Lost time is never found again;* and what we call *time-enough, always proves little enough:* Let us then up and be doing, and doing to the purpose; so by diligence shall we do more with less perplexity. *Sloth makes all things difficult, but industry all easy,* as *Poor Richard* says; and *He that riseth late, must trot all day, and shall scarce overtake his business at night.* While *laziness travels so slowly, that poverty soon overtakes him,* as we read in *Poor Richard,* who adds, *Drive thy business, let not that drive thee;* and *Early to bed, and early to rise, makes a man healthy, wealthy and wise.*

So much for industry, my friends, and attention to one's own business; but to these we must add *frugality,* if we would make our *industry* more certainly successful. A man may, if he knows not how to save as he gets, *keep his nose all his life to the grindstone,* and die not worth a *groat* at last. *A fat kitchen makes a lean will,* as *Poor Richard* says; and,

> *Many estates are spent in the getting,*
> *Since women for tea forsook spinning and knitting,*
> *And men for punch forsook hewing and splitting.*

This doctrine, my friends, is *reason* and *wisdom;* but after all, do not depend too much upon your own *industry,* and *frugality,* and *prudence,* though excellent things, for they may all be blasted without the blessing of Heaven; and therefore ask that blessing humbly, and be not uncharitable to those that at present seem to want it, but comfort and help them. Remember *Job* suffered, and was afterwards prosperous.

And now to conclude, *Experience keeps a dear school, but fools will learn in no other, and scarce in that;* for it is true, *we may give advice, but we cannot give conduct,* as *Poor Richard* says: However, remember this, *They that won't be counselled, can't be helped,* as *Poor Richard* says: And farther, That *if you will not hear Reason, she'll surely rap your knuckles.*

Thus the old gentleman ended his harangue. The people heard it, and approved the doctrine and immediately practised the contrary, just as if it had been a common sermon; for the vendue opened, and they began to buy extravagantly, notwithstanding all his cautions, and their own fear of taxes. I found the good man had thoroughly studied my Almanacks, and digested all I had dropt on those topicks during the course of five-and-twenty years. The frequent mention he made of me must have tired anyone else, but my vanity was wonderfully delighted with it, though I was conscious that not a tenth part of the wisdom was my own which he ascribed to me, but rather the *gleanings* I had made of the sense of all ages and nations. However, I resolved to be the better for the echo of it; and though I had at first determined to buy stuff for a new coat, I went away resolved to wear my old one a little longer. *Reader,* if thou wilt do the same, thy profit will be as great as mine.

I am, as ever, Thine to serve thee,

7 July 1757   RICHARD SAUNDERS

On arrival in England Benjamin wrote immediately to his wife:

To Deborah, Falmouth, 17 July 1757

The bell ringing for church, we went thither immediately, and with hearts full of gratitude, returned sincere thanks to God for the mercies we had received: were I a Roman Catholic, perhaps I should on this occasion vow to build a chapel to some saint; but as I am not, if I were to vow at all, it should be to build a lighthouse.

He then turned his sights on London. According to the Autobiography,

I set out immediately, with my son, for London, and we only stopped a little by the way to view Stonehenge on Salisbury Plain, and Lord Pembroke's house and gardens, with his very curious antiques at Wilton.

He arrived in London 27 July 1757. And so to business. Franklin recalled the purpose of his mission in Part IV of the Autobiography:

As soon as I was settled in a lodging Mr Charles had provided for me, I went to visit Dr Fothergill, to whom I was strongly recommended, and whose counsel respecting my proceedings I was advised to obtain. He was against an immediate complaint to government, and thought the proprietaries should first be personally applied to, who might possibly be induced by the interposition and persuasion of some private friends, to accommodate matters amicably. I then waited on my old friend and correspondent, Mr Peter Collinson, who told me that John Hanbury, the great Virginia merchant, had requested to be informed when I should arrive, that he might carry me to Lord Granville's, who was then President of the Council and wished to see me as soon as possible. I agreed to go with him the next morning. Accordingly Mr Hanbury called for me and took me in his carriage to that nobleman's, who received me with great civility; and after some questions respecting the present state of affairs in America and discourse thereupon, he said to me: 'You Americans have wrong ideas of the nature of your constitution; you contend that the king's instructions to his governors are not laws, and think yourselves at liberty to regard or disregard them at your own discretion. But those instructions are not like the pocket instructions given to a minister going abroad, for regulating his conduct in some trifling point of ceremony. They are first drawn up by judges learned in the laws; they are then considered, debated, and perhaps amended in Council, after which they are signed by the king. They are then, so far as they relate to you, the *law of the land,* for the king is the LEGISLATOR OF THE COLONIES.' I told his lordship this was new doctrine to me. I had always understood from our charters that our laws were to be made by our Assemblies, to be presented indeed to the king for his royal assent, but that being once given the king could not repeal or alter them. And as the Assemblies could not make permanent laws without his assent, so neither could he make a law for them without theirs. He assured me I was totally mistaken. I did not think so, however, and his lordship's conversation having a little alarmed me as to what might be the sentiments of the court concerning us, I wrote it down as soon as I returned to my lodgings. I recollected that about twenty years before, a clause in a bill brought into Parliament by the ministry had proposed to make the king's instructions laws in the colonies, but the clause was thrown out by the Commons, for which we adored them as our friends and friends of liberty, till by their conduct towards us in 1765 it seemed that they had refused that point of sovereignty to the king only that they might reserve it for themselves.

After some days, Dr Fothergill having spoken to the proprietaries, they agreed to a meeting with me at Mr T. Penn's house in Spring Garden. The conversation at first consisted of mutual declarations of disposition to reasonable accommodations, but I suppose each party had its own ideas of what should be meant by *reasonable.* We then went into consideration of our several points of complaint, which I enumerated. The proprietaries justified their conduct as well as they could, and I the Assembly's. We now appeared very wide, and so far from each other in our opinions as to discourage all hope of agreement. However, it was concluded that I should give them the heads of our complaints in writing, and they promised then to consider them. I did so soon after, but they put the paper into the hands of their solicitor, Ferdinand John Paris, who managed for them all their law business in their great suit with the neighbouring proprietary of Maryland, Lord Baltimore, which had subsisted seventy years, and wrote for them all their papers and messages in their dispute with the Assembly. He was a proud, angry man, and as I had occasionally in the answers of the Assembly treated his papers with some severity, they being really weak in point of argument and haughty in expression, he had conceived a mortal enmity to me, which discovering itself whenever we met, I declined the proprietary's proposal that he and I should discuss the heads of complaint between our two selves, and refused treating with anyone but them. They then by his advice put the paper into the hands of the Attorney- and Solicitor-General for their opinion and counsel upon it, where it lay unanswered a year wanting eight days, during which time I made frequent demands of an answer from the proprietaries, but without obtaining any other than that they had not yet received the opinion of the Attorney- and Solicitor-General. What it was when they did receive it I never learnt, for they did not communicate it to me, but sent a long message to the Assembly drawn and signed by Paris, reciting my paper, complaining of its want of formality, as a rudeness on my part, and giving a flimsy justification of their conduct, adding that they should be willing to accommodate matters if the Assembly would send out *some person of candour* to treat with them for that purpose, intimating thereby that I was not such.

The want of formality or rudeness was, probably, my not having addressed the paper to them with their assumed titles of True and Absolute Proprietaries of the Province of Pennsylvania, which I omitted as not thinking it necessary in a paper, the intention of which was only to reduce to a certainty by writing, what in conversation I had delivered *viva voce*.

But during this delay, the Assembly having prevailed with Governor Denny to pass an act taxing the proprietary estate in common with the estates of the people, which was the grand point in dispute, they omitted answering the message.

When this act, however, came over, the proprietaries, counselled by Paris, determined to oppose its receiving the royal assent. Accordingly they petitioned the king in Council, and a hearing was appointed in which two lawyers were employed by them against the act, and two by me in support of it. They alleged that the act was intended to load the proprietary estate in order to spare those of the people, and that if it were suffered to continue in force, and the proprietaries who were in odium with the people, left to their mercy in proportioning the taxes, they would inevitably be ruined. We replied that the act had no such intention, and would have no such effect. That the assessors were honest and discreet men under an oath to assess fairly and equitably, and that any advantage each of them might expect in lessening his own tax by augmenting that of the proprietaries was too trifling to induce them to perjure themselves. This is the purport of what I remember as urged by both sides, except that we insisted strongly on the mischievous consequences that must attend a repeal, for that the money, 100,000 pounds, being printed and given to the king's use, expended in his service, and now spread among the people, the repeal would strike it dead in their hands to the ruin of many, and the total discouragement of future grants, and the selfishness of the proprietors in soliciting such a general catastrophe, merely from a groundless fear of their estate being taxed too highly, was insisted on in the strongest terms. On this, Lord Mansfield, one of the counsel, rose, and beckoning me took me into the clerk's chamber, while the lawyers were pleading, and asked me if I was really of opinion that no injury would be done the proprietary estate in the execution of the act. I said certainly. 'Then', says he, 'you can have little objection to enter into an engagement to assure that point.' I answered, 'None at all.' He then called in Paris, and after some discourse, his lordship's proposition was accepted on both sides; a paper to the purpose was drawn up by the clerk of the Council, which I signed with Mr Charles, who was also an agent of the province for their ordinary affairs, when Lord Mansfield returned to the Council Chamber, where finally the law was allowed to pass. Some changes were however recommended and we also engaged they should be made by a subsequent law, but the Assembly did not think them necessary; for one year's tax having been levied by the act before the order of Council arrived, they appointed a committee to examine the proceedings of the assessors, and on this committee they put several particular friends of the proprietaries. After a full enquiry, they unanimously signed a report that they found the tax had been assessed with perfect equity.

The Assembly looked on my entering into the first part of the engagement, as an essential service to the province, since it secured the credit of the paper money then spread over all the country. They gave me their thanks in form when I returned. But the proprietaries were enraged at Governor Denny for having passed the act, and turned him out with threats of suing him for breach of instructions which he had given bond to observe. He, however, having done it at the instance of the general, and for his Majesty's service, and having some powerful interest at court, despised the threats and they were never put in execution.

It was not all work. Henry Home, known by the courtesy title of Lord Kames, was a judge of the Court of Session, and was host to both Franklins on their first Scottish trip in 1759. Benjamin wrote to him from London.

To Lord Kames, London, 5 January 1760

How unfortunate I was that I did not press you and Lady Kames more strongly to favour us with your company farther. How much more agreeable would our journey have been if we could have enjoyed you as far as York. We could have beguiled the way by discoursing on a thousand things that now we may never have an opportunity of considering together; for conversation warms the mind, enlivens the imagination, and is continually starting fresh game, that is immediately pursued and taken, and which would never have occurred in the duller intercourse of epistolary correspondence.

No one can more sincerely rejoice than I do on the reduction of Canada; and this is not merely as I am a colonist, but as I am a Briton. I have long been of opinion, that the *foundations of the future grandeur and stability of the British Empire lie in America;* and though, like other foundations, they are low and little now, they are, nevertheless, broad and strong enough to support the greatest political structure that human wisdom ever yet erected. I am, therefore, by no means for restoring Canada. If we keep it, all the country from the St Lawrence to the Mississippi will in another century be filled with British people. Britain itself will become vastly more populous, by the immense increase of its commerce; the Atlantic sea will be covered with your trading ships; and your naval power, thence continually increasing, will extend your influence round the whole globe, and awe the world! If the French remain in Canada, they will continually harass our colonies by the Indians, and impede if not prevent their growth; your progress to greatness will at best be slow, and give room for many accidents that may for ever prevent it. But I refrain, for I see you begin to think my notions extravagant, and look upon them as the ravings of a mad prophet.

My son joins with me in the most respectful compliments to you and Lady Kames. Our conversation, till we came to York, was chiefly a recollection of what we had seen and heard, the pleasures we had enjoyed, and the kindnesses we had received, in Scotland, and how far that country had exceeded our expectations. On the whole, I must say, I think the time we spent there was six weeks of the *densest* happiness I have met with in any part of my life; and the agreeable and instructive society we found there in such plenty has left so pleasing an impression on my memory that, did not strong connections draw me elsewhere, I believe Scotland would be the country I should choose to spend the remainder of my days in.

Franklin wrote faithfully to his wife:

London, 27 June 1760

MY DEAR CHILD,

I wrote a line to you by the pacquet, to let you know we were well, and I promised to write you fully by Captain Budden, and answer all your letters, which I accordingly now sit down to do. I am concerned that so much trouble should be given you by idle reports concerning me. Be satisfied, my dear, that while I have my senses, and God vouchsafes me his protection, I shall do nothing unworthy the character of an honest man, and one that loves his family . . .

Peter continues with me, and behaves as well as I can expect, in a country where there are many occasions of spoiling servants, if they are ever so good. He has as few faults as most of them, and I see with only one eye, and hear only with one ear; so we rub on pretty comfortably. King, that you enquire after, is not with us. He ran away from our house, near two years ago, while we were absent in the country; But was soon found in Suffolk, where he had been taken in the service of a lady, that was very fond of the merit of making him a Christian, and contributing to his education and improvement. As he was of little use, and often in mischief, Billy consented to her keeping him while we stay in England. So the lady sent him to school, has him taught to read and write, to play on the violin and french horn, with some other accomplishments more useful in a servant. Whether she will finally be willing to part with him, or persuade Billy to sell him to her, I know not. In the meantime he is no expence to us. The dried venison was very acceptable, and I thank you for it. We have had it constantly shaved to eat with our bread and butter for breakfast, and this week saw the last of it. The bacon still holds out, for we are choice of it. Some rashers of it, yesterday relished a dish of green pease. Mrs Stevenson thinks there was never any in England so good. The smoked beef was also excellent.

The accounts you give me of the marriages of our friends are very agreeable. I love to hear of everything that tends to increase the number of good people. You cannot conceive how shamefully the mode here is a single life. One can scarce be in the company of a dozen men of circumstance and fortune, but what it is odds that you find on enquiry eleven of them are single. The great complaint is the excessive expensiveness of English wives.

Franklin found England cold, and suffered from a severe chill soon after his arrival. On recovery, his scientific interests continued and soon a stove was designed and built in Craven Street. He also experimented with his armonica, the earliest American musical invention.

Franklin inherited his interest in music from his father; he himself played the violin, the harp and the guitar, and may even have composed string quartets. His tastes were for simple melodies and 'Scotch airs', and, as his letters to Lord Kames (1765) and to his elder brother, Peter (1762) reveal, he thought 'the reigning taste quite out of nature'.

'Musical glasses' were familiar enough, but in the 1740s they became something of a vogue, when an eccentric Irishman, Richard Pockrich (or Puckridge) gave concerts by striking the glasses with sticks, or by rubbing their rims with moistened fingers which gave their notes a more sustained quality. In 1746, the German composer Christoph Wilibald Gluck used the 'glasspiel' in a concert in London. An amateur performer was the scientist Edward Hussey Delaval, whom Franklin had helped elect to the Royal Society in 1759, and who brought them to Franklin's attention.

Franklin's interest was practical as well as musical. He devised a workable instrument, with clear instructions for blowing the glasses and tuning them, and for fitting them to a horizontal spindle running the length of a trough of water, in which their lower parts were submerged. By 1762, 'Franklin's glasschords' were being manufactured, and advertised for sale at forty guineas. He took one instrument back with him to Philadelphia. Indeed, in December 1762, he eased the strain of a meeting with Mrs Ann Graeme, the mother of William's jilted Betsy, by giving her a 'tune on the armonica'.

For some thirty years the musical glasses continued to be the rage in Europe. Mozart heard Friedrich Anton Mesmer play them, and composed one of his most delightful works, the Adagio and Rondo for Glass Armonica, with Flute, Oboe, Viola and Violincello (K 617) and an Adagio for Armonica solo (K 536); Beethoven wrote a fragment for it in Friedrich Dunker's opera Leonora Probaska (Op 202). Marianne Davies's concerts throughout Europe popularised the instrument, and Marie Antoinette became one of her pupils. A keyboard was devised in 1787 by Karl Leopold Rollig in Hamburg. Its fragility, however, prevented the armonica from becoming widely popular, and it was thought that it produced a nervous tremor in the hands and arms of its players.

Plate X.

Vol.VI.p.248.

ARMONICA.

Fig.1.

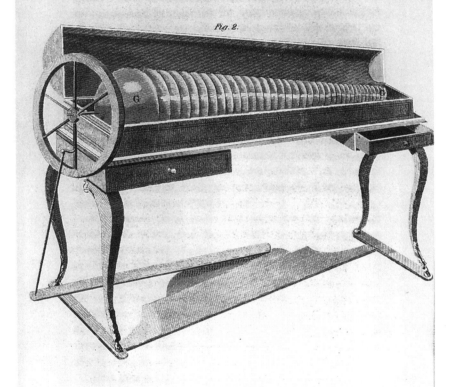

Fig.2.

Boston. Published by Hilliard, Gray & Co.

Franklin's armonica

*Mesmer found that its tone helped induce trances in his patients. The
proprietors took a different view. In April 1761, Thomas Penn wrote to
Governor James Hamilton (Denny's successor) that Franklin was happily
spending his time on 'philosophic matters and on musical performances
on glasses'.*

*Franklin himself described his new instrument to the Italian scientist,
Giambatista Beccaria:*

> London, 13 July 1762
>
> Perhaps, however, it may be agreeable to you, as you live in a
> musical country, to have an account of the new instrument
> lately added here to the great number that charming science
> was before possessed of. As it is an instrument that seems pe-
> culiarly adapted to Italian music, especially that of the soft and
> plaintive kind, I will endeavour to give you such a description
> of it, and of the manner of constructing it, that you or any of
> your friends may be enabled to imitate it, if you incline so to do,
> without being at the expense and trouble of the many experi-
> ments I have made in endeavouring to bring it to its present
> perfection.
>
> The glasses are blown as near as possible in the form of
> hemispheres, having each an open neck or socket in the middle.
> The thickness of the glass near the brim about a tenth of an
> inch, or hardly quite so much, but thicker as it comes nearer the
> neck, which in the largest glasses is about an inch deep, and an
> inch and half wide within, these dimensions lessening as the
> glasses themselves diminish in size, except that the neck of the
> smallest ought not to be shorter than half an inch. The largest
> glass is nine inches diameter, and the smallest three inches.
> Between these two are twenty-three different sizes, differing
> from each other a quarter of an inch in diameter. To make a
> single instrument there should be at least six glasses blown of
> each size; and out of this number one may probably pick thirty-
> seven glasses (which are sufficient for three octaves with all
> the semi-tones) that will be each either the note one wants or a
> little sharper than that note, and all fitting so well into each
> other as to taper pretty regularly from the largest to the small-
> est. It is true there are not thirty-seven sizes, but it often hap-
> pens that two of the same size differ a note or half-note in tone,

by reason of a difference in thickness, and these may be placed one in the other without sensibly hurting the regularity of the taper form . . .

The glasses being thus tuned, you are to be provided with a case for them, and a spindle on which they are to be fixed. My case is about three feet long, eleven inches every way wide within at the biggest end, and five inches at the smallest end; for it tapers all the way, to adapt it better to the conical figure of the set of glasses. This case opens in the middle of its height, and the upper part turns up by hinges fixed behind. The spindle, which is of hard iron, lies horizontally from end to end of the box within, exactly in the middle, and is made to turn on brass gudgeons at each end. It is round, an inch diameter at the thickest end, and tapering to a quarter of an inch at the smallest. A square shank comes from its thickest end through the box, on which shank a wheel is fixed by a screw. This wheel serves as a fly to make the motion equable, when the spindle, with the glasses, is turned by the foot like a spinning-wheel. My wheel is of mahogany, eighteen inches diameter, and pretty thick, so as to conceal near its circumference about twenty-five pounds of lead. An ivory pin is fixed in the face of this wheel, and about four inches from the axis. Over the neck of this pin is put the loop of the string that comes up from the movable step to give it motion. The case stands on a neat frame with four legs . . .

My largest glass is G, a little below the reach of a common voice, and my highest G, including three complete octaves. To distinguish the glasses the more readily to the eye, I have painted the apparent parts of the glasses within side, every semi-tone white, and the other notes of the octave with the seven prismatic colours, viz., C, red; D, orange; E, yellow; F, green; G, blue; A, indigo; B, purple; and C, red again; so that glasses of the same colour (the white excepted) are always octaves to each other.

This instrument is played upon, by sitting before the middle of the set of glasses as before the keys of a harpsichord, turning them with the foot, and wetting them now and then with a sponge and clean water. The fingers should be first a little soaked in water, and quite free from all greasiness; a little fine chalk upon them is sometimes useful, to make them catch the glass and bring out the tone more readily. Both hands are used, by which means different parts are played together. Observe, that the tones are best drawn out when the glasses turn *from* the ends of the fingers, not when they turn *to* them . . .

In honour of your musical language, I have borrowed from it the name of this instrument, calling it the Armonica.

In 1762 William Franklin became engaged to Elizabeth Downes from the West Indies, disappointing his father who had hoped that Polly Stevenson would become his daughter-in-law. He wrote to her from Portsmouth on his way back to Philadelphia.

Portsmouth, 11 August 1762

MY DEAR POLLY:

This is the best paper I can get at this wretched inn, but it will convey what is entrusted to it as faithfully as the finest. It will tell my Polly how much her friend is afflicted that he must, perhaps never again, see one for whom he has so sincere an affection joined to so perfect an esteem; who he once flattered himself might become his own, in the tender relation of a child, but can now entertain such pleasing hopes no more. Will it tell her *how much* he is afflicted? No, it cannot.

Adieu, my dearest child. I will call you so. Why should I not call you so, since I love you with all the tenderness, all the fondness of a father? Adieu. May the God of all goodness shower down his choicest blessings upon you, and make you infinitely happier than that event could have made you. Adieu. And wherever I am, believe me to be, with unalterable affection, my dear Polly, your sincere friend . . .

Contemplating his departure from England, Franklin wrote to his friend Strahan:

Portsmouth, Monday, 23 August 1762

DEAR SIR:

I have been two nights on board expecting to sail, but the wind continuing contrary, am just now on shore again, and have met with your kind letter of the 20th . . . I cannot, I assure you, quit even this disagreeable place without regret, as it carries me still farther away from those I love, and from the opportunities of hearing of their welfare. The attraction of reason is at present for the other side of the water, but that of inclination will be for this side. You know which usually prevails. I shall probably make but this one vibration and settle here for ever.

He wrote again to his friend when he reached home:

I got home well the 1st of November, and had the happiness to find my little family perfectly well, and that Dr Smith's reports of the diminution of my friends were all false. My house has been full of succession of them from morning to night ever since my arrival, congratulating me on my return with the utmost cordiality and affection. My fellow-citizens, while I was on the sea, had at the annual election chosen me unanimously, as they had done every year while I was in England, to be their representative in Assembly, and would, they say, if I had not disappointed them by coming privately to town, have met me with 500 horse.

In two years he would, he told Strahan, remove to England, 'provided we can persuade the good woman to cross the seas.'

The best survey of Franklin's two years in Philadelphia (1762–64) was given by Franklin himself in a letter to Lord Kames:

London, 2 June 1765

I left England about the end of August 1762, in company with ten sail of merchant ships, under a convoy of a man-of-war. We had a pleasant passage to Madeira, where we were kindly received and entertained: our nation being then in high honour with the Portuguese, on account of the protection we were then affording them against the united invasions of France and Spain. 'Tis a fertile island, and the different heights and situations among its mountains afford such temperaments of air that all the fruits of northern and southern countries are produced there: corn, grapes, apples, peaches, oranges, lemons, plantains, bananas, etc. Here we furnished ourselves with fresh provisions and refreshments of all kinds; and, after a few days, proceeded on our voyage, running southward until we got into the trade winds, and then with them westward till we drew near the coast of America. The weather was so favourable that there were few days in which we could not visit from ship to ship, dining with each other, and on board of the man-of-war; which made the time pass agreeably, much more so than when one goes in a single ship; for this was like travelling in a moving village, with all one's neighbours about one.

On the 1st of November, I arrived safe and well at my own home, after an absence of near six years; found my wife and daughter well; the latter grown quite a woman, with many amiable accomplishments acquired in my absence; and my friends as hearty and affectionate as ever, with whom my house was filled for many days, to congratulate me on my return. I had been chosen yearly during my absence to represent the city of Philadelphia in our provincial Assembly; and, on my appearance in the House, they voted me 3,000 pounds sterling for my services in England, and their thanks, delivered by the Speaker. In February following my son arrived with my new daughter; for, with my consent and approbation, he married soon after I left England a very agreeable West India lady with whom he is very happy. I accompanied him to his government, where he met with the kindest reception from the people of all ranks, and has lived with them ever since in the greatest harmony. A river only parts that province and ours, and his residence is within seventeen miles of me, so that we frequently see each other.

In the spring of 1763 I set out on a tour through all the northern colonies to inspect and regulate the post offices in the several provinces. In this journey I spent the summer, travelled about 1600 miles, and did not get home till the beginning of November. The Assembly sitting through the following winter, and warm disputes arising between them and the governor, I became wholly engaged in public affairs; for, besides my duty as an Assemblyman, I had another trust to execute, that of being one of the commissioners appointed by law to dispose of the public money appropriated to the raising and paying an army to act against the Indians, and defend the frontiers. And then in December, we had two insurrections of the back inhabitants of our province, by whom twenty poor Indians were murdered that had, from the first settlement of the province, lived among us under the protection of our government. This gave me a good deal of employment; for as the rioters threatened further mischief, and their actions seemed to be approved by an ever-acting party, I wrote a pamphlet entitled *A Narrative, etc.* (which I think I sent to you) to strengthen the hands of our weak government by rendering the proceedings of the rioters unpopular and odious. This had a good effect; and afterwards, when a great body of them with arms marched towards the capital, in defiance of the government . . . I formed an association at the governor's request, for his and their defence, we having no militia. Near a thousand of our citizens accordingly took arms . . . so that for about forty-eight hours, I was a very great man . . . But the fighting face we put on, and the reasonings we used with the insurgents (for I went at the request of the governor and Council, with three others, to meet and discourse with them) having turned them back and restored quiet to the city, I became a less man than ever; for I had, by this transaction, made myself many enemies among the populace; and the governor . . . joined the whole weight of the proprietary interest to get me out of the Assembly, which was accordingly effected at the last election, by a majority of about twenty-five in 4000 votes. The House, however, when they met in October, approved of the resolution taken, while I was Speaker, of petitioning the Crown for a change of government, and requested me to return to England to prosecute the petition, which service I accordingly undertook, and embarked at the beginning of November last, being accompanied to the ship, sixteen miles, by a cavalcade of 300 of my friends, who filled our sails with their good wishes, and I arrived in thirty days in London.

Franklin had stayed only two years in Philadelphia. Despite his enjoyment of his wife and daughter, and his new three-storeyed house set back from Market Street, and the proximity of his son (with his bride) at Burlington and Trenton, where William was Royal Governor of New Jersey (an appointment Franklin père attributed to the interest of Lord

Bute, former tutor to the new king, George III, and Prime Minister in
1761), the appeal of the Old Country was strong. He remembered her
people with admiration in a letter to Polly Stevenson in March 1763:

Of all the enviable things England has, I envy it most its people.
Why should that petty island, which compared to America, is
but like a stepping-stone in a brook, scarce enough of it above
water to keep one's shoes dry; why, I say, should that little
island enjoy in almost every neighbourhood, more sensible,
virtuous, and elegant minds, than we can collect in ranging
a hundred leagues of our vast forests? But 'tis said the arts
delight to travel westward. You have effectually defended us
in this glorious war, and in time you will improve us. After
the first cares for the necessaries of life are over, we shall
come to think of the embellishments. Already some of our
young geniuses begin to lisp attempts at painting, poetry, and
musick.

The acquisition of Canada in 1763 brought an uncertain peace on the
frontier, even though there was in that year an ugly if short war with
Pontiac and the Ottawa Indians, coupled with anxieties in the Western
Counties. Franklin was summoned to mediate in 1764, when angry
Scots-Irish frontiersmen from Paxton and Donegal murdered defence-
less Indians in Lancaster, and marched on Philadelphia to protect
against what they saw as Quaker indifference to frontier defence. His
account of the march of the 'Paxton boys' is very bitter—an eloquent and
savage account of the massacres which, for once, lacks Franklin's cus-
tomary urbanity.

They would have been safer among the *Moors* in *Spain*, though
they had been murderers of sons; if faith had once been
pledged to them, and a promise of protection given. But these
have had the faith of the *English* given to them many times by
the government, and, in reliance on that faith, they lived among
us, and gave us the opportunity of murdering them. However,
what was honourable in *Moors*, may not be a rule to us; for we
are *Christians!* They would have been safer it seems among
Popish Spaniards, even if enemies, and delivered into their hands
by a tempest. These were not enemies; they were born among

us, and yet we have killed them all. But shall we imitate *idolatrous Papists*, we that are *enlightened Protestants?* They would have even been safer among the *Negroes of Africa*, where at least one manly soul would have been found, with sense, spirit and humanity enough, to stand in their defence. But shall *Whitemen* and *Christians* act like a *Pagan Negroe?* In short it appears, that they would have been safe in any part of the known world, except in the neighbourhood of the CHRISTIAN WHITE SAVAGES of *Peckstang* and *Donegall!*

He campaigned openly now for an end of control by the Penns, and for the colony to cease to be a proprietary, and to become a royal colony, like the majority. When he was (narrowly) defeated at the polls in Philadelphia in 1764—his first defeat—he became aware that he had enemies. He mused on this predicament to his daughter, Sarah:

Reedy Island, 7 at night, 8 November 1764
You know I have many enemies, all indeed on the public account, (for I cannot recollect that I have in a private capacity given just cause of offence to anyone whatever,) yet they are enemies, and very bitter ones; and you must expect their enmity will extend in some degree to you, so that your slightest indiscretions will be magnified into crimes, in order the more sensibly to wound and afflict me. It is therefore the more necessary for you to be extremely circumspect in all your behaviour, that no advantage may be given to their malevolence.

Go constantly to church, whoever preaches. The act of devotion in the Common Prayer Book is your principal business there, and if properly attended to, will do more towards amending the heart than sermons generally can do. For they were composed by men of much greater piety and wisdom, than our common composers of sermons can pretend to be; and therefore I wish you would never miss the prayer days; yet I do not mean you should despise sermons, even of the preachers you dislike, for the discourse is often much better than the man, as sweet and clear waters come through very dirty earth. I am the more particular on this head, as you seemed to express a little before I came away some inclination to leave our church, which I would not have you do.

He was sent back to London by the Assembly to seek the end of proprietary rule. It was almost like going home.

His intense Anglophilia, however, did not lessen his asperity on learning from Richard Jackson that George Grenville had devised a new colonial policy, involving the tightening up of customs regulations, and the drafting of more troops to defend the newly-won lands in the West and on the Lakes. He wrote to Peter Collinson on 30 April 1764:

By the inclosed papers you will see that we are all to pieces again; and the general wish seems to be a king's government. If that is not to be obtained, many talk of quitting the province, and among them your old friend, who is tired of these contentions, and longs for philosophic ease and leisure.

I suppose by this time the wisdom of your Parliament has determined in the points you mention, of trade, duties, troops, and fortifications in America.

Our opinions or inclinations, if they had been known, would perhaps have weighed but little among you. We are in your hands as clay in the hands of the potter; and so in one more particular than is generally considered: for as the potter cannot waste or spoil his clay without injuring himself, so I think there is scarce anything you can do that may be hurtful to us but what will be as much or more so to you. This must be our chief security; for interest with you we have but little. The West Indians vastly outweigh us of the northern colonies. What we get above a subsistence we lay out with you for your manufactures.

Therefore what you get from us in taxes you must lose in trade. The cat can yield but her skin. And as you must have the whole hide, if you first cut thongs out of it, 'tis at your own expense. The same in regard to our trade with the foreign West India islands. If you restrain it in any degree, you restrain in the same proportion our power of making remittances to you, and of course our demand for your goods; for you will not clothe us out of charity, though to receive a hundred per cent for it in Heaven. In time perhaps mankind may be wise enough to let trade take its own course, find its own channels, and regulate its own proportions, etc. At present, most of the edicts of princes, placaerts, laws, and ordinances of kingdoms and states for that purpose prove political blunders. The advantages they produce not being *general* to the commonwealth, but *particular* to private persons or bodies in the state who procured them, and *at the expense of the rest of the people.* Does nobody see that if you confine us in America to your own Sugar Islands for that commodity, it must raise the price of it upon you in England? Just so much as the price advances, so much is every Englishman taxed to the West Indians.

The Old England Man was also a good American—descriptions that were not yet contradictory.

'THAT FINE AND NOBLE CHINA VASE, THE BRITISH EMPIRE'

The Britain to which Franklin returned was by that time preoccupied with other problems than Pennyslvania's form of government. Prime Minister George Grenville was worried over the size of the National Debt, now heavily increased by the cost of the war with France and the campaigns to liberate Canada. The war was won, he contended, primarily by British regulars. Their cost was borne by the British tax-payer, and by the steeply-increased land tax, to which an unrepresentative and heavily rural House of Commons was especially sensitive. In February 1764, long before Franklin landed, Grenville had proposed the imposition on the colonists of a Stamp Act on documents and newspapers—a tax that already obtained at home—and gave the colonial agents a year in which to suggest practical alternatives. Franklin, despite his earlier letters to Governor Shirley advocating colonial representation in London and claiming that the colonists were already heavily taxed (though indirectly), recognized that they had few sanctions. Always the realist, he promptly nominated two of his friends as stamp distributors. In America the news of the Stamp Act sparked off riots and demonstrations, and Franklin's critics in Philadelphia were not slow to portray him as a possible author of the act. For nine days Deborah and the family had to barricade themselves in against the crowd, and Debby hurriedly learned how to handle a musket. She reported to her husband:

'I sente to aske my brother to cume and bring his gun all so so we maid one room into a Magazin. I ordored sum sorte of defens up Stairs such as I cold manaig my self. I sed when I was advised to remove that I was verey shuer you had dun nothing to hurte aney body . . .'

To Lord Kames Franklin rehearsed, once more, the arguments for closer union between Mother Country and colonies:

SIR,

I have attentively perused the paper you sent me, and am of opinion, that the measure it proposes, of an union with the colonies, is a wise one; but I doubt it will hardly be thought so here, till it is too late to attempt it. The time has been, when the colonies would have esteemed it a great advantage, as well as honour to be permitted to send members to Parliament; and would have asked for that privilege, if they could have had the least hopes of obtaining it. The time is now come when they are indifferent about it, and will probably not ask it, though they might accept it if offered them; and the time will come, when they will certainly refuse it. But if such an union were now established (which methinks it highly imports this country to establish) it would probably subsist as long as Britain shall continue a nation. This people, however, is too proud, and too much despises the Americans, to bear the thought of admitting them to such an equitable participation in the government of the whole.

Then the next best thing seems to be, leaving them in the quiet enjoyment of their respective constitutions; and when money is wanted for any public service, in which they ought to bear a part, calling upon them by requisitorial letters from the Crown (according to the long-established custom) to grant such aids as their loyalty shall dictate, and their abilities permit.

Every year during the war, requisitions were made by the Crown on the colonies for raising money and men; that accordingly they made more extraordinary efforts, in proportion to their abilities, than Britain did; that they raised, paid, and clothed, for five or six years, near twenty-five thousand men, besides providing for other services, as building forts, equipping guard-ships, paying transports, etc. And that this was more than their fair proportion is not merely an opinion of mine, but was the judgment of government here, in full knowledge of all the facts; for the then ministry, to make the burthen more equal, recommended the case to Parliament, and obtained a reimbursement to the Americans of about 200,000 pounds sterling every year; which amounted only to about two fifths of their expense; and great part of the rest lies still a load of debt upon them; heavy taxes on all their estates, real and personal,

being laid by acts of their assemblies to discharge it, and yet will
not discharge it in many years.

While, then, these burdens continue; while Britain restrains
the colonies in every branch of commerce and manufactures
that she thinks interferes with her own; while she drains the
colonies, by her trade with them, of all the cash they can procure by every art and industry in any part of the world, and
thus keeps them always in her debt; (for they can make no law
to discourage the importation of your to *them* ruinous superfluities, as *you* do the superfluities of France; since such a law
would immediately be reported against by your Board of
Trade, and repealed by the Crown;) I say, while these circumstances continue, and while there subsists the established
method of royal requisitions for raising money on them by their
own assemblies on every proper occasion; can it be necessary or
prudent to distress and vex them by taxes laid here, in a Parliament wherein they have no representative, and in a manner
which they look upon to be unconstitutional and subversive of
their most valuable rights? And are they to be thought unreasonable and ungrateful if they oppose such taxes?

In my own private judgment, I think an immediate repeal of
the Stamp Act would be the best measure for this country; but
a suspension of it for three years, the best for that. The repeal
would fill them with joy and gratitude, re-establish their respect
and veneration for Parliament, restore at once their ancient
and natural love for this country, and their regard for everything that comes from it; hence the trade would be renewed in
all its branches; they would again indulge in all the expensive
superfluities you supply them with, and their own new-assumed
home industry would languish. But the suspension, though it
might continue their fears and anxieties, would at the same
time keep up their resolutions of industry and frugality; which
in two or three years would grow into habits, to their lasting
advantage. However, as the repeal will probably not be now
agreed to, from what I think a mistaken opinion, that the honour and dignity of government is better supported by persisting
in a wrong measure once entered into, than by rectifying an
error as soon as it is discovered; we must allow the next best
thing for the advantage of both countries, is the suspension;

for, as to executing the act by force, it is madness, and will be ruin to the whole.

Franklin the realist was also, however, Franklin the opportunist. If the protest was to be on the grand scale, then he was the one to voice it. Along with the merchants whose trade with America was being disrupted by widespread boycotts (notably among them the Anglo-American Barlow Trecothick, MP), Franklin organized the witnesses who, marshalled at the bar of the House of Commons, protested against the act in February 1766 and secured its repeal. He was prompt to print and circulate and send to America copies of his own brilliant answers (carefully rehearsed) to no fewer than 174 questions (carefully planted), for example:

Q.   What was the temper of America towards Great Britain before the year 1763?

A.   The best in the world. They submitted willingly to the government of the Crown, and paid, in all their courts, obedience to Acts of Parliament. Numerous as the people are in the several old provinces, they cost you nothing in forts, citadels, garrisons or armies, to keep them in subjection. They were governed by this country at the expense only of a little pen, ink and paper. They were led by a thread. They had not only a respect, but an affection, for Great Britain, for its laws, its customs and manners, and even a fondness for its fashions, that greatly increased the commerce. Natives of Britain were always treated with particular regard; to be an Old England man was, of itself, a character of some respect, and gave a kind of rank among us.

Q.   Don't you think they would submit to the Stamp Act, if it was modified, the obnoxious parts taken out, and the duty reduced to some particulars, of small moment?

A.   No; they will never submit to it.

Q.   Was it an opinion in America before 1763, that the Parliament had no right to lay taxes and duties there?

A.   I never heard any objection to the right of laying duties to

William Temple Franklin

Peter Collinson

regulate commerce; but a right to lay internal taxes was never supposed to be in Parliament, as we are not represented there.

Q.   Then no regulation with a tax would be submitted to?

A.   Their opinion is, that when aids to the Crown are wanted, they are to be asked of the several assemblies, according to the old established usage, who will, as they have always done, grant them freely. And that money ought not to be given away without their consent, by persons at a distance, unacquainted with their circumstances and abilities. The granting aids to the Crown is the only means they have of recommending themselves to their sovereign, and they think it extremely hard and unjust, that a body of men, in which they have no representatives, should make a merit to itself of giving and granting what is not its own, but theirs, and deprive them of a right they esteem of the utmost value and importance, as it is the security of all their other rights.

Q.   What used to be the pride of the Americans?

A.   To indulge in the fashions and manufactures of Great Britain.

Q.   What is now their pride?

A.   To wear their old clothes over again, till they can make new ones.

On the theme of clothes, Franklin celebrated the repeal appropriately. He wrote to his wife in April 1766:

As the Stamp Act is at length repealed, I am willing you should have a new gown, which you may suppose I did not send sooner, as I knew you would not like to be finer than your neighbours, unless in a gown of your own spinning. Had the trade between the two countries totally ceased, it was a comfort to me to recollect, that I had once been clothed from head to foot in woollen and linnen of my wife's manufacture, that I never was prouder of any dress in my life, and that she and her daughter might do it again if it was necessary . . . I have sent you a fine piece of pompador sattin, 14 yards, cost 11 shillings per yard;

a silk *negligee* and petticoat of brocaded lutestring for my dear
Sally, with two dozen gloves, 4 bottles of lavender water, and
two little reels.

Anglo-American concord continued to exercise him. He contributed a
piece to The Gazetteer *(in January 1766) that suggested an even*
wider rift.

Give me leave, Master John Bull, to remind you, that you are
related to all mankind; and therefore it less becomes you than
anybody, to affront and abuse other nations. But you have
mixed with your many virtues a pride, a haughtiness, and an
insolent contempt for all but yourself, that, I am afraid, will if
not abated, procure you one day or other a handsome drub-
bing. Besides your rudeness to foreigners, you are far from
being civil even to your own family. The Welch you have always
despised for submitting to your government: but why despise
your own English, who conquered and settled Ireland for you;
who conquered and settled America for you? Yet these you now
think you may treat as you please, because forsooth, they are a
conquered people. Why despise the Scotch, who fight and die
for you all over the world? Remember you courted Scotland for
one hundred years, and would fain have had your wicked will
of her. She virtuously resisted all your importunities; but at
length kindly consented to become your lawful wife. You then
solemnly promised to love, cherish, and honour her, as long as
you both should live; and yet you have ever since treated her
with the utmost contumely, which you now begin to extend to
your common children.

But, pray, when your enemies are uniting in a Family Compact against you, can it be descreet in you to kick up in your
own house a Family Quarrel? And at the very time you are
inviting foreigners to settle on your lands, and when you have
more to settle than ever you had before, is it prudent to suffer
your lawyer, Vindex, to abuse those who have settled there
already, because they cannot yet speak 'plain English'?—It is my
opinion Master Bull, that the Scotch and Irish, as well as the
colonists, are capable of speaking much plainer English than

they ever yet spoke, but which I hope they will never be provoked to speak.

*To Lord Kames he was frank about his political worries, and he was
clearly moving towards a commitment to what would later be called
'dominion status' for America.*

London, 11 April 1767

I send it [the copy of his cross-examination] you now, because
I apprehend some late incidents are likely to revive the contest
between the two countries. I fear it will be a mischievous one. It
becomes a matter of great importance that clear ideas should be
formed on solid principles, both in Britain and America, of the
true political relation between them, and the mutual duties
belonging to that relation. Till this is done, they will be often
jarring . . .

I am fully persuaded with you, that a *Consolidating Union*, by
a fair and equal representation of all the parts of this empire in
Parliament, is the only firm basis on which its political grandeur
and prosperity can be founded. Ireland once wished it, but now
rejects it. The time has been, when the colonies might have
been pleased with it: they are now *indifferent* about it; and if it
is much longer delayed, they too will *refuse* it. But the pride of
this people cannot bear the thought of it, and therefore it will
be delayed. Every man in England seems to consider himself as
a piece of a sovereign over America; seems to jostle himself into
the throne with the king, and talks of *our subjects in the colonies.*
The Parliament cannot well and wisely make laws suited to the
colonies, without being properly and truly informed of their
circumstances, abilities, temper, etc. This it cannot be, without
representatives from thence . . .

It is a common, but mistaken notion here, that the colonies
were planted at the expence of Parliament, and that therefore
the Parliament has a right to tax them, etc. The truth is, they
were planted at the expence of private adventurers, who went
over there to settle, with leave of the king, given by charter. On
receiving this leave, and those charters, the adventurers voluntarily engaged to remain the king's subjects, though in a foreign

country; a country which had not been conquered by either king or Parliament, but was possessed by a free people . . .

All the colonies acknowledge the king as their sovereign; his governors there represent his person: Laws are made by their Assemblies or little Parliaments, with the governor's assent, subject still to the king's pleasure to confirm or annul them: Suits arising in the colonies, and differences between colony and colony, are determined by the king in Council. In this view, they seem so many separate little states, subject to the same prince. The *sovereignty of the king* is therefore easily understood. But nothing is more common here than to talk of the *sovereignty* of PARLIMENT, and the *sovereignty of* THIS NATION over the colonies; a kind of sovereignty, the idea of which is not so clear, nor does it clearly appear on what foundation it is established. On the other hand, it seems necessary for the common good of the empire, that a power be lodged somewhere to regulate the general commerce; this, as things are at present circumstanced, can be placed nowhere so properly as in the Parliament of Great Britain.

Upon the whole, I have lived so great a part of my life in Britain, and have formed so many friendships in it, that I love it, and sincerely wish it prosperity; and therefore wish to see that union, on which alone I think it can be secured and established. As to America, the advantages of such a union to her are not so apparent. She may suffer at present under the arbitrary power of this country; she may suffer for a while in a separation from it; but these are temporary evils that she will outgrow. Scotland and Ireland are differently circumstanced. Confined by the sea, they can scarcely increase in numbers, wealth and strength, so as to overbalance England. But America, an immense territory, favoured by Nature with all advantages of climate, soil, great navigable rivers, and lakes, etc. must become a great country, populous and mighty; and will, in a less time than is generally conceived, be able to shake off any shackles that may be imposed on her, and perhaps place them on the imposers. In the meantime, every act of oppression will sour their tempers, lessen greatly, if not annihilate the profits of your commerce with them, and hasten their final revolt.

Franklin was obviously building up to write his Causes of the American Discontents, *which appeared in 1768. By now, sovereignty had
come to mean something different on different sides of the ocean.*

But a new kind of loyalty seems to be required of us, a loyalty
to Parliament; a loyalty that is to extend, it is said, to a surrender of all our properties, whenever a House of Commons, (in
which there is not a single member of our choosing) shall think
fit to grant them away without our consent; and to a patient
suffering the loss of our privileges as Englishmen, if we cannot
submit to make such surrender. We were separated too far
from Britain by the ocean, but we were united to it by respect
and love, so that we could at any time freely have spent our lives
and little fortunes in its cause: But this unhappy new system of
politics tends to dissolve those bands of union, and to sever us
for ever.

*The tensions did not prevent Franklin from travelling. He visited the
Low Countries in 1767, France in 1767 and 1769 (accompanied by
Sir John Pringle), Ireland in 1771, and Scotland recurrently. He
wrote to Polly Stevenson from Paris in 1767:*

The women we saw at Calais, on the road, at Bouloigne, and in
the inns and villages, were generally of dark complexions; but
arriving at Abbeville we found a sudden change, a multitude of
both women and men in that place appearing remarkably fair.
   As soon as we left Abbeville, the swarthiness returned. I speak
generally, for here are some fair women at Paris, who I think
are not whitened by art. As to rouge, they don't pretend to
imitate Nature in laying it on. There is no gradual diminution
of the colour, from the full bloom in the middle of the cheek to
the faint tint near the sides, nor does it show itself differently in
different faces. I have not had the honour of being at any lady's
toylette to see how it is laid on, but I fancy I can tell you how it
is or may be done. Cut a hole of three inches diameter in a piece
of paper; place it on the side of your face in such a manner as
that the top of the hole may be just under your eye; then with
a brush dipt in the colour, paint face and paper together; so
when the paper is taken off there will remain a round patch of

red exactly the form of the hole. This is the mode, from the actresses on the stage upwards through all ranks of ladies to the princesses of the blood, but it stops there, the queen not using it, having in the serenity, complacence, and benignity that shine so eminently in, or rather through her countenance, sufficient beauty, though now an old woman, to do extreamly well without it.

You see I speak of the queen as if I had seen her, and so I have; for you must know I have been at court. We went to Versailles last Sunday, and had the honour of being presented to the king; he spoke to both of us very graciously and chearfully, is a handsome man, has a very lively look, and appears younger than he is. The king talked a good deal to Sir John, asking many questions about our royal family; and did me too the honour of taking some notice of me; that's saying enough, for I would not have you think me so much pleased with this king and queen, as to have a whit less regard than I used to have for ours. No Frenchman shall go beyond me in thinking my own king and queen the very best in the world, and the most amiable.

Versailles has had infinite sums laid out in building it and supplying it with water. Some say the expences exceeded 80 millions sterling. The range of building is immense; the garden front most magnificent, all of hewn stone; the number of statues, figures, urns, etc., in marble and bronze of exquisite workmanship, is beyond conception. But the waterworks are out of repair, and so is great part of the front next the town, looking with its shabby half-brick walls, and broken windows, not much better than the houses in Durham Yard. There is, in short, both at Versailles and Paris, a prodigious mixture of magnificence and negligence, with every kind of elegance except that of cleanliness, and what we call *tidyness*. Though I must do Paris the justice to say, that in two points of cleanliness they exceed us. The water they drink, though from the river, they render as pure as that of the best spring, by filtring it through cisterns filled with sand; and the streets by constant sweeping are fit to walk in, though there is no paved footpath. Accordingly, many well-dressed people are constantly seen walking in them. The crowds of coaches and chairs for this reason is not so great.

Men, as well as women, carry umbrellas in their hands, which they extend in case of rain or two much sun; and a man with an umbrella not taking up more than three foot square, or nine square feet of the street, when, if in a coach, he would take up 240 square feet, you can easily conceive that though the streets here are narrower they may be much less encumbered. They are extreamly well paved, and the stones, being generally cubes, when worn on one side, may be turned and become new.

The civilities we everywhere receive give us the strongest impressions of the French politeness. It seems to be a point settled here universally, that strangers are to be treated with respect; and one has just the same deference shewn one here by being a stranger, as in England by being a lady. The custom-house officers at Port St Denis, as we entered Paris, were about to seize two doz. of excellent Bordeaux wine given us at Boulogne, and which we brought with us; but, as soon as they found we were strangers, it was immediately remitted on that account. At the Church of Notre Dame, where we went to see a magnificent illumination, with figures, etc., for the deceased dauphiness, we found an immense crowd, who were kept out by guards; but, the officer being told that we were strangers from England, he immediately admitted us, accompanied and showed us everything. Why don't we practise this urbanity to Frenchmen? Why should they be allowed to outdo us in anything?

Here is an exhibition of paintings like ours in London, to which multitudes flock daily. I am not connoisseur enough to judge which has most merit. Every night, Sundays not excepted here are plays or operas; and though the weather has been hot, and the houses full, one is not incommoded by the heat so much as with us in winter. They must have some way of changing the air, that we are not acquainted with. I shall enquire into it.

Travelling is one way of lengthening life, at least in appearance. It is but about a fortnight since we left London, but the variety of scenes we have gone through makes it seem equal to six months living in one place. Perhaps I have suffered a greater change, too, in my own person, than I could have done in six years at home. I had not been here six days, before my taylor and perruquier had transformed me into a Frenchman. Only think what a figure I make in a little bag-wig and naked ears! They told me I was become twenty years younger, and looked very galante.

So being in Paris where the mode is to be sacredly followed I was once very near making love to my friend's wife . . .

Back in Craven Street, Franklin kept a record of life there in a parody of a court gazette. His landlady was away for five days, leaving the household in charge of young Polly (newly married, in 1770, to William Hewson). It is a charming account of Franklin's domestic life in London.

Saturday, 22 September 1770

This morning Queen Margaret, accompanied by her first maid of honour, Miss Franklin, set out for Rochester. Immediately on their departure the whole street was in tears—from a heavy shower of rain. It is whispered that the new family administration, which took place on her Majesty's departure, promises, like all other new administrations, to govern much better than the old one.

We hear that the Great Person (so called from his enormous size) of a certain family in a certain street is grievously affected at the late changes, and could hardly be comforted this morning, though the new ministry promised him a roasted shoulder of mutton and potatoes for his dinner.

It is said that the same Great Person intended to pay his respects to another great personage this day at St James's, it being coronation day; hoping thereby a little to amuse his grief; but was prevented by an accident, Queen Margaret or her maid of honour having carried off the key of the drawers, so that the lady of the bedchamber could not come at a laced shirt for his Highness. Great clamours were made on this occasion against her Majesty.

Other accounts say that the shirts were afterwards found, though too late, in another place. And some suspect that the wanting a shirt from those drawers was only a ministerial pretence to excuse picking the locks, that the new administration might have everything at command.

We hear that the lady chamberlain of the household went to

market this morning by her own self, gave the butcher whatever he asked for the mutton, and had no dispute with the
potato-woman, to their great amazement at the change of times.

It is confidently asserted that this afternoon, the weather
being wet, the Great Person a little chilly, and nobody at home
to find fault with the expense of fuel, he was indulged with a
fire in his chamber. It seems the design is to make him contented by degrees with the absence of the queen.

A project has been under consideration of government to
take the opportunity of her Majesty's absence for doing a thing
she was always averse to, namely, fixing a new lock on the street
door, or getting a key made to the old one; it being found
extremely inconvenient that one or other of the great officers of
state should, whenever the maid goes out for a ha'penny worth
of sand or a pint of porter, be obliged to tend the door to let her
in again. But opinions being divided which of the two expedi-
ents to adopt, the project is for the present laid aside.

We have good authority to assure our readers that a Cabinet
Council was held this afternoon at tea; the subject of which was
a proposal for the reformation of manners and a more strict
observation of the Lord's day. The result was a unanimous
resolution that no meat should be dressed tomorrow; whereby
the cook and the first minister will both be at liberty to go to
church, the one having nothing to do, and the other no roast to
rule. It seems the cold shoulder of mutton and the apple pie
were thought sufficient for Sunday's dinner. All pious people
applaud this measure and it is thought the new ministry will
soon become popular.

Monday, 24 September

We are credibly informed that the Great Person dined this day
with the Club at the Cat and Bagpipes in the City on cold round
of boiled beef. This, it seems, he was under some necessity of
doing (though he rather dislikes beef) because truly the ministers were to be all abroad somewhere to dine on hot roast
venison. It is thought that if the queen had been at home he
would not have been so slighted. And though he shows out-
wardly no marks of dissatisfaction, it is suspected that he begins
to wish for her Majesty's return.

It is currently reported that poor nanny had nothing for dinner in the kitchen for herself and Puss but the scrapings of the bones of Saturday's mutton.

This evening there was high play at Craven Street House. The Great Person lost money. It is supposed the ministers, as is usually supposed of all ministers, shared the emoluments among them.

Even Franklin's bitter political exchanges with Lord Hillsborough (who from 1768 to 1772 was in effect minister for North American affairs) did not prevent a visit in 1771 to the earl's estate at Hillsborough in County Down—now a centre of acute political tension—where the son and heir was charged to act as guide.

In the same year, he paid two visits to Twyford in Hampshire to stay at the handsome Tudor house that his friend Jonathan Shipley, the Bishop of St Asaph, had inherited from his wife's family, and during the second of these visits the first part of The Autobiography *was written. The thank-you letters he wrote on his return to London are warm evidences of his uncanny and easy skills with people of all ages; to her mother, he describes his conversation with Kitty Shipley, at eleven the youngest of the five Shipley girls, whom he was accompanying back to her school in Marlborough Street, London, and from whom he coaxes— in the end—a voluble assessment of the men her sisters should marry, and who would best suit her.*

London, 12 August 1771

DEAR MADAM,

This is just to let you know that we arrived safe and well in Marlborough Street about six, where I delivered up my charge.

The above seems too short for a letter; so I will lengthen it by a little account of our journey. The first stage we were rather pensive. I tried several topics of conversation, but none of them would hold. But after breakfast, we began to recover spirits, and had a good deal of chat. Will you hear some of it? We talked of her brother, and she wished he was married. And don't you wish your sisters married too? Yes. All but Emily; I would not have her married. Why? Because I can't spare her, I can't part with her. The rest may marry as soon as they please, so they do but get good husbands. We then took upon us to consider for 'em what sort of husbands would be fittest for every one of them. We began with Georgiana. She thought a country gentleman, that loved travelling and would take her with him, that loved books and would hear her read to him; I added, that had a good estate and was a Member of Parliament and loved to see an experiment now and then. This she agreed to; so we set him down for Georgiana, and went on to Betsy. Betsy, says I, seems of a sweet mild temper, and if we should give her a country squire, and he should happen to be of a rough, passionate turn, and be angry now and then, it might break her heart. O, none of 'em must be so; for then they would not be good husbands. To make sure of this point, however, for Betsy, shall we give her a bishop? O no, that won't do. They all declare against the Church, and against the army; not one of them will marry either a clergyman or an officer; that they are resolved upon. What can be their reason for that? Why you know, that when a clergyman or an officer dies, the income goes with 'em; and then what is there to maintain the family? there's the point. Then suppose we give her a good, honest, sensible City merchant, who will love her dearly and is very rich? I don't know but that may do. We proceeded to Emily, her dear Emily, I was afraid we should hardly find anything good enough for Emily; but at last, after first settling that, if she did marry, Kitty was to live a good deal with her; we agreed that as Emily was very handsome we might expect an earl for her: So having fixed her, as I thought, a countess, we went on to Anna-Maria. She, says Kitty, should have a rich man that has a large family and a great many things to take care of; for she is very good at managing, helps my Mama very much, can look over bills, and order all sorts of family business. Very well; and as there is a grace and dignity in her manner that would become the station, what do you think of giving her a duke? O no! I'll have the duke for Emily. You may give the earl to Anna-Maria if you please: But Emily shall have the duke. I contested this matter some time; but at length was forced to give up the point, leave Emily in possession of the duke, and content myself with the earl for Anna-Maria. And now what shall we do for Kitty? We have forgot her, all this time. Well, and what will you do for her? I suppose that though the rest have resolved against the army, she may not yet have made so rash a resolution. Yes, but she has: Unless, now, an old one, an old general that has done fighting, and is rich, such a one as General Rufane; I like him a good deal; you must know I like an old man, indeed I do: And somehow or other all the old men take to me, all that come to our house like me better than my other sisters: I go to 'em and ask 'em how they do, and they like it mightily; and the maids take notice of it, and say when they see an old man come, there's a friend of yours, Miss Kitty. But then as you like an old general, hadn't you better take him while he's a young officer, and let him grow old upon your hands, because then, you'll like him better and better every year as he grows older and older. No, that won't do. He must be an old man of seventy or eighty, and take me when I am about thirty: And then you know I may be a rich young widow. We dined at Staines, she was Mrs Shipley, cut up the chicken pretty handily (with a little direction) and helped me in a very womanly manner. Now, says she, when I commended her, my father never likes to see me or Georgiana carve, because we do it, he says, so badly: But how should we learn if we never try? We drank good Papa and Mama's health, and the health's of the dutchess, the countess, the merchant's lady, the country gentlewoman, and our Welsh brother. This brought their affairs again under consideration. I doubt, says she, we have not done right for Betsy. I don't think a merchant will do for her. She is much inclined to be a fine gentlewoman; and is indeed already more of the fine gentlewoman, I think, than any of my other sisters; and therefore she shall be a vice countess.

Thus we chatted on, and she was very entertaining quite to town.

I have now made my letter as much too long as it was at first too short. The bishop would think it too trifling, therefore don't show it him. I am afraid too that you will think it so, and have a good mind not to send it. Only it tells you Kitty is well at school, and for that I let it go. My love to the whole amiable family, best respects to the bishop, and 1000 thanks for all your kindnesses, and for the happy days I enjoyed at Twyford. With the greatest esteem and respect, I am, madam, your most obedient humble servant

B. FRANKLIN

In fact, neither Kitty nor Betsy ever married, though Franklin's delight-
ful eleven-year-old companion lived to the ripe old age of eighty-one.
   The following year found Franklin condoling with Kitty's sister,
Georgiana, over the loss of a pet squirrel:

London, 26 September 1772

DEAR MISS,

   I lament with you most sincerely the unfortunate end of poor
MUNGO. Few squirrels were better accomplished; for he had
had a good education, had travelled far, and seen much of the
world. As he had the honour of being, for his virtues, your
favourite, he should not go, like common skuggs, without an
elegy or an epitaph. Let us give him one in the monumental
style and measure, which, being neither prose nor verse, is
perhaps the properest for grief; since to use common language
would look as it we were not affected, and to make rhymes
would seem trifling in sorrow.

EPITAPH

Alas! poor MUNGO!
Happy wert thou, hadst thou known
Thy own felicity.
Remote from the fierce bald eagle,
Tyrant of thy native woods,
Thou hadst nought to fear from his piercing talons,
Nor from the murdering gun
Of the thoughtless sportsman.
Safe in thy wired castle,
GRIMALKIN never could annoy thee.
Daily wert thou fed with the choicest viands,
By the fair hand of an indulgent mistress;
But, discontented,
Thou wouldst have more freedom.

Too soon, alas! didst thou obtain it;
And wandering,
Thou art fallen by the fangs of wanton, cruel RANGER!

Learn hence,
Ye who blindly seek more liberty,

Whether subjects, sons, squirrels or daughters,
That apparent restraint may be real protection;
Yielding peace and plenty
With security.

You see, my dear miss, how much more decent and proper this broken style is, than if we were to say, by way of epitaph,

Here SKUGG
Lies snug,
As a bug
In a rug.

and yet, perhaps there are people in the world of so little feeling as to think that this would be a good-enough epitaph for poor Mungo.

If you wish it, I shall procure another to succeed him; but perhaps you will now choose some other amusement.

Privately enjoyable, Craven Street was not only the base for many of Franklin's scientific experiments (where he built stoves, invented his armonica, designed clocks and studied lead poisoning) but also a journalist's office. There he wrote the two slashing satires which marked the start of his breach with the British Government. He gave an account of their reception in a letter to his son.

London, 6 October 1773
From a long and thorough consideration of the subject, I am indeed of opinion that the Parliament has no right to make any law whatever, binding on the colonies; that the king, and not the king, Lords, and Commons collectively, is their sovereign; and that the king, with their respective Parliaments, is their only legislator. I know your sentiments differ from mine on these subjects. You are a thorough government man, which I do not wonder at, nor do I aim at converting you. I only wish you to act uprightly and steadily, avoiding that duplicity which in Hutchinson adds contempt to indignation. If you can promote the prosperity of your people and leave them happier than you found them, whatever your political principles are, your memory will be honoured.

I have written two pieces here lately for the *Public Advertiser*, on American affairs, designed to expose the conduct of this country towards the colonies in a short, comprehensive, and striking view, and stated, therefore, in out-of-the-way forms, as most likely to take the general attention. The first was called *Rules by Which a Great Empire May Be Reduced to a Small One;* the second, *An Edict of the King of Prussia.* I sent you one of the first, but could not get enough of the second to spare you one, though my clerk went the next morning the printer's and wherever they were sold. They were all gone but two. In my own mind I preferred the first, as a composition, for the quantity and variety of the matter contained and a kind of spirited ending of each paragraph. But I find that others here generally prefer the second.

I am not suspected as the author except by one or two friends; and have heard the latter spoken of in the highest terms, as the keenest and severest piece that has appeared here for a long time. Lord Mansfield, I hear, said of it, that it *was very able and very artful indeed;* and would do mischief by giving here a bad impression of the measures of government; and in the colonies, by encouraging them in their contumacy. It is reprinted in the *Chronicle*, where you will see it, but stripped of all the capitaling and italicizing that intimate the allusions and mark the emphasis of written discourses, to bring them as near as possible to those spoken. Printing such a piece all in one even small character seems to me like repeating one of Whitefield's sermons in the monotony of a schoolboy.

What made it the more noticed here was that people in reading it were, as the phrase is, *taken in,* till they had got half through it, and imagined it a real edict, to which mistake I suppose the King of Prussia's *character* must have contributed. I was down at Lord Le Despencer's when the post brought that day's papers. Mr Whitehead was there, too (Paul Whitehead, the author of *Manners*), who runs early through all the papers and tells the company what he finds remarkable. He had them in another room, and we were chatting in the breakfast parlour, when he came running in to us out of breath, with the paper in his hand. 'Here!' says he, 'here's news for ye! Here's the King of Prussia claiming a right to this kingdom!' All stared, and I as much as anybody; and he went on to read it. When he had read two or three paragraphs, a gentleman present said: 'Damn his impudence; I dare say we shall hear by next post that he is upon his march with one hundred thousand men to back this.' Whitehead, who is very shrewd, soon after began to smoke it, and looking in my face, said: 'I'll be hanged if this is not some of your American jokes upon us.' The reading went on, and ended with abundance of laughing and a general verdict that it was a fair hit; and the piece was cut out of the paper and preserved in my lord's collection.

AN EDICT BY THE KING OF PRUSSIA

From the *Gentleman's Magazine*, October, 1773

Dantzic, 5 September

We have long wondered here at the supineness of the English nation, under the Prussian impositions upon its trade entering our port. We did not, till lately, know the claims, ancient and modern, that hang over that nation; and therefore could not suspect that it might submit to those impositions from a sense of duty or from principles of equity. The following Edict, just made publick, may, if serious, throw some light upon this matter.

'FREDERIC, by the grace of God, King of Prussia, etc. etc. etc., to all present and to come, (*à tous présens et à venir,*) Health. The peace now enjoyed throughout our dominions, having afforded us leisure to apply ourselves to the regulation of commerce, the improvement of our finances, and at the same time the easing our domestic subjects in their taxes: For these causes, and other good considerations us thereunto moving, we hereby make known, that, after having deliberated these affairs in our council, present our dear brothers, and other great officers of the state, members of the same, we, of our certain knowledge, full power, and authority royal, have made and issued this present Edict, viz.

'Whereas it is well known to all the world, that the first German settlements made in the island of Britain, were by colonies of people, subject to our renowned ducal ancestors, and drawn from their dominions, under the conduct of Hengist, Horsa, Hella, Uff, Cerdicus, Ida, and others; and that the said colonies have flourished under the protection of our august house for ages past; have never been emancipated therefrom; and yet have hitherto yielded little profit to the same: And whereas we ourself have in the last war fought for and defended the said colonies, against the power of France, and thereby enabled them to make conquests from the said power in America, for which we have not yet received adequate compensation: And whereas it is just and expedient that a revenue should be raised from the said colonies in Britain, towards our indemnification; and that those who are descendants of our ancient subjects, and thence still owe us due obedience, should contribute to the replenishing of our royal coffers as they must have done, had their ancestors remained in the territories now to us appertaining: We do therefore hereby ordain and command, that, from and after the date of these presents, there shall be levied and paid to our officers of the *customs*, on all goods, wares, and merchandizes, and on all grain and other produce of the earth, exported from the said island of Britain, and on all goods of whatever kind imported into the same, a duty of four and a half per cent *ad valorem*, for the use of us and our successors. And that the said duty may more effectually be collected, we do hereby ordain, that all ships or vessels bound from Great Britain to any other part of the world, or from any other part of the world to Great Britain, shall in their respective voyages touch at our port of Koningsberg, there to be unladen, searched, and charged with the said duties.

'And whereas there hath been from time to time discovered in the said island of Great Britain, by our colonists there, many mines or beds of iron-stone; and sundry subjects, of our ancient dominion, skilful in converting the said stone into metal, have in time past transported themselves thither, carrying with them and communicating that art; and the inhabitants of the said island, presuming that they had a natural right to make the best use they could of the natural productions of their country for their own benefit, have not only built furnaces for smelting the said stone into iron, but have erected plating-forges, slitting-mills, and steel-furnaces, for the more convenient manufacturing of the same; thereby endangering a diminution of the said manufacture in our ancient dominion; we do therefore hereby farther ordain, that, from and after the date hereof, no mill or other engine for slitting or rolling of iron, or any plating-forge to work with a tilt-hammer, or any furnace for making steel, shall be erected or continued in the said island of Great Britain: And the Lord Lieutenant of every county in the said island is hereby commanded, on information of any such erection within his county, to order and by force to cause the same to be abated and destroyed; as he shall answer the neglect thereof to us at his peril. But we are nevertheless graciously pleased to permit the inhabitants of the said island to transport their iron into Prussia, there to be manufactured, and to them returned; they paying our Prussian subjects for the workmanship, with all the costs of commission, freight, and risk, coming and returning; anything herein contained to the contrary notwithstanding.

'We do not, however, think fit to extend this our indulgence to the article of wool; but, meaning to encourage, not only the manufacturing of woollen cloth, but also the raising of wool, in our ancient dominions, and to prevent both, as much as may be, in our said island, we do hereby absolutely forbid the transportation of wool from thence, even to the Mother Country, Prussia; and that those islanders may be farther and more effectually restrained in making any advantage of their own wool in the way of manufacture, we command that none shall be carried out of one county into another; nor shall any worsted, bay, or woollen yarn, cloth, says, bays, kerseys, serges, frizes, druggets, cloth-serges, shalloons, or any other drapery stuffs, or woollen manufactures whatsoever, made up or mixed with wool in any of the said counties, be carried into any other county, or be waterborne even across the smallest river or creek, on penalty of forfeiture of the same, together with the boats, carriages, horses, etc., that shall be employed in removing them. Nevertheless, our loving subjects there are hereby permitted (if they think proper) to use all their wool as manure for the improvement of their lands.

'And whereas the art and mystery of making hats hath arrived at great perfection in Prussia, and the making of hats by our remoter subjects ought to be as much as possible restrained:

And forasmuch as the islanders before mentioned, being in possession of wool, beaver and other furs, have presumptuously conceived they had a right to make some advantage thereof, by manufacturing the same into hats, to the prejudice of our domestic manufacture: We do therefore hereby strictly command and ordain, that no hats or felts whatsoever, dyed or undyed, finished or unfinished, shall be loaded or put into or upon any vessel, cart, carriage, or horse, to be transported or conveyed out of one county in the said island into another county, or to any other place whatsoever, by any person or persons whatsoever; on pain of forfeiting the same, with a penalty of 500 pounds sterling for every offence. Nor shall any hat-maker, in any of the said counties, employ more than two apprentices, on penalty of 5 pounds sterling per month; we intending hereby, that such hatmakers, being so restrained, both in the production and sale of their commodity, may find no advantage in continuing their business. But, lest the said islanders should suffer inconveniency by the want of hats, we are farther graciously pleased to permit them to send their beaver furs to Prussia; and we also permit hats made thereof to be exported from Prussia to Britain; the people thus favoured to pay all costs and charges of manufacturing, interest, commission to our merchants, insurance and freight going and returning, as in the case of iron.

'And, lastly, being willing farther to favour our said colonies in Britain, we do hereby also ordain and command, that all the *thieves*, highway and street robbers, house-breakers, forgerers, murderers, s—d—tes, and villains of every denomination, who have forfeited their lives to the law in Prussia; but whom we, in our great clemency, do not think fit here to hang, shall be emptied out of our gaols into the said island of Great Britain, for the better peopling of that country.

'We flatter ourselves, that these our royal regulations and commands will be thought just and reasonable by our much-favoured colonists in England; the said regulations being copied from their statutes of 10 and 11 William III. c. 10, 5 George II. c. 22, 23, George II. c. 29, 4 George I. c. II, and from other equitable laws made by their Parliaments; or from instructions given by their princes; or from resolutions of both Houses, entered into for the good government of their *own colonies in Ireland and America.*

'And all persons in the said island are hereby cautioned not to oppose in any wise the execution of this our Edict, or any part thereof, such opposition being high treason; of which all who are suspected shall be transported in fetters from Britain to Prussia, there to be tried and executed according to the Prussian law.

'Such is our pleasure.

'Given at Potsdam, this twenty-fifth day of the month of August, one thousand seven hundred and seventy-three, and in the thirty-third year of our reign.

'By the King, in his Council.

'RECHTMAESSIG, *Sec.*'

Some take this edict to be merely one of the king's *jeux d'esprit:* others suppose it serious, and that he means a quarrel with England; but all here think the assertion it concludes with, 'that these regulations are copied from acts of the English Parliament respecting their colonies,' a very injurious one; it being impossible to believe, that a people distinguished for their love of liberty, a nation so wise, so liberal in its sentiments, so just and equitable towards its neighbours, should, from mean and injudicious views of petty immediate profit, treat its own children in a manner so arbitrary and tyrannical!

RULES BY WHICH A GREAT EMPIRE MAY BE REDUCED TO A SMALL ONE

Presented to a late minister, when he entered upon his
administration
From the *Gentleman's Magazine*, September 1773

An ancient sage boasted, that, though he could not fiddle, he knew how to make a *great city* of a *little one*. The science that I, a modern simpleton, am about to communicate, is the very reverse.

I address myself to all ministers who have the management of extensive dominions, which from their very greatness are become troublesome to govern, because the multiplicity of their affairs leaves no time for *fiddling*.

1. In the first place, gentlemen, you are to consider, that a great empire, like a great cake, is most easily diminished at the edges. Turn your attention, therefore, first to your *remotest* provinces; that, as you get rid of them, the next may follow in order.

2. That the possibility of this separation may always exist, take special care the provinces are never incorporated with the Mother Country; that they do not enjoy the same common rights, the same privileges in commerce; and that they are governed by *severer* laws, all of *your enacting*, without allowing them any share in the choice of the legislators. By carefully making and preserving such distinctions, you will (to keep to my simile of the cake) act like a wise ginger-bread-baker, who, to facilitate a division, cuts his dough half through in those places where, when baked, he would have it *broken to pieces.*

3. Those remote provinces have perhaps been acquired, purchased, or conquered, at the *sole expence* of the settlers, or their ancestors, without the aid of the Mother Country. If this should happen to increase her *strength*, by their growing numbers, ready to join in her wars; her *commerce*, by their growing demand for her manufactures; or her *naval power*, by greater employment for her ships and seamen, they may probably suppose some merit in this, and that it entitles them to some favour; you are therefore to *forget it all, or resent it,* as if they had done you injury. If they happen to be zealous whigs, friends of liberty, nurtured in revolution principles, *remember all that* to their prejudice, and resolve to punish it; for such principles, after a revolution is thoroughly established, are of *no more use;* they are even *odious* and *abominable.*

4. However peaceably your colonies have submitted to your government, shewn their affection to your interests, and patiently borne their grievances; you are to *suppose* them always inclined to revolt, and treat them accordingly. Quarter troops among them, who by their insolence may *provoke* the rising of mobs, and by their bullets and bayonets *suppress* them. By this means, like the husband who uses his wife ill *from suspicion,* you may in time convert your *suspicions* into *realities.*

5. Remote provinces must have *governors* and *judges*, to represent the Royal Person, and execute everywhere the delegated parts of his office and authority. You ministers know, that much of the strength of government depends on the *opinion* of the people; and much of that opinion on the *choice of rulers* placed immediately over them. If you send them wise and good men for governors, who study the interest of the colonists, and advance their prosperity, they will think their king wise and good, and that he wishes the welfare of his subjects. If you send them learned and upright men for judges, they will think him a lover of justice. This may attach your provinces more to his government. You are therefore to be careful whom you recommend for those offices. If you can find prodigals, who have ruined their fortunes, broken gamesters or stockjobbers, these may do well as *governors;* for they will probably be rapacious, and provoke the people by their extortions. Wrangling proctors and pettifogging lawyers, too, are not amiss; for they will be for ever disputing and quarrelling with their little Parliaments. If withal they should be ignorant, wrong-headed, and insolent, so much the better. Attornies' clerks and Newgate solicitors will do for *Chief Justices,* especially if they hold their places *during your pleasure;* and all will contribute to impress those ideas of your government, that are proper for a people *you would wish to renounce it.*

6. To confirm these impressions, and strike them deeper, whenever the injured come to the capital with complaints of maladministration, oppression, or injustice, punish such suitors with long delay, enormous expence, and a final judgment in favour of the oppressor. This will have an admirable effect every way. The trouble of future complaints will be prevented, and governors and judges will be encouraged to farther acts of oppression and injustice; and thence the people may become more disaffected, and at length desperate.

7. When such governors have crammed their coffers, and made themselves so odious to the people that they can no longer remain among them, with safety to their persons, *recall and reward* them with pensions. You may make them *baronets* too, if that respectable order should not think fit to resent it. All will contribute to encourage new governors in the same practice, and make the supreme government, *detestable.*

8. If, when you are engaged in war, your colonies should vie in liberal aids of men and money against the common enemy, upon your simple requisition, and give far beyond their abilities, reflect that a penny taken from them by your power is more honourable to you, than a pound presented by their benevolence; despise therefore their voluntary grants, and resolve to harass them with novel taxes. They will probably complain to your Parliaments, that they are taxed by a body in which they have no representative, and that this is contrary to common right. They will petition for redress. Let the Parliaments flout their claims, reject their petitions, refuse even to suffer the reading of them, and treat the petitioners with the utmost contempt. Nothing can have a better effect in producing the alienation proposed; for though many can forgive injuries, *none ever forgave contempt.*

9. In laying these taxes, never regard the heavy burthens those remote people already undergo, in defending their own frontiers, supporting their own provincial governments, making new roads, building bridges, churches, and other public edifices, which in old countries have been done to your hands by your ancestors, but which occasion constant calls and demands on the purses of a new people. Forget the *restraints* you lay on their trade for *your own* benefit, and the advantage a *monopoly* of this trade gives your exacting merchants. Think nothing of the wealth those merchants and your manufacturers acquire by the colony commerce; their encreased ability thereby to pay taxes at home; their accumulating, in the price of their commodities, most of those taxes, and so levying them from their consuming customers; all this, and the employment and support of thousands of your poor by the colonists, you are *intirely to forget.* But remember to make your arbitrary tax more grievous to your provinces, by public declarations importing that your power of taxing them has *no limits;* so that when you take from them without their consent one shilling in the pound, you have a clear right to the other nineteen. This will probably weaken every idea of *security in their property,* and convince them, that under such a government they *have nothing they can call their own;* which can scarce fail of producing the *happiest consequences!*

10. Possibly, indeed, some of them might still comfort them-

selves, and say, 'Though we have no property, we have yet *something* left that is valuable; we have constitutional *liberty*, both of person and of conscience. This king, these Lords, and these Commons, who it seems are too remote from us to know us, and feel for us, cannot take from us our *Habeas Corpus* right, or our right of trial *by a jury of our neighbours;* then cannot deprive us of the exercise of our religion, alter our ecclesiastical constitution, and compel us to be Papists, if they please, or Mahometans.' To annihilate this comfort, begin by laws to perplex their commerce with infinite regulations, impossible to be remembered and observed; ordain seizures of their property for every failure; take away the trial of such property by jury, and give it to arbitrary judges of your own appointing, and of the lowest characters in the country, whose salaries and emoluments are to arise out of the duties or condemnations, and whose appointments are *during pleasure*. Then let there be a formal declaration of both Houses, that opposition to your edicts is *treason*, and that any person suspected of treason in the provinces may, according to some obsolete law, be seized and sent to the metropolis of the empire for trial; and pass an act, that those there charged with certain other offences, shall be sent away in chains from their friends and country to be tried in the same manner for felony. Then erect a new Court of Inquisition among them, accompanied by an armed force, with instructions to transport all such suspected persons; to be ruined by the expence, if they bring over evidences to prove their innocence, or be found guilty and hanged, if they cannot afford it. And, lest the people should think you cannot possibly go any farther, pass another solemn declaratory act, 'that king, Lords, Commons had, hath, and of right ought to have, full power and authority to make statutes of sufficient force and validity to bind the unrepresented provinces IN ALL CASES WHATSOEVER.' This will include *spiritual* with temporal, and, taken together, must operate wonderfully to your purpose; by convincing them, that they are at present under a power something like that spoken of in the scriptures, which can not only *kill their bodies*, but *damn their souls* to all eternity, by compelling them, if it pleases, *to worship the Devil*.

11. To make your taxes more odious, and more likely to

procure resistance, send from the capital a board of officers to superintend the collection, composed of the most *indiscreet, ill-bred*, and *insolent* you can find. Let these have large salaries out of the extorted revenue, and live in open, grating luxury upon the sweat and blood of the industrious; whom they are to worry continually with groundless and expensive prosecutions before the above mentioned arbitrary revenue judges; *all at the cost of the party prosecuted*, though acquitted, because *the king is to pay no costs*. Let these men, *by your order*, be exempted from all the common taxes and burthens of the province, though they and their property are protected by its laws. If any revenue officers are *suspected* of the least tenderness for the people, discard them. If others are justly complained of, protect and reward them. If any of the under officers behave so as to provoke the people to drub them, promote those to better offices: this will encourage others to procure for themselves such profitable drubbings, by multiplying and enlarging such provocations, and *all will work towards the end you aim at*.

12. Another way to make your tax odious, is to misapply the produce of it. If it was originally appropriated for the *defence* of the provinces, the better support of government, and the administration of justice, where it may be *necessary*, then apply none of it to that *defence*, but bestow it where it is *not necessary*, in augmented salaries or pensions to every governor, who has distinguished himself by his enmity to the people, and by calumniating them to their sovereign. This will make them pay it more unwillingly, and be more apt to quarrel with those that collect it and those that imposed it, who will quarrel again with them, and all shall contribute to your *main purpose*, of making them *weary of your government*.

13. If the people of any province have been accustomed to support their own governors and judges to satisfaction, you are to apprehend that such governors and judges may be thereby influenced to treat the people kindly, and to do them justice. This is another reason for applying part of that revenue in larger salaries to such governors and judges, given, as their commissions are, *during your pleasure* only; forbidding them to take any salaries from their provinces; that thus the people may no longer hope any kindness from their governors, or (in

Crown cases) any justice from their judges. And, as the money thus misapplied in one province is extorted from all, probably *all will resent the misapplication.*

14. If the Parliaments of your provinces should dare to claim rights, or complain of your administration, order them to be harrassed with *repeated dissolutions.* If the same men are continually returned by new elections, adjourn their meetings to some country village, where they cannot be accommodated, and there keep them *during pleasure;* for this, you know, is your PREROGATIVE; and an excellent one it is, as you may manage it to promote discontents among the people, diminish their respect, and *increase their disaffection.*

15. Convert the brave, honest officers of your *navy* into pimping tide-waiters and colony officers of the *customs.* Let those, who in time of war fought gallantly in defence of the commerce of their countrymen, in peace be taught to prey upon it. Let them learn to be corrupted by great and real smugglers; but (to shew their diligence) scour with armed boats every bay, harbour, river, creek, cove, or nook throughout the coast of your colonies; stop and detain every coaster, every wood-boat, every fisherman, tumble their cargoes and even their ballast inside out and upside down; and, if a penn'orth of pins is found unentered, let the whole be seized and confiscated. Thus shall the trade of your colonists suffer more from their friends in time of peace, than it did from their enemies in war. Then let these boats crews land upon every farm in their way, rob the orchards, steal the pigs and the poultry, and insult the inhabitants. If the injured and exasperated farmers, unable to procure other justice, should attack the aggressors, drub them, and burn their boats; you are to call this *high treason and rebellion,* order fleets and armies into their country, and threaten to carry all the offenders 3000 miles to be hanged, drawn, and quartered. *O! this will work admirably!*

16. If you are told of discontents in your colonies, never believe that they are general, or that you have given occasion for them; therefore do not think of applying any remedy, or of changing any offensive measure. Redress no grievance, lest they should be encouraged to demand the redress of some other grievance. Grant no request that is just and reasonable, lest they should make another that is unreasonable. Take all your infor-

mations of the state of the colonies from your governors and officers in enmity with them. Encourage and reward these *leasing-makers;* secrete their lying accusations, lest they should be confuted; but act upon them as the clearest evidence; and believe nothing you hear from the friends of the people: suppose all *their* complaints to be invented and promoted by a few factious demagogues, whom if you could catch and hang, all would be quiet. Catch and hang a few of them accordingly; and the *blood of the Martyrs* shall *work miracles* in favour of your purpose.

17. If you see *rival nations* rejoicing at the prospect of your disunion with your provinces, and endeavouring to promote it; if they translate, publish, and applaud all the complaints of your discontented colonists, at the same time privately stimulating you to severer measures, let not that *alarm* or offend you. Why should it, since you all mean *the same thing?*

18. If any colony should at their own charge erect a fortress to secure their port against the fleets of a foreign enemy, get your governor to betray that fortress into your hands. Never think of paying what it cost the country, for that would look, at least, like some regard for justice; but turn it into a citadel to awe the inhabitants and curb their commerce. If they should have lodged in such fortress the very arms they bought and used to aid you in your conquests, seize them all; it will provoke like *ingratitude* added to *robbery*. One admirable effect of these operations will be, to discourage every other colony from erecting such defences, and so your enemies may more easily invade them; to the great disgrace of your government, and of course *the furtherance of your project*.

19. Send armies into their country under pretence of protecting the inhabitants; but, instead of garrisoning the forts on their frontiers with those troops, to prevent incursions, demolish those forts, and order the troops into the heart of the country, that the savages may be encouraged to attack the frontiers, and that the troops may be protected by the inhabitants. This will seem to proceed from your ill will or your ignorance, and contribute farther to produce and strengthen an opinion among them, *that you are no longer fit to govern them.*

20. Lastly, invest the general of your army in the provinces, with great and unconstitutional powers, and free him from the

control of even your own civil governors. Let him have troops enow under his command, with all the fortresses in his possession; and who knows but (like some provincial generals in the Roman Empire, and encouraged by the universal discontent you have produced) he may take it into his head to set up for himself? If he should, and you have carefully practised these few *excellent rules* of mine, take my word for it, all the provinces will immediately join him; and you will that day (if you have not done it sooner) get rid of the trouble of governing them, and all the *plagues* attending their *commerce* and connection from henceforth and for ever.

QED.

Once Lord Hillsborough had resigned as Secretary of State for the Colonies (in 1772), to be replaced by Lord Dartmouth, Franklin was a happier man.

As to my situation here, nothing can be more agreeable, especially as I hope for less embarrassment from the new minister; a general respect paid me by the learned, a number of friends and acquaintance among them, with whom I have a pleasing intercourse; a character of so much weight, that it has protected me when some in-power would have done me injury, and continued me in an office they would have deprived me of; my company so much desired, that I seldom dine at home in winter, and could spend the whole summer in the country-houses of inviting friends, if I chose it. Learned and ingenious foreigners, that come to England, almost all make a point of visiting me; for my reputation is still higher abroad than here. Several of the foreign ambassadors have assiduously cultivated my acquaintance, treating me as one of their corps, partly I believe from the desire they have, from time to time, of hearing something of American affairs, an object become of importance in foreign courts, who begin to hope Britain's alarming power will be diminished by the defection of her colonies; and partly that they may have an opportunity of introducing me to the gentlemen of their country who desire it. The king, too, has lately been heard to speak of me with great regard.

SIX

THE UNGRATEFUL INCENDIARY

Between 1767 and 1769 Thomas Hutchinson, then lieutenant-governor (later governor) and Andrew Oliver, then secretary of the province (but later lieutenant-governor) wrote a number of letters to Thomas Whateley, Grenville's former secretary, in which drastic measures against the colonies were urged. 'There must be an abridgement of what are called English liberties,' wrote Hutchinson. These letters were shown to Franklin by an unknown Member of Parliament—Franklin never revealed his source.

With the owner's permission, Franklin sent this correspondence, in December 1772 (by which time Whateley had died), to his friend in Boston, Thomas Cushing, Speaker of the Massachusetts House of Representatives. Franklin instructed Cushing to show the letters to the colonial leaders—not to copy or print them—and then to return them.

Despite this injunction, they were printed in Boston and circulated in London. The London news-sheets speculated on the source of the 'leak'. An inconclusive duel was fought in Hyde Park between William Whateley, his brother's executor, and John Temple—who was accused of stealing the letters. In order to exonerate Temple, Franklin revealed, on Christmas Day 1773, that he had been responsible for sending the correspondence to Boston.

TO THE PRINTER OF THE PUBLIC ADVERTISER

SIR:

Finding that two gentlemen have been unfortunately engaged in a duel about a transaction and its circumstance of which both of them are totally ignorant and innocent, I think it incumbent upon me to declare (for the prevention of further mischief, as far as such a declaration may contribute to prevent it) that I alone am the person who obtained and transmitted to Boston the letters in question. Mr W. could not communicate them, because they were never in his possession; and for the same reason, they could not be taken from him by Mr T. They were not of the nature of *private* letters between friends. They were written by public officers to persons in public stations, on public affairs, and intended to procure public measures; they were therefore handed to other public persons who might be influenced by them to produce those measures. Their tendency was to incense the Mother Country against her colonies and, by the steps recommended, to widen the breach, which they effected. The chief caution expressed with regard to privacy was to keep their contents from the colony agents who, the writers apprehended, might return them or copies of them to America. That apprehension was, it seems, well founded, for the first agent who laid his hands on them thought it his duty to transmit them to his constituents.

B. FRANKLIN
Agent for the House of Representatives of Massachusetts Bay
Craven Street, 25 December 1773

The opinions expressed by Hutchinson were neither especially inflammatory nor more outspoken than those which many of his circle were regularly expressing; and they were private. By revealing them to his Boston colleagues, Franklin thought to shift blame from London to Hutchinson. But now Franklin could be attacked. In the Privy Council in January 1774, Alexander Wedderburn, Solicitor General, referred to him as 'the true incendiary', 'the actor and secret spring' of the committee of correspondence in Boston. His petition for Hutchinson's removal from the governorship was rejected. He himself lost his post as deputy post-master general. He kept Thomas Cushing in close touch with developments in London.

London, 15 February 1774

SIR,

I wrote a line to you by the last packet, just to acquaint you there had been a hearing on our petition. I shall now give you the history of it as succintly as I can.

We had long imagined that the king would have considered that petition, as he had done the preceding one, in his cabinet, and have given an answer without a hearing, since it did not pray punishments or disabilities on the governors. But on Saturday, the 8th of January, in the afternoon, I received notice from the clerk of the Council, that the lords of the Committee for Plantation Affairs would, on the Tuesday following at twelve, meet at the Cockpit, to take into consideration the petition referred to them by his Majesty, and that my attendance was required.

I sent directly to Mr Arthur Lee, requesting a meeting, that we might consult upon it. He was not at his chambers, but my note was left for him. Sunday morning I went to Mr Bollan and communicated the affair to him. He had received a similar notice. We considered whether it was best to employ other counsel, since Mr Lee, he said, could not be admitted as such, not being yet called to the bar. He thought it not advisable. He had sometimes done it in colony cases, and found lawyers of little service. Those who are eminent, and hope to rise in their profession, are unwilling to offend the court; and its disposition on this occasion was well known. But he would move to be heard in behalf of the council of the province, and thence take occasion to support the petition himself.

I went and sent again to Mr Lee's chambers in the Temple, but could not meet with him; and it was not till near the end of the week that I learned he was at Bath. On Monday, very late in the afternoon, I received another notice, that Mr Mauduit, agent for the governor and lieutenant-governor, had asked and obtained leave to be heard by counsel on the morrow in their behalf. This very short notice seemed intended to surprize us. On Tuesday, we attended at the Cockpit, and the petition being read, I was called upon for what I had to offer in support of it; when, as had been concerted between us, I acquainted their lordships that Mr Bollan, then present, in pursuance of their notice, would speak to it.

He came forward and began to speak; but objection was immediately made by some of the lords, that he, being only agent for the Council, which was not a party to this petition, could not properly be heard on it. He however repeatedly endeavoured to obtain leave to speak, but without effect; they would scarce hear out a sentence, and finally set him aside. I then said that, with the petition of the House of Representatives, I had received their resolutions which preceded it, and a copy of the letters on which those resolutions were founded, which I would lay before their lordships in support of the petition.

The resolutions were accordingly read; but, when the letters were taken up, Mr Wedderburn, the Solicitor-General, brought there as counsel for the governors, began to object, and inquire how they were authenticated, as did also some of the lords. I said the authentications were annexed. They wanted to know the nature of them. I said that would appear when they were read, and prayed they would hear them. Lord Chief Justice de Grey asked whom the letters were directed to; and, taking them in his hand, observed there was no address prefixed to any of them. I said that, though it did not appear to whom they were directed, it appeared who had written them; their names were subscribed; the originals had been shown to the gentlemen themselves, and they had not denied their handwriting; and the testifications annexed proved these to be true copies.

With difficulty I obtained leave to have the authentications read; and the Solicitor-General proceeding to make observations as counsel for the governors, I said to their lordships, that it was some surprize to me to find counsel employed against the petition; that I had no notice of that intention till late in the preceding day; that I had not purposed troubling their lordships with the hearing of counsel, because I did not conceive that anything could possibly arise out of the petition, any point of law or of right, that might require the discussion of lawyers; that I apprehended this matter before their lordships was rather a question of civil or political prudence, whether, on the state of the fact that the governors had lost all trust and confidence with the people, and become universally obnoxious, it would be for the interest of his Majesty's service to continue them in those stations in that province, that I conceived this to be a question of which their lordships were already perfect judges, and could receive no assistance in it from the arguments of counsel; but, if counsel was to be heard on the other side, I must then request leave to bring counsel in behalf of the Assembly, and that their lordships would be pleased to appoint a further day for the hearing, to give time for preparing the counsel.

Mr Mauduit was then asked if he would waive the leave he had of being heard by counsel, that their lordships might proceed immediately to consider the petition. He said he was requested by the governors to defend them, and they had promised to defray the expense, by which he understood that they expected he should employ counsel; and then, making me some compliments, as if of superior abilities, said he should not against me hazard the defence of his friends by taking it upon himself. I said I had intended merely to lay the papers before their lordships without making a single comment on them. But this did not satisfy; he chose to be heard by counsel. So finally I had leave to be heard by counsel also in behalf of the petition. The Solicitor-General, finding his cavils against the admission of the letters were not supportable, at last said that, to save their lordships' time, he would admit the copies to be true transcripts of the originals, but he should reserve to himself a right, when the matter come on again, of asking certain questions, such as, how the Assembly came into possession of them, through what hands, and by what means they were procured? 'Certainly,' replied Lord Chief Justice de Grey, somewhat austerely, 'and to whom they were directed; for the perfect understanding of the passages may depend on that and other such circumstances. We can receive no charge against a man founded on letters directed to nobody, and perhaps received by nobody. The laws of this country have no such practice.' Lord President, near whom I stood, as I was putting up my papers, asked me if I intended to answer such questions. In that, I said, I shall take counsel. The day appointed for the hearing was the 29th of January.

Several friends now came to me and advised me to retain Mr Dunning, formerly Solicitor-General, and very able in his profession. I wished first to consult with Mr Lee, supposing he might rather be for his friend, Mr Sergeant Glynn. I found Mr Lee was expected in town about the latter end of the week, and thought to wait his coming; in the meantime I was urged to take Mr Dunning's advice as to my own conduct, if such questions should be asked me. I did so; and he was clear that I was not and could not be obliged to answer them, if I did not choose it, which I informed him was the case, being under a promise not to divulge from whom I received the letters. He said he would attend, however, if I desired it, and object in my behalf to their putting such questions.

A report now prevailed through the town that I had been grossly abused by the Solicitor-General, at the council board. But this was premature. He had only intended it, and mentioned that intention. I heard, too, from all quarters, that the ministry and all the courtiers were highly enraged against me for transmitting those letters. I was called an incendiary, and the papers were filled with invectives against me. Hints were given me that there was some thoughts of apprehending me, seizing my papers, and sending me to Newgate. I was well informed that a resolution was taken to deprive me of my place, it was only thought best to defer it till after the hearing; I suppose, because I was there to be so blackened that nobody should think it injustice. Many knew, too, how the petition was to be treated; and I was told, even before the first hearing, that it was to be rejected with some epithets, the Assembly to be censured, and some honour done the governors. How this could be known, one cannot say. It might be only conjecture.

The transactions relating to the tea had increased and strengthened the torrent of clamour against us. No one had the least expectation of success to the petition; and, though I had asked leave to use counsel, I was half inclined to waive it, and save you the expense; but Mr Bollan was now strongly for it, as they had refused to hear him. And, though fortified by his opinion, as he had long experience in your affairs, I would at first have ventured to deviate from the instructions you sent me in that particular, supposing you to allow some discretionary liberty to your agents; yet, now that he urged it as necessary, I employed a solicitor, and furnished him with what materials I could for framing a brief; and Mr Lee, coming to town, entered heartily into the business, and undertook to engage Sergeant Glynn, who would readily have served us, but, being in a fit of the gout, which made his attendance uncertain, the solicitor retained Mr Dunning and Mr John Lee, another able man of the profession.

While my mind was taken up with this business, I was harassed with a subpoena from the chancellor to attend his court the next day, at the suit of Mr William Whately concerning the letters. This man was under personal obligations to me, such as would have made it base in him to commence such a suit of his own motion against me, without any previous notice, claim, or demand; but, if he was capable of doing it at the instance of the ministry, whose banker he is for some pension money, he must be still baser.

The briefs being prepared and perused by our counsel, we had a consultation at Mr Dunning's chambers in Lincoln's Inn. I introduced Mr Arthur Lee as my friend and successor in the agency. The brief, as you will see by a copy I send you, pointed out the passages of the letters, which were applicable in support of the particular charges contained in the resolutions and petition. But, the counsel observed, we wanted evidence to prove those passages false; the counsel on the other side would say they were true representations of the state of the country; and, as to the political reflections of the writers, and their sentiments of government, their aims to extend and enforce the power of Parliament and diminish the privileges of their countrymen, though these might appear in the letters and need no other proof, yet they would never be considered here as offences, but as virtues and merits. The counsel therefore thought it would answer no good end to insist on those particulars; and that it was more advisable to state as facts the general discontent of the people, that the governors had lost all credit with them, and were become odious, etc.; facts of which the petition was itself full proof, because otherwise it could not have existed; and then show that it must in such a situation be necessary for his Majesty's service, as well as the peace of the province, to remove them. By this opinion, great part of the brief became unnecessary.

Notwithstanding the intimations I had received, I could not believe that the Solicitor-General would be permitted to wander from the question before their lordships into a new case, the accusation of another person for another matter, not cognizable before them, who could not expect to be there so accused, and therefore could not be prepared for his defence.

And yet all this happened, and in all probability was precon-
certed; for all the courtiers were invited, as to an entertainment, and there never was such an appearance of privy
counsellors on any occasion, not less than thirty-five, besides an
immense crowd of other auditors.

The hearing began by reading my letter to Lord Dartmouth,
enclosing the petition, then the petition itself, the resolves, and
lastly the letters, the Solicitor-General making no objections,
nor asking any of the questions he had talked of at the preceding board. Our counsel then opened the matter, upon their
general plan, and acquitted themselves very handsomely; only
Mr Dunning, having a disorder on his lungs that weakened his
voice exceedingly, was not so perfectly heard as one could have
wished. The Solicitor-General then went into what he called a
history of the province for the last ten years, and bestowed
plenty of abuse upon it, mingled with encomium on the governors. But the favourite part of his discourse was levelled at
your agent, who stood there the butt of his invective ribaldry
for near an hour, not a single lord adverting to the impropriety
and indecency of treating a public messenger in so ignominious
a manner, who was present only as the person delivering your
petition, with the consideration of which no part of *his* conduct
had any concern. If he had done a wrong, in obtaining and
transmitting the letters, that was not the tribunal where he was
to be accused and tried. The cause was already before the chancellor. Not one of their lordships checked and recalled the or-
ator to the business before them, but, on the contrary, a very
few excepted, they seemed to enjoy highly the entertainment,
and frequently burst out in loud applauses. This part of his
speech was thought so good that they have since printed it, in
order to defame me everywhere, and particularly to destroy my
reputation on your side of the water; but the grosser parts of
the abuse are omitted, appearing, I suppose, in their own eyes,
too foul to be seen on paper so that the speech, compared to
what it was, is now perfectly decent. I send you one of the
copies. My friends advise me to write an answer, which I purpose immediately.

The reply of Mr Dunning concluded. Being very ill, and
much incommoded by standing so long, his voice was so feeble

as to be scarce audible. What little I heard was very well said, but appeared to have little effect.

Their lordships' report, which I send you, is dated the same day. It contains a severe censure, as you will see, on the petition and the petitioners; and, as I think, a very unfair conclusion from my silence, that the charge of surreptitiously obtaining the letters was a true one; though the solicitor, as appears in the printed speech, had acquainted them that the matter was before the chancellor; and my counsel had stated the impropriety of my answering there to charges then trying in another court. In truth I came by them honourably, and my intention in sending them was virtuous, if an endeavour to lessen the breach between two states of the same empire be such, by showing that the injuries complained of by one of them did not proceed from the other, but from traitors among themselves.

It may be supposed that I am very angry on this occasion, and therefore I did purpose to add no reflections of mine on the treatment the Assembly and their agent have received, lest they should be thought the effects of resentment and a desire of exasperating. But, indeed, what I feel on my own account is half lost in what I feel for the public. When I see that all petitions and complaints of grievances are so odious to government, that even the mere pipe which conveys them becomes obnoxious, I am at a loss to know how peace and union are to be maintained or restored between the different parts of the empire. Grievances cannot be redressed unless they are known; and they cannot be known but through complaints and petitions. If these are deemed affronts, and the messengers punished as offenders, who will henceforth send petitions? And who will deliver them? It has been thought a dangerous thing in any state to stop up the vent of griefs. Wise governments have therefore generally received petitions with some indulgence, even when but slightly founded. Those who think themselves injured by their rulers are sometimes, by a mild and prudent answer, convinced of their error. But where complaining is a crime, hope becomes despair.

The day following I received a written notice from the secretary of the general post office, that his Majesty's postmaster general *found it necessary* to dismiss me from my office of deputy postmaster general in North America. The expression was well chosen, for in truth they were *under a necessity* of doing it; it was not their own inclination; they had no fault to find with my conduct in the office; they knew my merit in it, and that, if it was now an office of value, it had become such chiefly through my care and good management; that it was worth nothing, when given to me; it would not then pay the salary allowed me, and, unless it did, I was not to expect it; and that it now produces near 3000 pounds a year clear to the treasury here. They had beside a personal regard for me. But as the post offices in all the principal towns are growing daily more and more valuable, by the increase of correspondence, the officers being paid *commissions* instead of *salaries*, the ministers seem to intend, by directing me to be displaced on this occasion, to hold out to them all an example that, if they are not corrupted by their office to promote the measures of administration, though against the interests and rights of the colonies, they must not expect to be continued. This is the first act for extending the influence of government in this branch. But as orders have been some time since given to the American postmaster general, who used to have the disposition of all places under him, not to fill vacancies of value till notice of such vacancies had been sent hither, and instructions thereupon received from hence, it is plain that such influence is to be a part of the system; and probable, that those vacancies will for the future be filled by officers from this country. How safe the correspondence of your Assembly committees along the continent will be through the hands of such officers may now be worth consideration, especially as the Post Office Act of Parliament allows a postmaster to open letters, if warranted so to do by the order of a secretary of state, and every provincial secretary may be deemed a secretary of state in his own province.

It is not yet known what steps will be taken by government with regard to the colonies, or to our province in particular. But, as inquiries are making of all who come from thence concerning the late riot and the meetings that preceded it, and who were speakers and movers at these meetings, I suspect there is some intention of seizing persons, and perhaps of sending them hither. But of this I have no certainty. No motion has yet been made in the House of Commons concerning our affairs; and that made in the House of Lords was withdrawn for the present. It is not likely, however, that the session will pass over without some proceeding relating to us, though perhaps it is not yet settled what the measures shall be. With my best wishes for the prosperity of the province, I have the honour to be sir, etc.,

B. FRANKLIN

It was the end of Franklin's usefulness in London. 'Hence it has often happened to me that while I have been thought here too much of an American, I have in America been deemed too much of an Englishman.'

On 20 February 1775, Franklin learned that his wife had died, after a stroke, two months earlier in Philadelphia. On 20 March, he embarked at Portsmouth in the Pennsylvania packet; he reached home on 5 May.

On the journey, he mused on the misunderstandings between Great Britain and its North American colonies. He was now aware that his account, subsequently known as The Negotiations to Prevent the War, *would form an important part of his own story. He still cast it in autobiographical form, as a private letter to his son. It would be the last of his writings so inscribed.*

But there was much more on which to ponder. His public career as the most eminent of Imperial administrators—postmaster, colonial agent, diplomat—seemed in ruins. He had failed to overturn proprietary government, to obtain a new colony in the West, to restore harmony. Even his reputation as Mr Smooth-it-away was gone. He hated the war, and the separation that he had never sought was now all too likely. Given his age, sixty-nine, and his distaste for violence, he was not now likely to see further public service. But this was the public man. The private? Perhaps the most remarkable feature of Franklin's character—amid a superhuman addiction to letters and public prints, all carefully copied and kept—is his silence on the thoughts of the private man. Although he made his first reputation through his journalism, he was always master of the great rule phrased, not by Poor Richard, but by Edward Everett: 'If you want your secret kept, keep it.' We shall never know who was the mother of his son, or of his grandson; we shall never know the strength of his feelings for Katy Ray of Block Island (or of hers for him), or of the personal relationship with Polly Stevenson Hewson, hidden behind their correspondence on the working of the barometer, the effects of heat of the sun on clothing, the habits of insects or the movements of the tides in the rivers.

Only on one issue does his control crack: his break with William. His son's loyalty to the Crown as Royal Governor prevented this remaining a private hurt. As early as 1762, the father had been aware of the son's taste for being a government man. Yet not until their meeting in Philadelphia in 1775 did the gulf—for them as for so many other families— become unbridgeable. Yet the condemnatory phrase the father used of the son nine years later—'there are natural duties which precede political ones and cannot be extinguished by them'—comes as a novelty in the older man's writing. No one had been readier than he to put politics before family, and to use one to help the other. His own discovery of these 'natural duties' probably came in retrospective old age. Certainly, on his return journey to Philadelphia in 1775, he must have been very conscious of one natural duty of which he had been conspicuously neglectful: concern for his wife.

Of her last eighteen years he had been absent from her for fifteen. He had never, apparently, been aware of her ill-health and suffering in her last six years. The separation was, of course, a consequence of his diplomatic mission. But, behind the warmth of his letters and his gifts, he could not but have long been aware that she shared none of his intellectual, scientific or political interests, and that—had he persuaded her to overcome her fear of the sea—her presence in London would have been an embarrassment. There was no marriage of minds here, and perhaps never had been. Deborah clearly had been a competent house- and-home-and-shopkeeper, a good and tolerant mother, dedicated to her husband, and clearly proud of him. As he journeyed 'home', there could not but have been a profound sadness in his heart, and perhaps some guilt; but this type of confessional, however suitable to Rousseau, was not a matter for Franklin's very public form of record-keeping. Nor did such revelations come from any other of the Founders.

On the seas and in retrospect, in Philadelphia and then in France, for him an image of 'England' as corrupt and vindictive now emerges. Yet we know from his own records how happy he had been, for many years, in Craven Street. The real legacies of these years, his friendship with a host of English and Scottish public men, in the end made possible the peace-making and reconciliation in 1782–3. But in 1775, between Portsmouth in the Old Country and the Market Street Wharf on the Delaware in the New, busy though he was with his narrative, and sedulously plumbing the ocean depths to establish the course of the Gulf Stream, he was aware only that the long idyll was over.

> On board the Pennsylvania Packet,
> bound to Philadelphia, 22 March 1775

DEAR SON:

Having now a little leisure for writing, I will endeavour, as I promised you, to recollect what particulars I can of the negotiations I have lately been concerned in, with regard to the *misunderstandings between Great Britain and America.*

During the recess of the last Parliament, which had passed the severe acts against the province of the Massachusetts Bay, the minority having been sensible of their weakness as an effect of their want of union among themselves, began to think seriously of a coalition. For they saw in the violence of these American measures, if persisted in, a hazard of dismembering, weakening, and perhaps ruining the British Empire. This inclined some of them to propose such an union with each other as might be more respectable in the ensuing session, have more weight in opposition, and be a body out of which a new ministry might easily be formed, should the ill-success of the late measures and the firmness of the colonies in resisting them make a change appear necessary to the king.

I took some pains to promote this disposition, in conversations with several of the principal among the minority of both Houses, whom I beseeched and conjured most earnestly not to suffer, by their little misunderstandings, so glorious a fabric as the present British Empire to be demolished by these blunderers; and for their encouragement assured them, as far as my opinions could give any assurance, of the *firmness* and *unanimity* of America, the continuance of which was what they had frequent doubts of, and appeared extremely apprehensive and anxious concerning it . . .

The new Parliament was to meet the 29th of November [1774]. About the beginning of that month, being at the Royal Society, Mr Raper, one of our members, told me there was a certain lady who had a desire of playing with me at chess, fancying she could beat me, and had requested him to bring me to her. It was, he said, a lady with whose acquaintance he was sure I should be pleased,

a sister of Lord Howe, and he hoped I would not refuse the chal-
lenge. I said I had been long out of practice, but would wait upon
the lady when he and she should think fit. He told me where her
house was, and would have me call soon, and, without further
introduction, which I undertook to do; but thinking it a little awkward, I postponed it; and on the 30th, meeting him again at the
feast of the Society election, being the day after the Parliament
met, he put me in mind of my promise, and that I had not kept
it, and would have me name a day when he said he would call for
me, and conduct me. I named the Friday following. He called
accordingly. I went with him, played a few games with the lady,
whom I found of very sensible conversation and pleasing behaviour, which induced me to agree most readily to an appointment
for another meeting a few days after; though I had not the least
apprehension that any political business could have any connection with this new acquaintance.

On the Thursday preceding this chess party, Mr David Barclay
called on me to have some discourse concerning the meeting of
merchants to petition Parliament. When that was over, he spoke
of the dangerous situation of American affairs, the hazard that
a civil war might be brought on by the present measures, and the
great merit that person would have who could contrive some
means of preventing so terrible a calamity and bring about a reconciliation. He was then pleased to add that he was persuaded,
from my knowledge of both countries, my character and influence in one of them, and my abilities in business, no man had so
much in his power as myself. I naturally answered that I should
certainly be very happy if I could in any degree be instrumental
in so good a work, but that I saw no prospect of it; for though I
was sure the Americans were always willing and ready to agree
upon any equitable terms, yet I thought an accommodation impracticable unless both sides wished it; and by what I could judge
from the proceedings of the ministry, I did not believe they had
the least disposition towards it; that they rather wished to provoke the North American people into an open rebellion, which
might justify a military execution and thereby gratify a grounded
malice which I conceived to exist here against the Whigs and Dis-
senters of that country. Mr Barclay apprehended I judged too
harshly of the ministers; he was persuaded they were not all of

that temper, and he fancied they would be very glad to get out of their present embarrassment on any terms, only saving the honour and dignity of the government. He wished therefore that I would think of the matter, and he would call again and converse with me further upon it. I said I would do so, as he requested it, but I had no opinion of its answering any purpose. We parted upon this. But two days after I received a letter from him, enclosed in a note from Dr Fothergill, both of which follow:

'Youngsbury, near Ware, 3rd, 12th Month, 1774
'ESTEEMED FRIEND:

'After we parted on Thursday last I accidentally met our mutual friend Dr Fothergill, in my way home, and intimated to him the subject of our discourse; in consequence of which I have received from him an invitation to a further conference on this momentous affair, and I intend to be in town tomorrow accordingly to meet at his house between four and five o'clock; and we unite in the request of thy company. We are neither of us insensible that the affair is of that *magnitude* as should almost deter private persons from meddling with it; at the same time we are respectively such well-wishers to the cause that nothing in our power ought to be left undone, though the utmost of our efforts may be unavailable. I am thy respectful friend,

'DAVID BARCLAY'

'Dr Franklin, Craven Street.

'Dr Fothergill presents his respects to Dr Franklin, and hopes for the favour of his company in Harpur Street tomorrow evening, to meet their mutual friend David Barclay, to confer on American affairs. As near five o'clock as may be convenient.

'Harpur Street, 3rd inst.'

The time thus appointed was the evening of the day on which I was to have my second chess party with the agreeable Mrs Howe, whom I met accordingly. After playing as long as we liked, we fell into a little chat, partly on a mathematical problem,* and partly about the new Parliament, then just met,

* This lady (which is a little unusual in ladies) has a good deal of mathematical knowledge.

when she said: 'And what is to be done with this dispute between Great Britain and the colonies? I hope we are not to have
a civil war.' 'They should kiss and be friends,' said I; 'what can
they do better? Quarrelling can be of service to neither, but is
ruin to both.' 'I have often said,' replied she, 'that I wished
government would employ you to settle the dispute for 'em; I
am sure nobody could do it so well. Do not you think that the
thing is practicable?' 'Undoubtedly, madam, if the parties are
disposed to reconciliation; for the two countries have really no
clashing interests to differ about. 'Tis rather a matter of punc-
tilio which two or three reasonable people might settle in half
an hour. I thank you for the good opinion you are pleased to
express of me; but the ministers will never think of employing
me in that good work; they choose rather to abuse me.' 'Ay,'
said she, 'they have behaved shamefully to you. And indeed
some of them are now ashamed of it themselves.' I looked upon
this as accidental conversation, thought no more of it, and went
in the evening to the appointed meeting at Dr Fothergill's,
where I found Mr Barclay with him.

The doctor expatiated feelingly on the mischiefs likely to
ensue from the present difference, the necessity of accommo-
dating it, and the great merit of being instrumental in so good
a work, concluding with some compliments to me: that nobody
understood the subject so thoroughly and had a better head for
business of the kind; that it seemed therefore a duty incumbent
on me to do everything I could to accomplish a reconciliation;
and that, as he had with pleasure heard from David Barclay
that I had promised to think of it, he hoped I had put pen to
paper, and formed some plan for consideration, and brought it
with me. I answered that I had formed no plan, as the more I
thought of the proceedings against the colonies the more satisfied I was that there did not exist the least disposition in the
ministry to an accommodation; that therefore all plans must be
useless. He said I might be mistaken; that, whatever was the
violence of some, he had reason, *good reason*, to believe others
were differently disposed; and that if I would draw a plan which
we three upon considering should judge reasonable, it might be
made use of and answer some good purpose, since he believed
that either himself or David Barclay could get it communicated

to some of the most moderate among the ministers, who would consider it with attention; and what appeared reasonable to us, two of us being Englishmen, might appear so to them.

As they both urged this with great earnestness and, when I mentioned the impropriety of my doing anything of the kind at the time we were in daily expectation of hearing from the Congress who undoubtedly would be explicit on the means of restoring a good understanding, they seemed impatient, alleging that it was uncertain when we should receive the result of the Congress, and what it would be; that the least delay might be dangerous; that additional punishments for New England were in contemplation, and accidents might widen the breach and make it irreparable; therefore something preventive could not be too soon thought of and applied. I was therefore finally prevailed with to promise doing what they desired, and to meet them again on Tuesday evening at the same place, and bring with me something for their consideration.

Accordingly, at the time, I met with them and produced the following paper.

HINTS FOR CONVERSATION UPON THE SUBJECT OF TERMS THAT MIGHT PROBABLY PRODUCE A DURABLE UNION BETWEEN BRITAIN AND THE COLONIES

1. The tea destroyed to be paid for.

2. The Tea Duty Act to be repealed, and all the duties that have been received upon it to be repaid into the treasuries of the several provinces from which they have been collected.

3. The Acts of Navigation to be all re-enacted in the colonies.

4. A naval officer, appointed by the Crown, to reside in each colony to see that those acts are observed.

5. All the acts restraining manufactures in the colonies to be repealed.

6. All duties arising on the acts for regulating trade with the colonies to be for the public use of the respective colonies and paid into their treasuries. The collectors and custom-house officers to be appointed by each governor, and not sent from England.

7. In consideration of the Americans maintaining their own peace establishment, and the monopoly Britain is to have of their commerce, no requisition to be made from them in time of peace.

8. No troops to enter and quarter in any colony, but with the consent of its legislature.

9. In time of war, on requisition made by the king, with the consent of Parliament, every colony shall raise money by the following rules or proportions, viz.: If Britain, on account of the war, raises 3 shillings in the pound to its land tax, then the colonies to add to their last general provincial peace tax a sum equal to one-fourth thereof; and if Britain, on the same account, pays 4 shillings in the pound, then the colonies to add to their said last peace tax a sum equal to half thereof, which additional tax is to be granted to his Majesty, and to be employed in raising and paying men for land or sea service, furnishing provisions, transports, or for such other purposes as the king shall require and direct. And though no colony may contribute less, each may add as much by voluntary grant as they shall think proper.

10. Castle William to be restored to the province of the Massachusetts Bay, and no fortress built by the Crown in any province, but with the consent of its legislature.

11. The late Massachusetts and Quebec Acts to be repealed, and a free government granted to Canada.

12. All judges to be appointed during good behaviour, with equally permanent salaries, to be paid out of the province revenues by appointment of the Assemblies. Or, if the judges are to be appointed during the pleasure of the Crown, let the salaries be during the pleasure of the Assemblies, as heretofore.

13. Governors to be supported by the Assemblies of each province.

14. If Britain will give up its monopoly of the American commerce, then the aid above mentioned to be given by America in time of peace as well as in time of war.

15. The extension of the act of Henry the Eighth, concerning treasons to the colonies, to be formally disowned by Parliament.

16. The American admiralty courts reduced to the same

powers they have in England, and the acts establishing them to be re-enacted in America.

17. All powers of internal legislation in the colonies to be disclaimed by Parliament.

In the following week arrived the proceedings of the Congress, which had been long and anxiously expected both by the friends and adversaries of America.

The petition of Congress to the king was inclosed to me, and accompanied by the following letter from their president, addressed to the American agents in London as follows:

TO PAUL WENTWORTH, ESQUIRE, DR BENJAMIN
FRANKLIN, WILLIAM BOLLAN, ESQUIRE, DR ARTHUR
LEE, THOMAS LIFE, ESQUIRE, EDMUND BURKE, ESQUIRE,
CHARLES GARTH, ESQUIRE

'Philadelphia, 26 October 1774

'GENTLEMEN:

'We give you the strongest proof of our reliance on your zeal and attachment to the happiness of America and the cause of liberty, when we commit the inclosed papers to your care.

'We desire you will deliver the petition into the hands of his Majesty, and after it has been presented, we wish it may be made public through the press, together with the list of grievances. And as we hope for great assistance from the spirit, virtue, and justice of the nation, it is our earnest desire that the most effectual care be taken, as early as possible, to furnish the trading cities and manufacturing towns throughout the United Kingdom with our memorial to the people of Great Britain.

'We doubt not but that your good sense and discernment will lead you to avail yourselves of every assistance that may be derived from the advice and friendship of all great and good men who may incline to aid the cause of liberty and mankind.

'The gratitude of America, expressed in the inclosed vote of thanks, we desire may be conveyed to the deserving objects of it, in the manner that you think will be most acceptable to them.

'It is proposed that another Congress be held on the 10th of May next, at this place, but in the meantime we beg the favour

of you, gentlemen, to transmit to the Speakers of the several
Assemblies the earliest information of the most authentic accounts you can collect, of all such conduct and designs of ministry or Parliament as it may concern America to know. We are,
with unfeigned esteem and regard, gentlemen, etc.

'By order of the Congress.

'HENRY MIDDLETON, PRESIDENT'

The first impression made by them (the proceedings of the
American Congress) on the people in general was greatly in our
favour. Administration seemed to be staggered, were impatient
to know whether the *Petition* mentioned in the proceedings was
come to my hands, and took a roundabout method of obtaining
that information, by getting a ministerial merchant, a known
intimate of the Solicitor-General, to write me a letter importing
that he heard I had received such a petition, that I was to be
attended in presenting it by the merchants, and begging to
know the time, that he might attend 'on so important an occasion and give his testimony to so good a work'. Before these
proceedings arrived, it had been given out that no petition
from the Congress could be received, as they were an illegal
body; but the secretary of state after a day's perusal (during
which a council was held) told us it was a decent and proper
petition, and cheerfully undertook to present it to his Majesty,
who he afterwards assured us was pleased to receive it very
graciously, and to promise to lay it, as soon as they met, before
his two Houses of Parliament; and we had reason to believe that
at that time the petition was intended to be made the foundation of some change of measures; but that purpose, if such
there were, did not long continue.

On Christmas Day evening, visiting Mrs Howe, she told me as
soon as I came in that her brother Lord Howe wished to be
acquainted with me; that he was a very good man, and she was
sure we should like each other. I said I had always heard a good
character of Lord Howe, and should be proud of the honour of
being known to him. 'He is but just by,' said she; 'will you give
me leave to send for him?' 'By all means, madam, if you think
proper.' She rang for a servant, wrote a note, and Lord Howe
came in a few minutes.

After some extremely polite compliments as to the general motives for his desiring an acquaintance with me, he said he had a particular one at this time, which was the alarming situation of our affairs with America, which no one, he was persuaded, understood better than myself; that it was the opinion of some friends of his that no man could do more towards reconciling our differences than I could, if I would undertake it; that he was sensible that I had been very ill-treated by the ministry, but he hoped that would not be considered by me in the present case; that he himself, though not in opposition, had much disapproved of their conduct towards me; that some of them, he was sure, were ashamed of it and sorry it had happened; which he supposed must be sufficient to abate resentment in a great and generous mind; that if he were himself in administration, he should be ready to make me ample satisfaction, which he was persuaded would one day or other be done; that he was unconnected with the ministry except by some personal friendships, wished well however to government, was anxious for the general welfare of the whole empire, and had a particular regard for New England, which had shown a very endearing respect to his family; that he was merely an independent Member of Parliament desirous of doing what good he could, agreeably to his duty in that station; that he therefore had wished for an opportunity of obtaining my sentiments on the means of reconciling our differences, which he saw must be attended with the most mischievous consequences if not speedily accommodated; that he hoped his zeal for the public welfare would with me excuse the impertinence of a mere stranger who could have otherwise no reason to expect, or right to request, me to open my mind to him on these topics; but he did conceive that, if I would indulge him with my ideas of the means proper to bring about a reconciliation, it might be of some use; that perhaps I might not be willing myself to have any *direct* communication with this ministry on this occasion; that I might likewise not care to have it known that I had any *indirect* communication with them, till I could be well assured of their good dispositions; that being himself upon no ill terms with them, he thought it not impossible that he might, by conveying my sentiments to them and theirs to me, be a means of bringing on a good understanding, without committing either them or me if his negotiation should not succeed; and that I might rely on his keeping perfectly secret everything I should wish to remain so . . .

I begged him, in the first place, to give me credit for a sincere desire of healing the breach between the two countries; that I would cheerfully and heartily do everything in my small power to accomplish it; but that I apprehended from the king's speech, and from the measures talked of as well as those already determined on, no intention or disposition of the kind existed in the present ministry, and therefore no accomodation could be expected till we saw a change. That as to what his lordship mentioned of the *personal injuries* done me, those done my country were so much greater that I did not think the other, at this time, worth mentioning; that besides, it was a fixed rule with me not to mix my private affairs with those of the public; that I could join with my personal enemy in serving the public, or, when it was for its interest with the public in serving that enemy; these being my sentiments, his lordship might be assured that no private considerations of the kind should prevent my being as useful in the present case as my small abilities would permit.

He appeared satisfied and pleased with these declarations, and gave it me as his sincere opinion that some of the ministry were extremely well disposed to any reasonable accommodation, preserving only the dignity of government; and he wished me to draw up in writing some propositions containing the terms on which I conceived a good understanding might be obtained and established, and the mode of proceeding to accomplish it; which propositions, as soon as prepared, we might meet to consider . . .

I had promised Lord Chatham to communicate to him the first important news I should receive from America. I therefore sent him the proceedings of the Congress as soon as I received them; but a whole week passed after I received the petition before I could, as I wished to do, wait upon him with it in order to obtain his sentiments on the *whole;* for my time was taken up in meetings with the other agents to consult about presenting the petition, in waiting three different days with them on Lord

Lord Chatham

Dartmouth, in consulting upon and writing letters to the Speakers of Assemblies, and other business, which did not allow me a day to go to Hayes.

At last, on Monday the 26th, I got out and was there about one o'clock. He received me with an affectionate kind of respect that from so great a man was extremely engaging; but the opinion he expressed of the Congress was still more so. They had acted, he said, with so much temper, moderation, and wisdom that he thought it the most honourable assembly of statesmen since those of the ancient Greeks and Romans, in the most virtuous times. That there were not in their whole proceedings above one or two things he could have wished otherwise; perhaps but one, and that was their assertion that the keeping up a standing army in the colonies in time of peace, without consent of their legislatures, was against law. He doubted that was not well-founded, and that the law alluded to did not extend to the colonies. The rest he admired and honoured. He thought the petition decent, manly, and properly expressed. He inquired much and particularly concerning the state of America, the probability of their perseverance, the difficulties they must meet with in adhering for any long time to their resolutions, the resources they might have to supply the deficiency of commerce; to all which I gave him answers with which he seemed well-satisfied. He expressed a great regard and warm affection for that country, with hearty wishes for their prosperity; and that government here might soon come to see its mistakes and rectify them; and intimated that possibly he might, if his health permitted, prepare something for its consideration when the Parliament should meet after the holidays; on which he should wish to have previously my sentiments . . .

I returned to town the next morning in time to meet at the hour appointed by Lord Howe. I apologized for my not being ready with the paper I had promised, by my having been kept longer than I intended in the country. We had, however, a good deal of conversation on the subject, and his lordship told me he could now assure me, of a certainty, that there was a sincere disposition in Lord North and Lord Dartmouth to accommodate the differences with America, and to listen favourably to any propositions that might have a probable tendency to answer that salutary purpose. He then asked me what I thought of sending some person or persons over, commissioned to inquire into the grievances of America upon the spot, converse with the leading people, and endeavour with them to agree upon some means of composing our differences. I said that a person of rank and dignity who had a character of candour, integrity, and wisdom, might possibly, if employed in that service, be of great use.

He seemed to be of the same opinion, and that whoever was employed should go with a hearty desire of promoting a sincere reconciliation on the foundation of mutual interests and mutual good will; that he should endeavour, not only to remove their prejudices against government, but equally the prejudices of government against them, and bring on a perfect good understanding, etc. Mrs Howe said: 'I wish, brother, you were to be sent thither on such a service; I should like that much better than General Howe's going to command the army there.' 'I think, madam,' said I, 'they ought to provide for General Howe some more honourable employment.' Lord Howe here took out of his pocket a paper and offering it to me said, smiling: 'If it is not an unfair question, may I ask whether you know anything of this paper?' Upon looking at it, I saw it was a copy, in David Barclay's hand, of the *Hints* before recited, and said that I had seen it; adding, a little after, that since I perceived his lordship was acquainted with a transaction my concern in which I had understood was to have been kept a secret, I should make no difficulty in owning to him that I had been consulted on the subject and had drawn up that paper. He said he was rather sorry to find that the sentiments expressed in it were mine, as it gave him less hopes of promoting, by my assistance, the wished-for reconciliation; since he had reason to think there was no likelihood of the admission of those propositions. He hoped, however, that I would reconsider the subject, and form some plan that would be acceptable here. He expatiated on the infinite service it would be to the nation, and the great merit in being instrumental in so good a work; that he should not think of influencing me by any selfish motive, but certainly I might with reason expect any reward in the power of the government to bestow.

This to me was what the French vulgarly call *spitting in the soup*. However, I promised to draw some sketch of a plan at his request, though I much doubted, I said, whether it would be thought preferable to that he had in his hand. But he was willing to hope that it would; and, as he considered my situation, that I had friends here and constituents in America to keep well with, that I might possibly propose something improper to be seen in my handwriting; therefore it would be better to send it to Mrs Howe, who would copy it, send the copy to him to be communicated to the ministry, and return me the original. This I agreed to, though I did not apprehend the inconvenience he mentioned. In general, I liked much his manner, and found myself disposed to place great confidence in him on occasion; but in this particular the secrecy he proposed seemed not of much importance.

In a day or two I sent the following paper, enclosed in a cover directed to the Honourable Mrs Howe.

'It is supposed to be the wish on both sides not merely to put a stop to the mischief at present threatening the general welfare, but to cement a *cordial union*, and remove, not only every real grievance, but every cause of jealousy and suspicion.

'With this view, the first thing necessary is to know what is, by the different parties in the dispute, thought essentially necessary for the obtaining such a union.

'The American Congress in their petition to the king have been explicit, declaring that by a repeal of the oppressive acts therein complained of, *the harmony between Great Britain and the colonies, so necessary to the happiness of both and so ardently desired of them, will, with the usual intercourse, be immediately restored.*

'If it has been thought reasonable here to expect that, previous to an alteration of measures, the colonies should make some declaration respecting their future conduct, they have also done that by adding: *That when the causes of their apprehensions are removed, their future conduct will prove them not unworthy of the regard they have been accustomed in their happier days to enjoy.*

'For their sincerity in these declarations, they solemnly call to witness the Searcher of all hearts.

'If Britain can have any reliance on these declarations (and perhaps none to be extorted by force can be more relied on than these, which are thus freely made), she may without hazard to herself try the expedient proposed, since if it fails she has it in her power at any time to resume her present measures.

'It is then proposed: That Britain should show some confidence in these declarations, by repealing all the laws, or parts of laws, that are requested to be repealed in the petition of the Congress to the king; And that at the same time, orders should be given to withdraw the fleet from Boston, and remove all the troops to Quebec or the Floridas, that the colonies may be left at perfect liberty in their future stipulations.

'That this may, for the honour of Britain, appear not the effect of any apprehension from the measures entered into and recommended to the people by the Congress, but from good will, and a change of disposition towards the colonies, with a sincere desire of reconciliation, let some of their other grievances, which in their petition they have left to the magnanimity and justice of the king and Parliament, be at the same time removed, such as those relating to the payment of governors' and judges' salaries, and the instructions for dissolving Assemblies, etc., with the declarations concerning the statue of Henry the Eighth.

'And to give the colonies an immediate opportunity of demonstrating the reality of their professions, let their proposed ensuing Congress be authorized by government (as was that held at Albany in 1754), and a person of weight and dignity of character be appointed to preside at it on behalf of the Crown.

'And then let requisition be made to the Congress, of such points as government wishes to obtain for its future security, for aids, for the advantage of general commerce, for reparation to the India Company, etc., etc.

'A generous confidence thus placed in the colonies will give ground to the friends of government there, in their endeavours to procure from America every reasonable concession or engagement, and every substantial aid that can fairly be desired.'

On the Saturday evening I saw Mrs Howe, who informed me she had transcribed and sent the paper to Lord Howe in the country, and she returned me the original . . .

His lordship had, in his last conversation with me, acknowledged a communication between him and the ministry, to whom he wished to make my sentiments known. In this letter from the country he owns the receipt of them, and mentions his intention of forwarding them, that is, as I understood it, to the ministers; but expresses his apprehensions that such propositions were not likely to produce any good effect. Some time after, perhaps a week, I received a note from Mrs Howe, desiring to see me. I waited upon her immediately, when she showed me a letter from her brother, of which having no copy, I can only give from the best of my recollection the purport of it, which I think was this: that he desired to know from their friend, meaning me, through her means, whether it might not be expected that, if that friend would engage for their payment of the tea as a preliminary, relying on a promised redress of their grievances on future petitions from their Assembly, they would approve of his making such engagement; and whether the proposition in the former paper (the *Hints*) relating to aids, was still in contemplation of the author. As Mrs Howe proposed sending to her brother that evening, I wrote immediately the following answer which she transcribed and forwarded:

'The proposition in the former paper relating to aids is still in contemplation of the author, and, as he thinks, is included in the last article of the present paper.

'The people of America, conceiving that Parliament has no right to tax them, and that therefore all that has been extorted from them by the operation of the duty acts, with the assistance of an armed force, *preceding* the destruction of the tea, is so much injury which ought in order of time to be first repaired before a demand on the tea account can be justly made of them, are not, he thinks, likely to approve of the measure proposed, and pay *in the first place* the value demanded, especially as twenty times as much injury has since been done them by blocking up their port; and their castle also, seized before by the Crown, has not been restored nor any satisfaction offered them for the same.'

At the meeting of Parliament after the holidays, which was on the 19th of January (1775), Lord Howe returned to town, when we had another meeting at which he lamented that my propositions were not such as probably could be accepted; intimated that it was thought I had such powers or instructions from the Congress to make concessions on occasion, that would be more satisfactory. I disclaimed the having any of any kind but what related to the presenting of their petition. We talked over all the particulars in my paper, which I supported with reasons; and finally said that, if what I had proposed would not do, I should be glad to hear what would do; I wished to see some propositions from the ministers themselves. His lordship was not, he said, as yet fully acquainted with their sentiments, but should learn more in a few days. It was, however, some weeks before I heard anything further from him . . .

On the 19th of January I received a card from Lord Stanhope, acquainting me that Lord Chatham, having a motion to make on the morrow in the House of Lords concerning America, greatly desired that I might be in the House, into which Lord Stanhope would endeavour to procure me admittance. At this time it was a rule of the House that no person could introduce more than one friend. The next morning his lordship let me know by another card that, if I attended at two o'clock in the lobby, Lord Chatham would be there about that time, and would himself introduce me. I attended, and met him there accordingly. On my mentioning to him what Lord Stanhope had written to me, he said: 'Certainly; and I shall do it with the more pleasure, as I am sure your being present at this day's debate will be of more service to America than mine'; and so taking me by the arm was leading me along the passage to the door that enters near the throne, when one of the door-keepers followed and acquainted him that, by the order, none were to be carried in at that door but the eldest sons or brothers of peers; on which he limped back with me to the door near the bar, where were standing a number of gentlemen waiting for the peers who were to introduce them, and some peers waiting for friends they expected to introduce; among whom he delivered me to the door-keepers, saying aloud: 'This is Dr Franklin, whom I would have admitted into the House'; when they readily opened the door for me accordingly.

As it had not been publicly known that there was any communication between his lordship and me, this I found occasioned some speculation. His appearance in the House, I observed, caused a kind of bustle among the officers, who were hurried in sending messengers for members, I suppose those in connection with the ministry, something of importance being expected when that great man appears; it being but seldom that his infirmities permit his attendance. I had great satisfaction in hearing his motion and the debate upon it, which I shall not attempt to give here an account of, as you may find a better in the papers of the time. It was his motion for withdrawing the troops from Boston, as the first step towards an accommodation.

The day following, I received a note from Lord Stanhope expressing that, 'at the desire of Lord Chatham, was sent me inclosed the motion he made in the House of Lords, that I might be possessed of it in the most authentic manner, by the communication of the individual paper which was read to the House by the mover himself.' I sent copies of this motion to America, and was the more pleased with it as I conceived it had partly taken its rise from a hint I had given his lordship in a former conversation. It follows in these words.

LORD CHATHAM'S MOTION, 20 JANUARY 1775

That an humble address be presented to his Majesty, most humbly to advise and beseech his Majesty that, in order to open the way towards a happy settlement of the dangerous troubles in America, by beginning to allay ferments and soften animosities there, and above all, for presenting in the meantime any sudden and fatal catastrophe at Boston, now suffering under the daily irritation of an army before their eyes, posted in their town, it may graciously please his Majesty that immediate orders may be despatched to General Gage for removing his Majesty's forces from the town of Boston, as soon as the rigour of the season and other circumstances, indispensable to the safety and accommodation of the said troops, may render the same practicable.

. . . On the Sunday following, being the 29th, his lordship came to town and called upon me in Craven Street. He brought with him his plan, transcribed in the form of an Act of Parliament, which he put into my hands, requesting me to consider it carefully and communicate to him such remarks upon it as should occur to me. His reason for desiring to give me that trouble was, as he was pleased to say, that he knew no man so thoroughly acquainted with the subject, or so capable of giving advice upon it; that he thought the errors of ministers in American affairs had been often owing to their not obtaining the best information; that, therefore, though he had considered the business thoroughly in all its parts, he was not confident of his own judgment, but that he came to set it right by mine, as men set their watches by a regulator. He had not determined when he should produce it in the House of Lords; but in the course of our conversation, considering the precarious situation of his health, and that if presenting it was delayed some intelligence might arrive which would make it seem less seasonable, or in all parts not so proper, or the ministry might engage in different measures, and then say: 'If you had produced your plan sooner, we might have attended to it,' he concluded to offer it the Wednesday following; and therefore wished to see me about it the preceding Tuesday, when he would again call upon me, unless I could conveniently come to Hayes. I chose the latter, in respect to his lordship, and because there was less likelihood of interruptions; and I promised to be with him early, that we might have more time. He stayed with me near two hours, his equipage waiting at the door; and being there while people were coming from church, it was much taken notice of, and talked of, as at that time was every little circumstance that men thought might possibly any way affect American affairs. Such a visit from so great a man, on so important a business, flattered not a little my vanity; and the honour of it gave me the more pleasure as it happened on the very day twelve-month that the ministry had taken so much pains to disgrace me before the Privy Council . . .

I put down upon paper, as I went along, some short memorandums for my future discourse with him upon it which follow, that you may, if you please, compare them with the plan; and if you do so, you will see their drift and purpose, which otherwise would take me much writing to explain.

NOTES FOR DISCOURSE WITH LORD CHATHAM ON
HIS PLAN

Tuesday, 31 January 1775

Voluntary grants and forced taxes not to be expected of the same people at the same time.

Permanent revenue will be objected to. Would not a temporary agreement be best, suppose for one hundred years?

Does the whole of the rights claimed in the Petition of Rights relate to England only?

The American Naturalization Act gives all the rights of natural-born subjects to foreigners residing there seven years. Can it be supposed that the natives there have them not?

If the king should raise armies in America, would Britain like their being brought hither as the king might bring them when he pleased?

An Act of Parliament requires the colonies to furnish sundry articles of provision and accommodation to troops quartered among them; this may be made very burdensome to colonies that are out of favour.

If a permanent revenue, why not the same privileges in trade with Scotland?

Should not the lands conquered by Britain and the colonies in conjunction be given them (reserving a quit-rent), from whence they might form funds to enable them to pay?

Instructions about agents to be withdrawn.

Grants to be for three years, at the end of which a new Congress; and so from three to three years.

Congress to have the general defence of frontiers, making and regulating new settlements.

Protection mutual.

We go into all your wars.

Our settlements cost you nothing.

Take the plan of union.

'Defence, extension, and prosperity of.' The late Canada Act prevents their extension, and may check their prosperity.

Laws should be secure as well as charters.

Perhaps if the legislative power of Parliament is owned in the colonies, they may make a law to forbid the meeting of any Congress, etc . . .

On Wednesday, Lord Stanhope at Lord Chatham's request called upon me, and carried me down to the House of Lords, which was soon very full. Lord Chatham, in a most excellent speech, introduced, explained, and supported his plan. When he sat down, Lord Dartmouth rose and very properly said it contained matter of such weight and magnitude as to require much consideration; and he therefore hoped the noble earl did not expect their lordships to decide upon it by an immediate vote, but would be willing it should lie upon the table for consideration. Lord Chatham answered readily that he expected nothing more.

But Lord Sandwich rose, and in a petulant, vehement speech opposed its being received at all, and gave his opinion that it ought to be immediately *rejected* with the contempt it deserved; that he could never believe it to be the production of any British peer; that it appeared to him rather the work of some American; and turning his face towards me, who was leaning on the bar, said he fancied he had in his eye the person who drew it up, one of the bitterest and most mischievous enemies this country had ever known. This drew the eyes of many lords upon me, but as I had no inducement to take it to myself, I kept my countenance as immovable as if my features had been made of wood . . .

Lord Chatham, in his reply to Lord Sandwich, took notice of his illiberal insinuation that the plan was not the person's who proposed it; declared that it was entirely his own; a declaration he thought himself the more obliged to make, as many of their lordships appeared to have so mean an opinion of it; for if it was so weak or so bad a thing, it was proper in him to take care that no other person should unjustly share in the censure it deserved. That it had been heretofore reckoned his vice, not to be apt to take advice; but he made no scruple to declare that if he were the first minister of this country, and had the care of settling this momentous business, he should not be ashamed of publicly calling to his assistance a person so perfectly acquainted with the whole of American affairs as the gentleman alluded to, and so injuriously reflected on; one, he was pleased to say, whom all Europe held in high estimation for his knowledge and wisdom, and ranked with our Boyles and Newtons, who was an honour, not to the English nation only, but to human nature! I found it harder to stand this extravagant compliment than the preceding equally extravagant abuse; but kept as well as I could an unconcerned countenance, as not conceiving it to relate to me . . .

I was told that conferences had been held upon the *Hints*, and the paper being produced, was read, that I might hear the observations that had been made upon them separately, which were as follows:

1. The first article was approved.

2. The second agreed to, so far as related to the repeal of the Tea Act, but repayment of the duties that had been collected was refused.

3. The third not approved, as it implied a deficiency of power in the Parliament that made those acts.

4. The fourth approved.

5. The fifth agreed to, but with a reserve that no change prejudicial to Britain was to be expected.

6. The sixth agreed to, so far as related to the appropriation of the duties, but the appointment of the officers and their salaries to remain as at present.

7. The seventh, relating to aids in time of peace, agreed to.

8. The eighth, relating to the troops, was inadmissible.

9. The ninth could be agreed to, with this difference, that no proportion should be observed with regard to preceding taxes, but each colony should give at pleasure.

10. The tenth agreed to, as to the restitution of Castle William, but the restriction on the Crown in building fortresses refused.

11. The eleventh refused absolutely, except as to the Boston Port Bill, which would be repealed; and the Quebec Act might be so far amended as to reduce that province to its ancient limits. The other Massachusetts acts, being real amendments of their constitution, must for that reason be continued, as well as to be a standing example of the power of Parliament.

12. The twelfth agreed to, that the judges should be appointed during good behaviour, on the Assemblies providing permanent salaries such as the Crown should approve of.

13. The thirteenth agreed to, provided the Assemblies make provision as in the preceding article.

14. The fourteenth was totally inadmissible.

15. The fifteenth agreed to.

16. The sixteenth agreed to, supposing the duties paid to the colony treasuries.

17. The seventeenth inadmissible.

. . . Lord Chatham's rejected plan being printed, for the public judgment, I received six copies from Lord Mahon, his son-in-law, which I sent to different persons in America.

A week and more passed in which I heard nothing further of any negotiation, and my time was much taken up among the members of Parliament, when Mr Barclay sent me a note to say that he was indisposed but desirous of seeing me, and should be glad if I would call on him. I waited upon him the next morning, when he told me that he had seen Lord Hyde and had some further discourse with him on the articles; that he thought himself now fully possessed of what would do in this business; that he therefore wished another meeting with me and Dr Fothergill, when he would endeavour to bring prepared a draft conformable chiefly to what had been proposed and conceded on both sides . . .

Weighing now the present dangerous situation of affairs in America, and the daily hazard of widening the breach there irreparably, I embraced the idea proposed in the paper of sending over a commissioner, as it might be a means of suspending military operations, and bring on a treaty whereby mischief would be prevented and an agreement by degrees be formed and established. I also concluded to do what had been desired of me as to the engagement, and essayed a draft of a memorial to lord Dartmouth for that purpose simply, to be signed only by myself . . .

TO THE RIGHT HONOURABLE LORD DARTMOUTH

MY LORD:

Being deeply apprehensive of the impending calamities that threaten the nation and its colonies through the present unhappy dissensions, I have attentively considered by what possible means those calamities may be prevented. The great importance of a business which concerns us all, will I hope in some degree excuse me to your lordship if I presume, unasked, to offer my humble opinion that should his Majesty think fit to authorize delegates from the several provinces to meet at such convenient time and place as in his wisdom shall seem meet, then and there to confer with a commission or commissioners to be appointed and empowered by his Majesty, on the means of establishing a firm and lasting union between Britain and the American provinces, such a measure might be effectual for that purpose. I cannot, therefore, but wish it may be adopted, as no one can more ardently and sincerely desire the general prosperity of the British dominions than, my lord, your lordship's most obedient, etc.,

B. FRANKLIN

REMARKS ON THE PROPOSITIONS

Art. 1. In consequence of that engagement, all the Boston and Massachusetts acts to be suspended and, in compliance with that engagement, to be totally repealed.

By this amendment article fourth will become unnecessary.

Arts. 4 and 5. The numerous petitions heretofore sent home by the colony Assemblies, and either refused to be received, or received and neglected, or answered harshly, and the petitioners rebuked for making them, have I conceive totally discouraged that method of application; and if even their friends were now to propose to them the recurring again to petitioning, such friends would be thought to trifle with them. Besides, *all* they desire is now before government in the petition of the Congress, and the whole or parts may be granted or refused at pleasure. The sense of the colonies cannot be better obtained by petition from different colonies than it is by that general petition.

Art. 7. Read, *such as they may think necessary.*

Art. 11. As it stands, of little importance. The first proposition was that they should be repealed as unjust. But they may remain, for they will probably not be executed.

Even with the amendment proposed above to article first, I

cannot think it stands as it should do. If the object be merely the preventing present bloodshed, and the other mischiefs to fall on that country in war, it may possibly answer that end; but if a thorough, hearty reconciliation is wished for all cause of heart-burning should be removed, and strict justice be done on both sides. Thus the tea should not only be paid for on the side of Boston, but the damage done to Boston by the Port Act should be repaired, because it was done contrary to the custom of all nations, savage as well as civilized, of first demanding satisfaction.

Art. 14. The judges should receive nothing from the king.

As to the other two acts, the Massachusetts must suffer all the hazards and mischiefs of war rather than admit the alteration of their charters and laws by Parliament. 'They who can give up essential liberty to obtain a little temporary safety, deserve neither liberty nor safety.'

B. FRANKLIN

HINTS

I doubt the regulating duties will not be accepted, without enacting them, and having the power of appointing the collectors in the colonies.

If we mean a hearty reconciliation, we must deal candidly, and use no tricks.

The Assemblies are many of them in a state of dissolution. It will require time to make new elections; then to meet and choose delegates, supposing all could meet. But the Assembly of the Massachusetts Bay cannot act under the new constitution, nor meet the new Council for that purpose, without acknowledging the power of Parliament to alter their charter, which they never will do. The language of the proposal is: *Try on my fetters first, and then, if you don't like 'em, petition and we will consider.*

Establishing salaries for judges may be a general law. For governors not so, the constitution of colonies differing. It is possible troops may be sent to *particular* provinces, to burden them when they are out of favour.

Canada. We cannot endure despotism over any of our fellow-subjects. We must all be free, or none.

... On the morning of 20 February, it was currently and industriously reported all over the town that Lord North would that day make a pacific motion in the House of Commons for healing all differences between Britain and America. The House was accordingly very full, and the members full of expectation ...

LORD NORTH'S MOTION, 20 FEBRUARY 1775

That it is the opinion of this committee, that when the governor, Council, and Assembly, or the General Court of his Majesty's provinces or colonies shall propose to make provision according to their respective conditions, circumstances, and situations, for contributing their proportion to the common defence, such proportion to be raised under the authority of the General Court or General Assembly of such province or colony, and disposable by Parliament, and shall engage to make provision also for the support of the civil government and the administration of justice in such province or colony, it will be proper, if such proposal shall be approved by his Majesty in Parliament, and for so long as such provision shall be made accordingly, to forbear, in respect of such province or colony, to levy any duties, tax, or assessment, or to impose any further duty, tax, or assessment; except only such duties as it may be expedient to impose for the regulation of commerce; the net produce of the duties last mentioned to be carried to the account of such province, colony, or plantation, exclusively.

After a good deal of wild debate, in which this motion was supported upon various and inconsistent principles by the ministerial people, and even met with an opposition from some of them, which showed a want of concert, probably from the suddenness of the alterations above supposed, they all agreed at length, as usual, in voting it by a large majority ...

Three or four days after I received the following note from Mrs Howe:

Mrs Howe's compliments to Dr Franklin: Lord Howe begs to have the pleasure of meeting him once more before he goes, at her house; he is at present out of town, but returns on Monday;

and any day or hour after that, that the Doctor will name, he
will be very glad to attend him.
Grafton Street, Saturday. [4 March]

I answered that I would do myself the honour of waiting on
Lord Howe, at her house, the Tuesday following at eleven
o'clock. We met accordingly. He began by saying that I had
been a better prophet than himself in foreseeing that my in-
terview with Lord Hyde would be of no great use; and then said
that he hoped I would excuse the trouble he had given me, as
his intentions had been good both towards me and the public.
He was sorry that at present there was no appearance of things
going into the train he had wished, but that possibly they might
yet take a more favourable turn; and as he understood I was
going soon to America, if he should chance to be sent thither on
that important business, he hoped he might still expect my
assistance. I assured him of my readiness at all times of co-
operating with him in so good a work; and so, taking my leave,
and receiving his good wishes, ended the negotiations with Lord
Howe.
     A little before I left London, being at the House of Lords
during a debate in which Lord Camden was to speak, and who
indeed spoke admirably on American affairs, I was much disgusted, from the ministerial side, by many base reflections on
American courage, religion, understanding, etc., in which we
were treated with the utmost contempt, as the lowest of mankind, and almost of a different species from the English of
Britain; but particularly the American honesty was abused by
some of the Lords who asserted that we were all knaves, and
wanted only by this dispute to avoid paying our debts; that if we
had any sense of equity or justice, we should offer payment of
the tea, etc. I went home somewhat irritated and heated; and
partly to retort upon this nation, on the article of *equity*, drew
up a memorial to present to Lord Dartmouth before my departure; but consulting my friend, Mr Thomas Walpole, upon
it, who is a member of the House of Commons, he looked at it
and at me several times alternately, as if he apprehended me a
little out of my senses. As I was in the hurry of packing up, I
requested him to take the trouble of showing it to his neigh-

bour, Lord Camden, and ask his advice upon it, which he kindly undertook to do; and returned it to me with a note, which here follows the proposed memorial:

TO THE RIGHT HONOURABLE THE EARL OF
DARTMOUTH, ONE OF HIS MAJESTY'S PRINCIPAL
SECRETARIES OF STATE: A MEMORIAL FROM BENJAMIN
FRANKLIN, AGENT TO THE PROVINCE OF
MASSACHUSETTS BAY

Whereas an injury done can only give the party injured a right to full reparation; or in case that be refused, a right to return an equal injury; and whereas the blockade of Boston, now continued nine months, hath every week of its continuance done damage to that town equal to what was suffered there by the India Company; it follows that such *exceeding* damage is an *injury* done by this government for which reparation ought to be made; and whereas reparation of injuries ought always (agreeably to the custom of all nations, savage as well as civilized) to be first required before satisfaction is taken by a return of damage to the aggressors which was not done by Great Britain in the instance above mentioned; I the underwritten do therefore, as their agent, in the behalf of my country and the said town of Boston, protest against the continuance of the said blockade; and I do hereby solemnly demand satisfaction for the accumulated injury done them, beyond the value of the India Company's tea destroyed.

And whereas the conquest of the Gulf of St Lawrence, the coasts of Labrador and Nova Scotia, and the fisheries possessed by the French there and on the Banks of Newfoundland, so far as they were more extended than at present, was made by the *joint forces* of Britain and the colonies, the latter having nearly an equal number of men in that service with the former, it follows that the colonies have an equitable and just right to participate in the advantage of those fisheries; I do, therefore, in the behalf of the colony of the Massachusetts Bay, protest against the act now under consideration in Parliament, for depriving that province, with others, of that fishery (on pretence of their refusing to purchase British commodities), as an act highly unjust and injurious, and I give notice that satisfaction will probably one day be demanded for all the injury that may be done and suffered in the execution of such act; and that the injustice of the proceeding is likely to give such umbrage to *all the colonies* that in no future war, wherein other conquests may be meditated, either a man or a shilling will be obtained from any of them to aid such conquests, till full satisfaction be made as aforesaid.

B. FRANKLIN

Given in London, this 16th day of March, 1775

To Dr Franklin

DEAR SIR:

I return you the memorial, which it is thought might be attended with dangerous consequences to your person, and contribute to exasperate the nation.

I heartily wish you a prosperous voyage, and long health, and am, with the sincerest regard, your most faithful and obedient servant,

THOMAS WALPOLE

Lincoln's Inn Fields, 16 March 1775

In retrospect, the scale of British Parliamentary corruption left its mark. In the 1774 elections the American tensions had little impact, except in Bristol, where the American trade mattered, and where Edmund Burke and the American-born Henry Cruger were elected MPs. Seats were bought and sold, as was the fashion. Later, Franklin would tell his French friends that if the people of the United States had given him one-quarter of the cost of the war to be used in bribery, he could have bought independence for them.

By the time Franklin reached Philadelphia, the shots fired at Lexington Green and Concord Bridge were at least echoing round his own state. He was appointed a delegate of Pennsylvania to the Second Continental Congress which assembled on 9 May 1775. The fundamental matter was the relationship of this illegal assembly with the Mother Country. Most of the delegates were against independence, and a final appeal—John Dickinson's Olive Branch Petition—was drafted.

Feelings were running high. Franklin wrote to his old friend William Strahan on 5 July:

MR STRAHAN,

You are a Member of Parliament, and one of that majority which has doomed my country to destruction. You have begun to burn our towns, and murder our people. Look upon your hands! They are stained with the blood of your relations! You and I were long friends: You are now my enemy, and I am

Yours

B. FRANKLIN

But he did not post the letter.

Franklin was commissioner as well as committee man. Along with Thomas Lynch and Benjamin Harrison, he visited Washington's command at Cambridge. In the spring of 1776, he went north in the company of Samuel Chase and Charles Carroll to seek by persuasion to induce the Canadians to join their brothers in the south. He could not be expected to do by words what two invading armies had failed to do: they had been defeated at Quebec, one of their leaders—Richard Montgomery—killed, and the other, Benedict Arnold, wounded. His force, ravaged by smallpox, continued a siege through a long Canadian winter.

Franklin, now seventy, reached Montreal in April 1776. He stayed only a few days, near exhaustion and his legs swollen with dropsy. He reported adversely; Canada stayed firmly loyal.

On 24 June 1776, Congress passed the Allegiance and Treason Resolves, branding the king an enemy. A committee was set up to draft a Declaration of Independence 'in case the Congress agree thereto'. The draft was Jefferson's, and altered but slightly. Franklin was responsible for Jefferson's truths being described as self-evident rather than as 'sacred and undeniable'.

The draft was presented to the Congress on 1 July. After nine hours of debate, four colonies still were not in favour: Pennsylvania and South Carolina opposed it; Delaware was divided; the New York delegation was unable to vote because they awaited instructions from home. It was decided to postpone the final vote for a day. By the evening of 2 July—Caesar Rodney having ridden eighty miles on horseback and in pain from Dover to break the deadlock in his delegation—Delaware had voted in support. South Carolina had come in, and Pennsylvania also, but by a very narrow margin. New York alone, of all the colonies, failed to vote. The resolution was thus approved on 2 July, and on the fourth the Declaration was formally adopted. On 8 July, it was read in public in the State House yard, the Liberty Bell clanged lustily, and the royal coat of arms was torn down from the State House wall and burned in a great bonfire. The Declaration was not signed until 2 August, when a fair copy had been engrossed on parchment; and when Franklin said—or is said to have said—'Gentlemen, we must now all hang together, or we shall most assuredly hang separately.'

When Lord Howe, now in command of the British fleet sent against the rebels, wrote to Franklin suggesting offers of pardon, the reply was rough:

Philadelphia, 20 July 1776

It is impossible we should think of submission to a government that has with the most wanton barbarity and cruelty burnt our defenceless towns in the midst of winter, excited the savages to massacre our farmers and our slaves to murder their masters, and is even now bringing foreign mercenaries to deluge our settlements with blood. These atrocious injuries have extinguished every remaining spark of affection for that parent country we once held so dear; but were it possible for *us* to forget and forgive them, it is not possible for *you* (I mean the British nation) to forgive the people you have so heavily injured. You can never confide again in those as fellow-subjects, and permit them to enjoy equal freedom, to whom you know you have given such just cause of lasting enmity. And this must impel you, were we again under your government, to endeavor the breaking our spirit by the severest tyranny, and obstructing by every means in your power our growing strength and prosperity.

Long did I endeavour, with unfeigned and unwearied zeal, to preserve from breaking that fine and noble china vase, the British Empire for I knew that, being once broken, the separate parts could not retain even their shares of the strength or value that existed in the whole, and that a perfect reunion of those parts could scarce ever be hoped for. Your lordship may possibly remember the tears of joy that wet my cheek when, at your good sister's in London, you once gave me expectations that a reconciliation might soon take place. I had the misfortune to find those expectations disappointed, and to be treated as the cause of the mischief I was labouring to prevent.

I consider this war against us, therefore, as both unjust and unwise; and I am persuaded that cool, dispassionate posterity will condemn to infamy those who advised it; and that even success will not save from some degree of dishonour those who voluntarily engaged to conduct it. I know your great motive in coming hither was the hope of being instrumental in a reconciliation; and I believe, when you find *that* to be impossible on any terms given you to propose, you will relinquish so odious a command and return to a more honourable private station.

SEVEN

BONHOMME RICHARD

In September 1776, Franklin was chosen by Congress to be one of three Commissioners to the Court of France, with Jefferson and Silas Deane. He was already a familiar figure: he had visited the country in 1767 and in 1769; he was known as the author of Poor Richard's Almanack (Le Bonhomme Richard) *and of scientific papers, as a defender of colonial rights before the House of Commons in 1766, and was already an associate of the French Academy of Sciences. His paper, 'Observations and Experiments on Electricity' (published in England in 1769), was translated by Barbeu-Dubourg and published in two volumes as* Oeuvres de M. Franklin *in 1773. He was the friend of the Encyclopaedists and Physiocrats, and he had an admiring court of his own in the Hôtel Valentinois in Passy, the palatial residence of the Duc de Chaumont, with whom he stayed. When Franklin met Voltaire in the Academy in 1778, many saw their embrace as the high point of the Enlightment.*

In public terms, Franklin was more than philosophe. *In an aristocratic world, he dressed plainly, his hair unpowdered, his bifocals his own invention; his fur cap (worn to hide his eczema) seemed a badge of the frontier. His portrait appeared on medallions, rings and snuffboxes, and even chamber pots. His face, he told his daughter, was 'as well known as that of the moon'.*

Since the death of his wife in 1774 and the estrangement of his son William (who remained a Loyalist and was thus an enemy) Franklin counted as his closest of kin his sister Jane Mecom in Boston and his daughter Sarah in Philadelphia. William's illegitimate son, Temple, was his secretary in Paris—'Temple is my right hand,' he said—and for a time, Sarah's son, Benjamin Bache, was also there.

Temple was only seventeen, and not a very competent secretary, or

*filer of papers. He tied his wagon to his grandfather's, not his father's,
star, and would become, forty years later, the first to edit (and profit
from the sale of) his grandfather's papers. He never ceased to be a
playboy, and fathered two illegitimate children—like father, like
grandfather?—the latter by the sister of his father's landlady and second
wife, Mary D'Evelin. That child, baptized as Ellen Franklin, was in the
end to look after her grandfather (who was also her uncle) in his last
years.*

*'Benny' Bache was a boy of seven, and, lest he be contaminated by
Paris, was packed off to Geneva to be a 'Presbyterian and a Republi-
can'. There he spent four and a half years, never once allowed back for
a holiday in Paris, never visited by grandfather or by uncle, and never
complaining. He rejoined his grandfather in Paris in 1783. Like his
grandfather, he became a journalist (earning the nickname of 'Lightning Rod Junior'); he edited the Philadelphia* Aurora, *which in the
1790s was bitterly critical of President Washington, and—thanks to his
acquaintance with the great—won many scoops. He died of yellow fever
in 1798.*

*Franklin was presented to Vergennes in January 1777 and asked for
loans and ships for America. He received none of the latter, but via the
fictitious company of Roderigue Hortalez (behind which the adventurer
and tale-spinner, Beaumarchais, was the moving spirit) indirect, and
strictly illegal, French aid was already bound for America. Franklin
was also busy as an author (often anonymously) of propaganda, often
in the form of squibs and attacks on Britain which appeared in the
French and Dutch press. He was bedevilled by applications for aid in
getting to America from would-be volunteers: over 400 of them and was
driven to pen a 'Model of a Letter of Recommendation':*

Paris, 2 April 1777

SIR:

The bearer of this, who is going to America, presses me to
give him a Letter of Recommendation, though I know nothing
of him, not even his name. This may seem extraordinary, but I
assure you it is not uncommon here. Sometimes, indeed, one
unknown person brings another equally unknown, to recommend him; and sometimes they recommend one another! As to
this gentleman, I must refer you to himself for his character
and merits, with which he is certainly better acquainted than I

can possibly be. I recommend him however to those civilities, which every stranger, of whom one knows no harm, has a right to; and I request you will do him all the good offices, and show him all the favour that, on further acquaintance, you shall find him to deserve. I have the honour to be, etc.

To his friend Barbeu-Duborg he confessed (in October 1777) that he could not help him to meet such a request.

These applications are my perpetual torment. People will believe, notwithstanding my repeated declarations to the contrary, that I am sent hither to engage officers. In truth, I never had any such orders. It was never so much as intimated to me that it would be agreeable to my constituents. I have even received for what I have done of the kind, not indeed an absolute rebuke, but some pretty strong *hints* of disapprobation. Not a day passes in which I have not a number of soliciting visits, besides letters. If I could gratify them all, or any of them, it would be a pleasure. I might, indeed, give them the recommendation and the promises they desire, and thereby please them for the present; but when the certain disappointment of the expectations with which they will so obstinately flatter themselves shall arrive, they must curse me for complying with their mad requests and not undeceiving them; and will become so many enemies to our cause and country.

You can have no conception how I am harassed. All my friends are sought out and teased to tease me. Great officers of all ranks, in all departments; ladies, great and small, besides professed solicitors, worry me from morning to night. The noise of every coach now that enters my court terrifies me. I am afraid to accept an invitation to dine abroad, being almost sure of meeting with some officer or officer's friend who, as soon as I am put in good humour by a glass or two of champagne, begins his attack upon me. Luckily I do not often in my sleep dream of these vexatious situations, or I should be afraid of what are now my only hours of comfort. If, therefore, you have the least remaining kindness for me, if you would not help to drive me out of France, for God's sake, my dear friend, let this, your twenty-third application, be your last. Yours, etc . . .

Franklin assessed the position shrewdly in a letter to Samuel Cooper in May 1777.

All Europe is on our side of the question, as far as applause and good wishes can carry them. Those who live under arbitrary power do nevertheless approve of liberty, and wish for it; they almost despair of recovering it in Europe; they read the translations of our separate colony constitutions with rapture; and there are such numbers everywhere, who talk of removing to America, with their families and fortunes, as soon as peace and our independence shall be established, that 'tis generally believed we shall have a prodigious addition of strength, wealth, and arts, from the emigrations of Europe; and 'tis thought that, to lessen or prevent such emigrations, the tyrannies established there must relax, and allow more liberty to their people. Hence, 'tis a common observation here, that our cause is the cause of all mankind, and that we are fighting for their liberty in defending our own.

Franklin never told the story of his part in the forging of the Alliance with France, but afterwards—once he and Deane had jointly drafted their report to the Continental Congress—he wrote a personal letter to his old friend Thomas Cushing in Massachusetts:

Passy, near Paris, 27 February 1778

SIR:

I received your favour by Mr Austin, with your most agreeable congratulations on the success of the American arms in the Northern Department. In return, give me leave to congratulate you on the success of our negotiations here, in the completion of two treaties with his Most Christian Majesty: the one of amity and commerce, on the plan of that projected in Congress, with some good additions; the other of alliance for mutual defence, in which the Most Christian King agrees to make a common cause with the United States, if England attempts to obstruct the commerce of his subjects with them; and guarantees to the United States their liberties, sovereignty, and independence, absolute and unlimited, with the possessions they now have, or may have at the conclusion of the war; and the States in return

Madame Helvetius

guarantees to him his possession in the West Indies. The great principle in both treaties is a perfect equality and reciprocity; no advantage being demanded by France, or privileges in commerce, which the States may not grant to any and every other nation.

In short, the king has treated us generously and magnanimously: taking no advantage of our present difficulties to exact terms which we would not willingly grant when established in prosperity and power. I may add that he has acted wisely in wishing the friendship contracted by these treaties may be durable, which probably it might not be if a contrary conduct had been observed.

Several of our American ships, with stores for the Congress, are now about sailing under the protection of a French squadron. England is in great consternation, and the minister on the 17th instant, confessing in a long speech that all his measures had been wrong and that peace was necessary, proposed two bills for quieting America; but they are full of artifice and deceit and will, I am confident, be treated accordingly by our country . . .

P.S. The treaties were signed by the plenipotentiaries on both sides 6 February, but are still for some reason kept secret, though soon to be published. It is understood that Spain will soon accede to the same. The treaties are forwarded to Congress by this conveyance.

In April 1779, writing to John Adams, then at Brest and about to return to America, Franklin described his audience with Louis XVI in his new role as Minister from the United States.

Passy, 3 April 1779

SIR:

I received the letter you did me the honour to write me of the 24th past. I am glad you have been at Brest, as your presence there has contributed to expedite the operations of Captain Landais in refitting his ship. I think with you that more has been made of the conspiracy than was necessary; but that it would have been well if some of the most guilty could have received a proper punishment. As that was impracticable under our present naval code, I hope you will, on your return, obtain an amendment of it. I approve of clothing the midshipmen and petty officers agreeably to their request to you, and hope you have ordered it, without waiting to hear from me; and I now desire that whatever else you may judge for the good of the service, our friends and circumstances considered, you would in my behalf give directions for, as the great distance makes it inconvenient to send to me on every occasion; and I can confide in your prudence that you will allow no expense that is unnecessary.

My gout continues to disable me from walking longer than formerly; but on Tuesday the 23rd past I thought myself able to go through the ceremony, and accordingly went to court, had my audience of the king in the new character, presented my letter of credence, and was received very graciously. After which I went the rounds with the other foreign ministers, in visiting all the royal family. The fatigue, however, was a little too much for my feet, and disabled me for near another week. Upon the whole I can assure you that I do not think the good will of this court to the good cause of America is at all diminished by the late little reverses in the fortune of war; and I hope Spain, who has now forty-nine ships of the line and thirty-one frigates ready for service, will soon, by declaring, turn the scale. Remember me affectionately to Master Johnny, and believe me, with great esteem, sir, your most obedient and most humble servant . . .

By 1779, Spain was an ally of France but not of an independent America; she was reluctant to see a new and strong republic in North America lest it threaten her own colonies to the south. The great powers of Europe—Vergennes hoped—might arbitrate and limit the new state to the Atlantic coast. To John Jay, sent to Spain as minister in 1780, Franklin voiced his fears:

Spain owes us nothing; therefore, whatever friendship she shows us in lending money or furnishing clothes, etc., though not equal to our wants and wishes, is however *tant de gagné*. Those who have begun to assist us are more likely to continue than to decline, and we are still so much obliged as their aids amount to. But I hope, and am confident, that court will be wiser than to take advantage of our distress, and insist on our making sacrifices by an agreement which the circumstances of such distress would hereafter weaken, and the very proposition can only give disgust at present. Poor as we are, yet as I know we shall be rich, I would rather agree with them to buy at a great price the whole of their right on the Mississippi than sell a drop of its waters. A neighbour might as well ask me to sell my street door.

Busy as he was, as consul, as diplomat and negotiator and—always—as propagandist and persuader, Franklin was also spymaster and spied-upon.

Agents were everywhere. Viscount Stormont, the British ambassador, watched every move he made. Edward Bancroft, a confidant of Silas Deane and later secretary of the American Commissioners, was in British pay throughout the seven years of war, and never discovered in his lifetime. When Franklin was warned that he was surrounded by spies, he replied (January 1777):

As it is impossible to discover in every case the falsity of pretended friends who would know our affairs; and more so to prevent being watched by spies when interested people may think proper to place them for that purpose; I have long observed one rule which prevents any inconvenience from such practices. It is simply this: to be concerned in no affairs that I should blush to have made public, and to do nothing but what spies may see, and welcome . . . If I was sure, therefore, that my *valet de place* was a spy, as probably he is, I think I should not discharge him for that, if in other respects I liked him.

Despite this, he found time to enjoy the lighter things of life. He lived well, as the Duc de Chaumont's paying guest in his great house at Passy (then a lovely village on the Seine just outside Paris). The house had a well-stocked cellar and a printing press—which allowed Franklin to keep his hand in by sending the ladies of the salons *his playful and ironic* bagatelles. *His favourite among the ladies was Madame Brillon, to whom he wrote letters full of innuendo.*

People commonly speak of Ten Commandments. I have been taught that there are twelve. The first was, increase and multiply and replenish the earth. The twelfth is, a new Command-ment I give unto you, *that you love one another.* It seems to me that they are a little misplaced, and that the last should have been the first. However, I never made any difficulty about that, but was always willing to obey them both whenever I had an opportunity. Pray tell me, my dear Casuist, whether my keep-ing religiously these two commandments, though not in the Decalogue, may not be accepted in compensation for my break-ing so often one of the ten, I mean that which forbids coveting my neighbour's wife, and which I confess I break constantly, God forgive me, as often as I see or think of my lovely Con-fessor, and I am afraid I should never be able to repent of the sin even if I had the full possession of her.

And now I am consulting you upon a case of conscience, I will mention the opinion of a certain father of the church which I find myself willing to adopt though I am not sure it is orthodox. It is this, that the most effectual way to get rid of a certain temptation is, as often as it returns, to comply with and satisfy it.

Pray instruct me how far I may venture to practise upon this principle?

But why should I be so scrupulous when you have promised to absolve me of the future?

Adieu my charming conductress, and belive me ever with the sincerest esteem and affection.

Your most obed't hum. serv.

To his sister Jane, however, he contrived to sound becomingly modest:

I enjoy here an exceeding good state of health, I live in a fine airy house upon a hill, which has a large garden with fine walks in it, about half an hour's drive from the city of Paris. I walk a little every day in the garden, have a good appetite and sleep well. I think the French cookery agrees with me better than the English; I suppose because there is little or no butter in their sauces; for I have never once had the heartburn since my being here though I eat heartily, which shows that my digestion is good. I have got into a good neighbourhood, of very agreeable people who appear very fond of me; at least they are pleasingly civil: so that upon the whole I live as comfortably as a man can well do so far from his home and his family.

And to his daughter Sally, the delight of his heart, he had no hesitation in pointing out to her the error of her ways, when he deemed it necessary:

I was charmed with the account you give me of your industry, the table-cloths of your own spinning, etc. but the latter part of the paragraph, that you had sent for linen from France because weaving and flax were grown dear; alas, that dissolved the charm; and your sending for long black pins, and lace, and *feathers!* disgusted me as much as if you had put salt into my strawberries. The spinning, I see, is laid aside, and you are to be dressed for the ball! you seem not to know, my dear daughter, that of all the dear things in this world, idleness is the dearest, except mischief.

He also wrote a paper on the 'Morals of Chess'. He was a devotee of the game, seeing it as a model of diplomacy. In writing 'Morals' he must have remembered his games in London with Lord Howe's sister.

The game of Chess is not merely an idle amusement. Several very valuable qualities of the mind, useful in the course of human life, are to be acquired or strengthened by it, so as to become habits, ready on all occasions.

1. *Foresight,* which looks a little into futurity, and considers the consequences that may attend an action; for it is continually occuring to the player, 'If I move this piece, what will be the advantages or disadvantages of my new situation? What use can my adversary make of it to annoy me? What other moves can I make to support it, and to defend myself from his attacks?

2. *Circumspection,* which surveys the whole chessboard, or scene of action; the relations of the several pieces and situations, the dangers they are respectively exposed to, the several possibilities of their aiding each other, the probabilities that the adversary may make this or that move, and attack this or the other piece, and what different means can be used to avoid his stroke, or turn its consequences against him.

3. *Caution,* not to make our moves too hastily. This habit is best acquired, by observing strictly the laws of the game; such as, *If you touch a piece, you must move it somewhere; if you set it down, you must let it stand.* And it is therefore best that these rules should be observed, as the game becomes thereby more the image of human life, and particularly of war . . .

And *lastly,* we learn by Chess the habit of not being discouraged by present appearances in the state of our affairs, the habit of hoping for a favourable change, and that of persevering in the search of resources. The game is so full of events, there is such a variety of turns in it, the fortune of it is so subject to sudden vicissitudes, and one so frequently, after long contemplation, discovers the means of extricating one's self from a supposed insurmountable difficulty, that one is encouraged to continue the contest to the last, in hopes of victory from our own skill, or at least of getting a stalemate from the negligence of our adversary . . .

If your adversary is long in playing, you ought not to hurry him, or express any uneasiness at his delay. You should not sing, nor whistle, nor look at your watch, not take up a book to read, nor make a tapping with your feet on the floor, or with your fingers on the table, nor do anything that may disturb his attention. For all these things displease; and they do not show your skill in playing, but your craftiness or your rudeness.

You ought not to endeavour to amuse and deceive your adversary, by pretending to have made bad moves, and saying that you have now lost the game, in order to make him secure and careless, and inattentive to your schemes: for this is fraud and deceit, not skill in the game.

You must not, when you have gained a victory, use any triumphing or insulting expression, nor show too much pleasure; but endeavour to console your adversary, and make him less dissatisfied with himself, by every kind of civil expression that may be used with truth, such as 'you understand the game better than I, but you are a little inattentive;' or, 'you play too fast;' or, 'you had the best of the game, but something happened to divert your thoughts, and that turned it in my favour.'

If you are a spectator while others play, observe the most perfect silence. For, if you give advice, you offend both parties, him against whom you give it, because it may cause the loss of his game, him in whose favour you give it, because, though it be good, and he follows it, he loses the pleasure he might have had, if you had permitted him to think until it had occurred to himself. Even after a move or moves, you must not, by replacing the pieces, show how they might have been placed better; for that displeases, and may occasion disputes and doubts about their true situation. All talking to the players lessens or diverts their attention, and is therefore unpleasing.

Lastly, if the game is not to be played rigorously, according to the rules above mentioned, then moderate your desire of victory over your adversary, and be pleased with one over yourself. Snatch not eagerly at every advantage offered by his unskilfulness or inattention; but point out to him kindly, that by such a move he places or leaves a piece in danger and unsupported; that by another he will put his king in a perilous situation, etc. By this generous civility (so opposite to the unfairness above forbidden) you may, indeed, happen to lose the game to your opponent; but you will win what is better, his esteem, his respect, and his affection, together with the silent approbation and goodwill of impartial spectators.

In March 1780 Franklin wrote to his friend Dr Thomas Bond, member of the American Philosophical Society and of the Pennsylvania Society.

Passy, 16 March 1780

DEAR SIR:

I received your kind letter of September the 22nd, and I thank you for the pleasing account you give me of the health and welfare of my old friends, Hugh Roberts, Luke Morris, Philip Syng, Samuel Rhoads, etc., with the same of yourself and family. Shake the old ones by the hand for me, and give the young ones my blessing. For my own part, I do not find that I grow any older. Being arrived at seventy, and considering that my travelling farther in the same road I should probably be led to the grave, I stopped short, turned about, and walked back again; which having done these four years, you may now call me sixty-six. Advise those old friends of ours to follow my example; keep up your spirits, and that will keep up your bod-

ies; you will no more stoop under the weight of age than if you
had swallowed a handspike.

*Despite his protestations of good health, in March 1781 Franklin sub-
mitted his resignation to the Congress. He had been in France for nearly
five years.*

I have passed my seventy-fifth year, and I find that the long and
severe fit of the gout which I had the last winter has shaken me
exceedingly, and I am yet far from having recovered the bodily
strength I before enjoyed. I do not know that my mental faculties are impaired; perhaps I shall be the last to discover that;
but I am sensible of great diminution in my activity, a quality I
think particularly necessary in your minister for this court. I am
afraid therefore that your affairs may, some time or other,
suffer by my deficiency . . .
   And as I cannot at present undergo the fatigues of a sea
voyage (the last having been almost too much for me) and
would not again expose myself to the hazard of capture and
imprisonment in this time of war, I purpose to remain here at
least 'till the peace; perhaps may be for the remainder of my
life; and if any knowledge or experience I have acquired here
may be thought of use to my successor, I shall freely communicate it, and assist him with any influence I may be supposed
to have, or counsel that may be desired of me.

   *He was still enjoying his correspondence with the ladies of Paris—
Madame Helvetius, the widow of a rich official, presided over a famous
and merry salon and appeared to be one of the objects of Franklin's
devotion.*

And now I mention your friends, let me tell you that I have in
my way been trying to form some hypothesis to account for
your having so many and of such various kinds. I see that
statesmen, philosophers, historians, poets, and men of learning
of all sorts are drawn around you, and seem as willing to attach
themselves to you as straws about a fine piece of amber. It is not
that you make pretensions to any of their sciences; and if you
did, similarity of studies does not always make people love one

another. It is not that you take pains to engage them; artless simplicity is a striking part of your character. I would not attempt to explain it by the story of the ancient who, being asked why philosophers sought the acquaintance of kings and kings not that of philosophers, replied that philosophers knew what they wanted, which was not always the case with kings. Yet thus far the comparison may go, that we find in your sweet society that charming benevolence, that amiable attention to oblige, that disposition to please and be pleased, which we do not always find in the society of one another. It springs from you; it has its influence on us all; and in your company we are not only pleased with you, but better pleased with one another and with ourselves.

I am ever, with great respect and affection, etc . . .

But Madame Brillon remained his favourite.

THE EPHEMERA

An Emblem of Human Life (Written in 1778)
TO MADAME BRILLON, of Passy

You may remember, my dear friend, that when we lately spent that happy day in the delightful garden and sweet society of the Moulin Joly, I stopped a little in one of our walks, and staid some time behind the company. We had been shown numberless skeletons of a kind of little fly, called an ephemera, whose successive generations, we were told, were bred and expired within the day. I happened to see a living company of them on a leaf, who appeared to be engaged in conversation. You know I understand all the inferior animal tongues: my too great application to the study of them is the best excuse I can give for the little progress I have made in your charming language. I listened through curiosity to the discourse of these little creatures; but as they, in their national vivacity, spoke three or four together, I could make but little of their conversation. I found, however, by some broken expressions that I heard now and then, they were disputing warmly on the merit of two foreign musicians, one a *cousin,* the other a *moscheto;* in which dispute they spent their time, seemingly as regardless of the shortness of life as if they had been sure of living a month. Happy people! thought I, you live certainly under a wise, just, and mild government, since you have no public grievances to complain of, nor any subject of contention but the perfections and imperfections of foreign music. I turned my head from them to an old grey-headed one who was single on another leaf, and talking to himself. Being amused with his soliloquy, I put it down in writing, in hopes it will likewise amuse her to whom I am so much indebted for the most pleasing of all amusements, her delicious company and heavenly harmony.

'It was', said he, 'the opinion of learned philosophers of our race, who lived and flourished long before my time, that this vast world, the Moulin Joly, could not itself subsist more than eighteen hours; and I think there was some foundation for that opinion, since, by the apparent motion of the great luminary that gives life to all nature, and which in my time has evidently declined considerably towards the ocean at the end of our earth, it must then finish its course, be extinguished in the waters that surround us, and leave the world in cold and darkness, necessarily producing universal death and destruction. I have lived seven of those hours, a great age, being no less than four hundred and twenty minutes of time. How very few of us continue so long! I have seen generations born, flourish, and expire. My present friends are the children and grand-children of the friends of my youth, who are now, alas, no more! And I must soon follow them; for, by the course of nature, though still in health, I cannot expect to live above seven or eight minutes longer. What now avails all my toil and labour, in amassing honey-dew on this leaf, which I cannot live to enjoy! What the political struggles I have been engaged in, for the good of my compatriot inhabitants of this bush, or my philosophical studies for the benefit of our race in general! for in politics, what can laws do without morals? Our present race of ephemerae will in a course of minutes become corrupt, like those of other and older bushes, and consequently as wretched: and in philosophy how small our progress! Alas! art is long, and life is short! My friends would comfort me with the idea of a name, they say, I shall leave behind me; and they tell me I have lived long enough to nature and to glory. But what will fame be to an ephemera who no longer exists? and what will become of all history in the eighteenth hour, when the world itself, even the whole Moulin Joly, shall come to its end, and be buried in universal ruin?'

To me, after all my eager pursuits, no solid pleasures now remain, but the reflection of a long life spent in meaning well, the sensible conversation of a few good lady ephemera, and now and then a kind smile and a tune from the ever amiable *Brilliante.*

B. FRANKLIN

Franklin's request to resign was turned down. Three months later he was appointed one of the five commissioners to negotiate peace with Great Britain.

EIGHT

OLD, HEAVY AND A LITTLE INDOLENT

The negotiations for peace, including the recognition of American in-
dependence, were long and involved—with Franklin, John Adams and
John Jay as America's principal agents. Franklin kept a journal of the
discussions and included in it letters from his colleagues; but it was
erratically compiled over some four months, mainly in diary form, and
was never completed.

The preliminary treaty of peace between British and American com-
missioners, was signed on St Andrew's Day, 30 November 1782—a
date that pleased Richard Oswald, the chief agent of Lord Shelburne,
and his fellow-Scot, Caleb Whitefoord, the secretary of the British team
and Franklin's old Craven Street neighbour. Franklin gave a personal
account of the proceedings to Robert Livingston in December 1782.

Passy, 5 December 1782

SIR:

I am honoured by your several letters dated September 5, 13,
15, and 18. I believe that the complaints you make in them, of
my not writing, may ere now have appeared less necessary, as
many of my letters written before those complaints must have
since come to hand. I will nevertheless mention some of the
difficulties your ministers meet with, in keeping up a regular
and punctual correspondence. We are far from the seaports,
and not well informed, and often misinformed, about the sailing of vessels. Frequently we are told they are to sail in a week
or two, and often they lie in the ports for months after, with our
letters on board, either waiting for convoy or for other reasons.
The post office here is an unsafe conveyance; many of the
letters we receive by it have evidently been opened, and doubt-

less the same happens to those we send; and at this time particularly there is so violent a curiosity in all kinds of people to know something relating to the negotiations, and whether peace may be expected or a continuance of the war, that there are few private hands or travellers that we can trust with carrying our despatches to the sea coast; and I imagine that they may sometimes be opened and destroyed, because they cannot be well sealed.

Again, the observation you make that the Congress ministers in Europe seem to form themselves into a Privy Council, transacting affairs without the privity or concurrence of the sovereign, may be in some respects just; but it should be considered that, if they do not write as frequently as other ministers here do to their respective courts, or if, when they write, their letters are not regularly received, the greater distance of the seat of war and the extreme irregularity of conveyances may be the causes, and not a desire of acting without the knowledge or orders of their constituents. There is no European court to which an express cannot be sent from Paris in ten or fifteen days, and from most of them answers may be obtained in that time. There is, I imagine, no minister, who would not think it safer to act by orders than from his own discretion; and yet, unless you leave more to the discretion of your ministers in Europe than courts usually do, your affairs may sometimes suffer extremely from the distance, which, in the time of war especially, may make it five or six months before the answer to a letter shall be received. I suppose the minister from this court will acquaint Congress with the king's sentiments respecting their very handsome present of a ship of the line. People in general here are much pleased with it.

It is in vain for me to repeat again what I have so often written, and what I find taken so little notice of, that there are bounds to everything, and that the faculties of this nation are limited like those of all other nations. Some of you seem to have established as maxims the suppositions that France has money enough for all her occasions and all ours besides, and that if she does not supply us it is owing to her want of will, or to my negligence. As to the first, I am sure it is not true; and to the second, I can only say I should rejoice as much as any man in being able to obtain more; and I shall also rejoice in the greater success of those who may take my place. You desire to be very particularly acquainted with 'every step which tends to negotiation'. I am, therefore, encouraged to send you the first part of the *Journal,* which accidents and a long, severe illness interrupted, but which, from notes I have by me, may be continued if thought proper. In its present state it is hardly fit for the inspection of Congress, certainly not for public view. I confide it therefore to your prudence.

The arrival of Mr Jay, Mr Adams, and Mr Laurens has relieved me from much anxiety, which must have continued if I had been left to finish the treaty alone; and it has given me the more satisfaction, as I am sure the business has profited by their assistance . . .

The British minister struggled hard for two points: that the favours granted to the Loyalists should be extended, and all our fishery contracted. We silenced them on the first by threatening to produce an account of the mischief done by those people; and as to the second, when they told us they could not possibly agree to it as we requested it, and must refer it to the ministry in London, we produced a new article to be referred at the same time, with a note of facts in support of it, which you have, C. Apparently, it seemed that to avoid the discussion of this they suddenly changed their minds, dropped the design of recurring to London, and agreed to follow the fishery as demanded . . .

Every one of the present British ministry had, while in the ministry, declared the war against us as unjust, and nothing is clearer in reason than those who injure others by an unjust war should make full reparation. They have stipulated too, in these preliminaries, that in evacuating our towns they shall carry off no plunder, which is a kind of acknowledgment that they ought not to have done it before.

They wanted to bring their boundary down to the Ohio, and to settle their Loyalists in the Illinois country. We did not choose such neighbours. We communicated all the articles as soon as they were signed to Count de Vergennes (except the separate one), who thinks we have managed well, and told me that we had settled what was most apprehended as a difficulty in the work of a general peace, by obtaining the declaration of our independency.

14 December: I have this day learned that the principal preliminaries between France and England are agreed on, to wit:

1. France is to enjoy the right of fishing and drying on all the west coast of Newfoundland, down to Cape Ray. Miquelon and St Pierre to be restored, and may be fortified.

2. Senegal remains to France, and Goree to be restored. The Gambia entirely to England.

3. All the places taken from France in the East Indies to be restored, with a certain quantity of territory round them.

4. In the West Indies, Grenada and the Grenadines, St Christopher's, Nevis, and Montserrat, to be restored to England; St Lucia to France. Dominique to remain with France, and St Vincent's to be neutralized.

5. No commissioner at Dunkirk.

I am now entering on my seventy-eighth year; public business has engrossed fifty of them; I wish now to be, for the little time I have left, my own master. If I live to see this peace concluded, I shall beg leave to remind Congress, of their promise then to dismiss me. I shall be happy to sing with old Simeon: 'Now lettest thou thy servant depart in peace, for mine eyes have seen thy salvation.' With great esteem, etc . . .

On a more personal note, Franklin wrote to Jonathan Shipley, the Bishop of St Asaph:

Passy, 17 March 1783

I received with great pleasure my dear and respected friend's letter of the 5th instant, as it informed me of the welfare of a family I so much esteem and love.

The clamour against the peace in your Parliament would alarm me for its duration, if I were not of opinion with you that the attack is rather against the minister. I am confident none of the opposition would have made a better peace for England, if they had been in his place; at least, I am sure that Lord Stormont, who seems loudest in railing at it, is not the man that could have mended it. My reasons I will give you, when I have, what I hope to have, the great happiness of seeing you once more, and conversing with you.

They talk much of there being no *reciprocity* in our treaty. They think nothing, then, of our passing over in silence the atrocities committed by their troops, and demanding no satisfaction for their wanton burnings and devastations of our fair towns and countries. They have heretofore confessed the war to be unjust, and nothing is plainer in reasoning than that the mischiefs done in an unjust war should be repaired. Can Englishmen be so partial to themselves as to imagine they have a right to plunder and destroy as much as they please, and then, without satisfying for the injuries they have done, to have peace on equal terms? We were favourable, and did not demand what justice entitled us to. We shall probably be blamed for it by our constituents; and I still think it would be the interest of England voluntarily to offer reparation of those injuries, and effect it as much as may be in her power. But this is an interest she will never see.

Let us now forgive and forget. Let each country seek its advancement in its own internal advantages of arts and agriculture, not in retarding or preventing the prosperity of the other. America will, with God's blessing, become a great and happy country; and England, if she has at length gained wisdom, will have gained something more valuable, and more essential to her prosperity, than all she has lost; and will still be a great and respectable nation. Her great disease at present is the number and enormous salaries and emoluments of office. Avarice and ambition are strong passions, and, separately, act with great force on the human mind; but, when both are united, and may be gratified in the same object, their violence is almost irresistible, and they hurry men headlong into factions and contentions, destructive of all good government. As long, therefore, as these great emoluments subsist, your Parliament will be a stormy sea, and your public councils confounded by private interests. But it requires much public spirit and virtue to abolish them; more perhaps than can now be found in a nation so long corrupted.

I am, etc.

B. FRANKLIN

The American Commissioners of the preliminary peace negotiations with Great Britain. (From left to right: John Jay, John Adams, Franklin, Laurens and Temple Franklin.) Benjamin West, the artist, left space for British Commissioners Oswald and Whitefoord, but they never sat for him.

Caleb Whitefoord, the secretary to the British team

And to David Hartley MP, another of his English friends who had been sounding him out on peace proposals since 1778, he wrote:

Passy, 22 October 1783

. . . What would you think of a proposition, if I should make it, of a family compact between England, France, and America? America would be as happy as the Sabine girls, if she could be the means of uniting in perpetual peace her father and her husband. What repeated follies are these repeated wars! You do not want to conquer and govern one another. Why then should you continually be employed in injuring and destroying one another? How many excellent things might have been done to promote the internal welfare of each country; what bridges, roads, canals, and other useful public works and institutions, tending to the common felicity, might have been made and established with the money and men foolishly spent during the last seven centuries by our mad wars in doing one another mischief! You are near neighbours, and each have very respectable qualities. Learn to be quiet and to respect each other's rights. You are all Christians. One is *The Most Christian King,* and the other *Defender of the Faith.* Manifest the propriety of these titles by your future conduct. 'By this', says Christ, 'shall all men know that ye are my Disciples, if ye love one another.' 'Seek peace, and ensue it.' Adieu. Yours most affectionately,

B. FRANKLIN

The years were passing. In January 1783, Franklin heard from Polly Hewson that her mother had died on New Year's Day. 'I know you will pay the tribute of a sigh for the loss of one who loved you with the most ardent affection.' He wrote, 'Thus the ties I had to that country and indeed to the world in general are loosened one by one and I shall soon have no attachment left to make me unwilling to follow.'

By December 1783, when all parties had finally agreed to the terms of peace, Franklin was very infirm. But nothing would keep him from witnessing the second ascent of human passengers in a hot air balloon. He gave an account of the experiment to Sir Joseph Banks, president of The Royal Society in London.

The morning was foggy, but about one o'clock the air became tolerably clear, to the great satisfaction of the spectators, who

were infinite, notice having been given of the intended experiment several days before in the papers, so that all Paris was out,
either about the Tuileries, on the quays and bridges, in the
fields, the streets, at the windows, or on the tops of houses,
besides the inhabitants of all the towns and villages of the en-
virons. Never before was a philosophical experiment so mag-
nificently attended. Some guns were fired to give notice that the
departure of the great balloon was near, and a small one was
discharged, which went to an amazing height, there being but
little wind to make it deviate from its perpendicular course, and
at length the sight of it was lost. Means were used, I am told, to
prevent the great balloon's rising so high as might endanger its
bursting. Several bags of sand were taken on board before the
cord that held it down was cut, and the whole weight being then
too much to be lifted, such a quantity was discharged as to
permit its rising slowly. Thus it would sooner arrive at that
region where it would be in equilibrio with the surrounding air,
and by discharging more sand afterwards, it might go higher if
desired. Between one and two o'clock all eyes were gratified
with seeing it rise majestically from among the trees, and as-
cend gradually above the buildings, a most beautiful spectacle.
When it was about two hundred feet high, the brave adventurers held out and waved a little white pennant, on both sides
their car, to salute the spectators, who returned loud claps of
applause. The wind was very little, so that the object, though
moving to the northward, continued long in view; and it was a
great while before the admiring people began to disperse. The
persons embarked were Mr Charles, professor of experimental
philosophy and a zealous promoter of that science; and one of
the Messieurs Robert, the very ingenious constructors of the
machine. When it arrived at its height, which I suppose might
be three hundred or four hundred toises, it appeared to have
only horizontal motion. I had a pocket-glass with which I followed it, till I lost sight, first of the men, then of the car, and
when I last saw the balloon it appeared no bigger than a walnut.
I write this at seven in the evening. What became of them is not
yet known here. I hope they descended by daylight, so as to see
and avoid falling among trees or on houses, and that the experiment was completed without any mischievous accident,

which the novelty of it and the want of experience might well occasion. I am the more anxious for the event, because I am not well informed of the means provided for letting themselves gently down, and the loss of these very ingenious men would not only be a discouragement to the progress of art, but be a sensible loss to science and society.

William Franklin, who had been imprisoned in 1776 was, by 1784, living in London and had written to his father. He received an affectionate but unforgiving reply:

Passy, 16 August 1784

DEAR SON:

I received your letter of the 22nd past, and am glad to find that you desire to revive the affectionate intercourse that formerly existed between us. It will be very agreeable to me; indeed, nothing has ever hurt me so much and affected me with such keen sensations as to find myself deserted in my old age by my only son; and not only deserted, but to find him taking up arms against me in a cause wherein my good fame, fortune, and life were all at stake. You conceived, you say, that your duty to your king and regard for your country required this. I ought not to blame you for differing in sentiment with me in public affairs. We are men, all subject to errors. Our opinions are not in our own power; they are formed and governed much by circumstances that are often as inexplicable as they are irresistible. Your situation was such that few would have censured your remaining neuter, *though there are natural duties which precede political ones and cannot be extinguished by them.*

I did intend returning this year; but the Congress, instead of giving me leave to do so, have sent me another commission, which will keep me here at least a year longer; and perhaps I may then be too old and feeble to bear the voyage. I am here among a people that love and respect me, a most amiable nation to live with; and perhaps I may conclude to die among them; for my friends in America are dying off, one after another, and I have been so long abroad that I should now be almost a stranger in my own country.

On 12 July 1785 Franklin left Passy, carried in one of the royal litters because of the pain from his gout. It took five days to cover 150 miles, a sad but triumphal procession, interrupted by receptions in his honour. He carried with him a royal gift: a miniature of the French king encircled by 400 diamonds. When Sally inherited it, she sold it to finance a trip for her husband and herself to the France of which she had heard so much. 128 crates of luggage went by barge down the Seine.

Franklin wrote to his sister in Boston on the first leg of his journey home:

St Germain, 12 miles from Paris, 13 July 1785

DEAR SISTER:

I left Passy yesterday afternoon and am here on my way to Havre de Grace, a seaport, in order to embark for America. I make use of one of the king's litters carried by mules, who walk steadily and easily so that I bear the motion very well. I am to be taken on board a Philadelphia ship on the coast of England (Captain Truxton) the beginning of next month. Not having written to you since that which contained a bill for you on Mr Vernon, and as I may not have another opportunity before my arrival in Philadelphia (if it pleases God I do arrive), I write these particulars to go by way of England, that you may be less uneasy about me. I did my last public act in this country just before I set out, which was signing a treaty of amity and commerce with Prussia. I have continued to work till late in the day; 'tis time I should go home and go to bed.

To his dear 'Helvetia', Madame Helvetius, he wrote from Le Havre on 19 July:

... we shall leave France, the country that I love best in the world ... I am not sure that I shall be happy in America, but I must go. It seems to me that things are badly managed in the world, when I see that beings so made to be happy together are obliged to separate.

After eight and a half years in France, he sailed from Le Havre on 23 July. In Southampton, he met his son—alas, a cool reunion—and the

Shipleys. The whole family came on board to dine, and spent the night on the ship. On Thursday 28 July 'when I waked in the morning I found the company gone and the ship under sail'.

He left France in a golden glow, four years before the outbreak of the Revolution. He was spared knowledge of the fate in store for many of his friends. Bailly, the mayor of Paris; Lavoisier, the chemist; Le Veillard, neighbour, mayor of Passy and translator of many of his writings; Madame Rosalie Filleul, painter of his portrait . . . all were guillotined, as was Dr Guillotin himself. Condorcet would commit suicide in prison, and the Duc de la Rochefoucauld, whom Franklin persuaded to translate the Declaration of Independence into French, was stoned to death by a mob before his mother's eyes. Madame Helvetius survived the turmoil, but prudently buried her treasures in the garden at Auteuil.

The voyage was—as always—put to use. Franklin wrote three long scientific papers: 'Maritime Observations' (mainly the plotting of the Gulf Stream, 'the river in the ocean'), 'The Curses and Cure of Smoky Chimneys', and 'On a New Stove'. The Autobiogrophy *itself he felt he could not continue without his public papers. But there was always his diary:*

Wednesday, *14 September*. With the flood in the morning came a light breeze, which brought us above Gloucester Point, in full view of dear Philadelphia! when we again cast anchor to wait for the health officer, who, having made his visit and finding no sickness, gave us leave to land. My son-in-law came with a boat for us; we landed at Market Street Wharf, where we were received by a crowd of people with huzzas, and accompanied with acclamations quite to my door. Found my family well.

God be praised and thanked for all his mercies!

Aged seventy-nine, Franklin served as president of the Supreme Executive Council of Pennsylvania. He favoured a strong government, a single chamber, a plural executive and non-payment of salaries to executive officials. He had, in other words, faith in America but less faith in individuals. He expressed this in his 'Information to Those Who Would Remove to America' (written in 1784).

The truth is that though there are in that country few people so miserable as the poor of Europe, there are also very few that in

Europe would be called rich; it is rather a general happy mediocrity that prevails ... people do not inquire concerning a stranger, 'What is he?' but 'What can he do?' If he has any useful art, he is welcome; and if he exercises it and behaves well, he will be respected by all that know him; but a mere man of quality, who on that account wants to live upon the public by some office or salary, will be despised and disregarded. The husbandman is in honour there, and even the mechanic, because their employments are useful. The people have a saying that God Almighty is himself a mechanic, the greatest in the universe; and he is respected and admired more for the variety, ingenuity, and utility of his handiworks than for the antiquity of his family. They are pleased with the observation of a Negro, and frequently mention it, that "Boccarora" (meaning the white man) make de black man workee, make de horse workee, make de ox workee, make ebery ting workee, only de hog. He de hog, no workee; he eat, he drink, he walk about, he go to sleep when he please, he libb like a gentleman.' According to these opinions of the Americans, one of them would think himself more obliged to a genealogist who could prove for him that his ancestors and relations for ten generations had been ploughmen, smiths, carpenters, turners, weavers, tanners, or even shoemakers, and consequently that they were useful members of society; than if he could only prove that they were gentlemen, doing nothing of value, but living idly on the labour of others, mere *fruges consumere nati,* and otherwise *good for nothing,* till by their death their estates, like the carcass of the Negro's gentleman hog, 'come to be *cut up*'.

In his final speech, in 1787, read for him by James Wilson, Scottish immigrant Philadelphia lawyer and Supreme Court lawyer-to-be, he appealed to the Convention to adopt the Constitution:

Mr President: I confess, that I do not entirely approve of this Constitution at present; but, sir, I am not sure I shall never approve it; for, having lived long, I have experienced many instances of being obliged, by better information or fuller consideration, to change my opinions even on important subjects, which I once thought right, but found to be otherwise. It is therefore that, the older I grow, the more apt I am to doubt my own judgment of others . . . Thus I consent sir, to this Constitution, because I expect no better, and because I am not sure that it is not the best. The opinions I have had of its *errors* I sacrifice to the public good. I have never whispered a syllable of them abroad. Within these walls they were born, and here they shall die. I hope, therefore, for our own sakes, as a part of the people, and for the sake of our posterity, that we shall act heartily and unanimously in recommending this Constitution, wherever our influence may extend, and turn our future thoughts and endeavours to the means of having it *well administered.*

On the whole, sir, I cannot help expressing a wish, that every member of the Convention who may still have objections to it, would with me on this occasion doubt a little of his own infallibility, and, to make *manifest* our *unanimity,* put his name to this instrument.

Franklin lived with his daughter, surrounded by her children, and the neighbours and friends who came to salute him. The meetings of the American Philosophical Society were held in his home near Market Street. It had been extended for him, to ensure him privacy and to house his library. He was still writing to friends across the world and at home and trying to complete his memoirs—but without success; he brought the story only to 1757. His last public act in February 1790 was to sign a memorial to Congress for the abolition of slavery. He now suffered acutely and took drugs.

Franklin died 17 April 1790 after a long illness, aged eighty-four. He was buried in Christ Church Burial Ground, attended by a crowd of some 20,000, the largest ever to assemble in Philadelphia. The tomb has his own simple wording, as his will directed: Benjamin and Deborah Franklin: 1790.

But the epitaph by which he is remembered, he had written himself, with wry humour, sixty-two years before:

The body of
B. Franklin, Printer
(Like the Cover of an Old Book
Its Contents Torn Out

And Stript of its Lettering and Gilding)
Lies Here, Food for Worms.
But the Work shall not be Lost;
For it will (as he Believ'd) Appear once More
In a New and More Elegant Edition
Revised and Corrected
By the Author.

WHO'S WHO

ALLEN, WILLIAM (1704–80) merchant, public servant, chief justice, 1750–74. Born in Philadelphia, educated at Cambridge and the Middle Temple in London, he was Philadelphia's wealthiest citizen, leading philanthropist, social arbiter, and the political boss of the proprietary party. He recommended Franklin for deputy postmaster general, agreeing with him on defence matters, but later breaking with him over the issue of proprietary government. He opposed the Stamp Act in 1765 but ended as a Loyalist.

AMHERST, JEFFERY (1717–97) cr. Baron 1776, British general, succeeded Loudoun as commander-in-chief in North America, 1758–63, and as titular governor of Virginia, 1759–68. He captured Louisbourg, 1758; Ticonderoga and Crown Point, 1759; and Montreal, 1760, ending French resistance in North America. Though he declined active command in America in 1776, he was commander-in-chief in Great Britain in 1778 and again in 1793–95.

BACHE, RICHARD (1737–1811) b. Settle, Yorkshire, m. Sarah Franklin, journalist.

BACHE, BENJAMIN FRANKLIN (1769–98) son of above. Accompanied his grandfather to France 1776, attended school in Geneva until 1783; became anti-federalist journalist.

BARBEU-DUBOURG, JACQUES (1709–79) physician and botanist. One of Franklin's earliest friends and correspondents in France. Dedicated his *Code de la raison humaine* (1774) to Franklin, his *'cher maître'*.

BEAUMARCHAIS, PIERRE AUGUSTIN CARON (1732–99) author of *The Barber of Seville* and *The Marriage of Figaro*. Gave financial support to the American Revolutionary cause.

BECCARIA, GIOVANNI BATTISTA (1716–81) Italian physicist. Took religious orders. Professor of Experimental Physics at Palermo, Rome, and Turin. Fellow of English Royal Society. Spread knowledge of electrical experiments carried out by Franklin and others.

BENGER, ELLIOTT (d. 1751), a Scot who emigrated to Virginia before 1728, entered the service of Col. Alexander Spotswood, and lived on his estate at New Post on the Rappahannock River near Fredericksburg. He married Spotswood's sister-in-law, and was appointed deputy postmaster general for North America, 1743.

BRADDOCK, EDWARD (1695–1755) landed in Virginia, 1755, as commander-in-chief with the widest powers ever given to a British officer in America. His initial objective was the capture of Fort Duquesne (Pittsburg), but, without experience or even conception of wilderness warfare, and contemptuous of advice, he was defeated by French and Indians and fatally wounded in battle near the Monongahela River, July 9, 1755. Among his aides were George Washington, Horatio Gates and Charles Lee.

BRADFORD, ANDREW (1686–1742) son and partner of William Bradford, Franklin's competitor. He published the first Pennsylvania newspaper, *The American Weekly Mercury*, begun in 1719, as well as books, pamphlets, and almanacs; and was official printer to Pennsylvania.

BRADFORD, WILLIAM (1663–1732) pioneer American printer, father of Franklin's competitor Andrew, said to have come to Pennsylvania with William Penn. He displeased the Quaker leaders by printing some of George Keith's writings, was tried but not convicted, and in 1693 moved to New York, where he became royal printer.

BREINTNALL, JOSEPH (d. 1746) Quaker, merchant, copyist, original member of the Junto, versifier; secretary of the Library Co., 1731–36.

BRILLON, M. HARDANCOURT BRILLON de Jouy (née 1742) neighbour of Franklin in Passy.

BUFFON, GEORGE-LOUIS-LECLERC, Comte de (1707–88) most famous naturalist of his time. Wrote *Natural History* (1749–1804) in forty-four quarto volumes. Keeper of the Jardin du Roi and the royal museum. Author of the famous essay on style which contains the passage *Le style est l'homme même*. Member of the Academy, the Royal Society, and most of the distinguished learned societies in Europe. Corresponded with Franklin on scientific matters.

BURGOYNE, JOHN (1722–92) general, politician and dramatist. In 1777 commanded northern army, invading from Canada and reoccupied Crown Point and Ticonderoga. When Clinton failed to meet him and he was heavily outnumbered, he surrendered to Horatio Gates at Saratoga, Oct 17, 1777.

BURNET, WILLIAM (1688–1729) eldest son of Gilbert Burnet, bishop of Salisbury. From 1720 to 1728 Captain General and Governor-in-Chief of New York and New Jersey. Governor of New Hampshire, Nov 1727, and of Massachusetts Bay.

CABANIS, PIERRE-JEAN-GEORGE (1757–1808) eminent physiologist and administrator in the Paris hospitals. Professor at the Paris medical school, 1795–99.

Personal physician to Mirabeau. Member of the Council of Five Hundred and the Senate. Political career ended when Napoleon came to power.

CAVE, EDWARD (1691–1754) printer, journalist, founder and publisher of *The Gentleman's Magazine*, especially notable for the space it gave to American and Scientific news.

CHARLES, ROBERT (committed suicide 1770) agent for New York 1748. He and Franklin shared the agency 1757 to 1761, when Charles withdrew. He obtained accommodation for Franklin in Craven Street before his arrival in London.

CHASTELLUX, FRANCOIS-JEAN, Marquis de (1734–99) writer, explorer, soldier. Colonel in the French expeditionary force to the colonies in 1780. Composed light verse and comedies.

CHAUMONT, DONATIEN-LERAY Comte de (?–1803) Grand Master of the Woods and Forests of France. Honorary superintendent of the Hôtel des Invalides. Owner of the Hôtel de Valentinois, in which Franklin lived at Passy. Spent about two million francs, four-fifths of his entire fortune, in helping the American cause.

COLDEN, CADWALLADER (1688–1776) born in Ireland and migrated to Philadelphia in 1710 where he practised medicine and worked as a merchant. Moved to New York 1718. Acting Governor of New York on five occasions.

COLEMAN, WILLIAM (1704–69) Philadelphia merchant, original member of the Junto, held many civic and governmental posts, including that of associate justice of the Supreme Court, 1758–69. One of Franklin's closest friends, he helped him become an independent printer and was named executor in his will of 1757.

COLLINSON, PETER (1694–1763) London Quaker Merchant, FRS, one of the most important people in Franklin's life. A man of wide interests, he was a noted botanist who corresponded with Linnaeus and with colonial scientists, especially the botanist John Bartram. He was a great help to the Library Co. of Philadelphia and was responsible for the first publication, 1751, of Franklin's *Experiments and Observations on Electricity.*

CONDORCET, MARIE-JEAN-ANTOINE-NICHOLAS-CARITA (1743–94) mathematician and philosopher. Friend to most of the distinguished men of his time. Well known for his lives of Voltaire and Turgot. His most famous work, *Esquisse d'un tableau historique.* During the revolution Condorcet voted against the death penalty for the King. He became suspect and had to flee for his life. Found dead in prison—either from the effects of exhaustion or poison.

CROGHAN, GEORGE (d. 1782) Indian interpreter, trader, and land speculator, who came from Ireland in 1741. Though chronically in debt, he was indispensable at Indian conferences, assisted Washington and Braddock, and became deputy superintendent of Indian affairs under Sir William Johnson.

Le Docteur Francklin couronné par la Liberté

DALIBARD, THOMAS-FRANCOIS (1703–99) French physicist and botanist. After translating *Experiments and Observations on Electricity*, he arranged, and an assistant performed for the first time, May 10, 1752, Franklin's proposed experiment to prove the identity of lightning and electricity.

DARTMOUTH, WILLIAM LEGGE 2nd Earl (1731–1801) Secretary of State for the colonies (1772–75), stepbrother of Lord North, and Lord Privy Seal 1775–82.

DENHAM, THOMAS (d. 1728) Philadelphia merchant, Franklin's benefactor, half-owner of the *Berkshire* on which Franklin returned from England. In his will he cancelled the debt of £10.3s.5d. due for passage.

DIDEROT, DENIS (1713–84) famous French writer, spent most of his life editing the Encyclopedia. Frequently attended the dinners given by Baron d'Holbach, at which Franklin was also often present.

DINWIDDIE, ROBERT (1693–1770) governor of Virginia, 1751–58. Born near Glasgow, began a long and successful career in the colonial customs service in 1727, and, as surveyor general for the Southern District, in 1738 made his home in Virginia. His service as lieutenant governor and acting governor was distinguished by great energy and executive ability, especially in frontier and Indian affairs, but was marred by a quarrel with the Assembly over fees for land grants.

DUMAS, CHARLES-WILHELM-FREDERIC (1721–96) German-born, but of French Huguenot family, settled in the Hague, 1750, as tutor and translator; correspondent and agent of Franklin; strongly pro-American and always longed to settle there.

EGREMONT, CHARLES WYNDHAM, 2nd Earl (1710–63) son of Sir William; succeeded to the earldom on the death of an uncle, 1750. As Secretary of State for the Southern District, succeeding Pitt in 1761, he had charge of colonial affairs, which brought him into contact with Franklin.

ESTAING, CHARLES-HECTOR, Comte d' (1729–94) French admiral. Commander of the French fleet that assisted the colonies against Great Britain. In command of the combined French-American fleet when the treaty was signed in 1783. Gave testimony favouring Marie Antoinette in 1793 and was executed the following year.

FOLGER, PETER (1617–99) Benjamin's grandfather, born in Norwich, Norfolk, migrated to Boston, 1635, to Martha's Vineyard, and to Nantucket 1664. He married an indentured servant, Mary Morrill. He was a weaver, schoolmaster, miller, public official, and versifier.

FOTHERGILL, JOHN (1712–80) MD, Edinburgh, 1736; FRS, attended Franklin professionally in 1757. A strong Quaker, he was in constant touch with Friends in Pennsylvania and advised their withdrawal from the Assembly in 1756 because of the war with France. He wrote the preface for Franklin's *Experiments and Observations on Electricity*, 1751, and saw it through the press.

FRANKLIN, ABIAH FOLGER (1667–1752) Benjamin's mother. Only her children and her epitaph record details of her history. A memorial marks the site of her birth on Nantucket.

FRANKLIN, BENJAMIN ('THE ELDER') (1650–1727) the uncle after whom Benjamin Franklin was named; London silk dyer; came to Boston in 1715, widowed, and having lost nine of his ten children; lived for four years with his brother Josiah's family.

FRANKLIN, DEBORAH READ ROGERS (1708–74) married John Rogers, 1725, was deserted by him, and became Franklin's plain, sensible wife and competent helper in business. Though she could not share his intellectual or social life, he cherished her and was usually indulgent, affectionate, and generous. She did not accompany him on his two English missions, and she died, after a stroke, having not seen him for ten years.

FRANKLIN, FRANCIS FOLGER (1732–36) son of Benjamin and Deborah. 'The DE-LIGHT of all that knew him' his parents described him on his gravestone. Franklin wrote to his sister Jane in 1772 mentioning the boy, 'whom I have seldom seen equall'd in anything, and whom to this Day I cannot think of without a Sigh.'

FRANKLIN, JAMES (1697–1735) Benjamin's brother, learned the printer's trade in England. Brought back a press, types, and supplies, and started *The New England Courant*, 1721, a new and too lively kind of journalism for Boston. In about 1726 he went to Newport, where he published briefly the *Rhode Island Gazette*, 1732–33, and became the public printer.

FRANKLIN, JOHN (1643–91) Benjamin's uncle, dyer in Banbury, whose great-granddaughter Sarah (c.1753–81) occasionally stayed with Franklin in London 1766–70.

FRANKLIN, JOHN (1690–1756) Benjamin's favourite brother, moved to Rhode Island and set up as a soap boiler and candle maker. Subsequently he became postmaster of Boston and co-founder of a glass factory in Braintree.

FRANKLIN, JOSIAH (1657–1745) Benjamin's father, silk dyer in Banbury before migrating to Boston in 1683, where he became a tallow chandler. By his first wife, Ann Child, he had seven children; by his second, Abiah Folger, Benjamin's mother, ten.

FRANKLIN, JOSIAH (1685–c.1715) Benjamin's half-brother; broke away from home and went to sea, returned after nine years, was finally lost at sea.

FRANKLIN, WILLIAM (c.1731–1813) son of Benjamin. In 1750 his father described him as 'a tall proper Youth and much of a Beau'. A close companion in many activities, he succeeded the older man as a clerk of the Assembly and post-master of Philadelphia, had a brief military career, went to England with his father in 1757, and entered the Middle Temple to study law. He was appointed royal governor of New Jersey, 1762. They took opposite sides in the events leading to the Revolution; as a loyalist, William was arrested and confined in Connecticut, but was exchanged after two years, remained with the British Army in New York for nearly four years, and then went to England. Though there was an attempted reconciliation in 1785, Franklin almost wholly excluded William in his last will: 'The part he acted against me in the late War, which is of public Notoriety, will account for my leaving him no more of an Estate he endeavoured to deprive me of.'

GODFREY, THOMAS (1704–49) glazier, self-taught mathematician and astronomer, original member of the Junto. In 1730 he invented a new mariner's quadrant, known as Hadley's, for which the Royal Society gave him belated recognition.

GRACE, ROBERT (1709–66) proprietor of the Warwick Iron Works, which he acquired by marriage, and where Franklin's fireplaces were cast; an original member of the Junto, which met at his house, and director of the Library Co. He lent Franklin money to set up independently, refused payment of the debt, and Franklin in turn gave him the model of his fireplace to manufacture and sell without royalty. Grace rented his Market Street house to Franklin in 1739; here the 'New Printing Office' was maintained for thirty-seven years and here the Franklin family lived until 1748.

GRANVILLE, JOHN CARTERET, 1st Earl (1690–1763) Lord President of the Privy Council (1751–63). He was related by marriage to the Penn family and sympathetic to the Quakers.

HALL, DAVID (1714–72) born in Edinburgh, journeyman with Watts (where Franklin had worked) in London, then with William Strahan, who sent him to Franklin in 1744. Instead of setting up Hall in the West Indies, as he had intended, Franklin made him his foreman and then his partner, 1748, and their close relationship lasted until Hall's death.

HAMILTON, ANDREW (c.1676–1714) lawyer and office holder. A powerful, able and controversial figure in Pennsylvania, politically independent, he was speaker of the Assembly, 1729–33, 1734–39. His most famous legal case was his successful defence of John Peter Zenger when tried for seditious libel in New York, 1735. Franklin regarded him as a most 'useful' friend.

HANBURY, JOHN (1700–58) important and well-connected London Quaker, 'the greatest tobacco merchant of his day, perhaps in the world'. In association with John Thomlinson he was money contractor for the British armies in North America.

HELVETIUS, CLAUDE-ADRIAN, Baron de (1715–71) philosopher. Held office of *fermier général*, which brought him an income of 300,000 francs per year. His book *De l'Esprit* was banned by the parliament of Paris for its freedom of opinion. Fled to England, thence to Sans Souci (Berlin). Returned to France in 1771.

HELVETIUS, MME DE, *née* Anne-Catherine de Ligniville, widow of the Baron. Lived at Auteuil, near Passy. Hostess to and friend of the *philosophes*.

HEMPHILL, SAMUEL, Presbyterian minister from Ireland, received by the Synod of Philadelphia in 1734 as assistant to Andrews. To explain and urge the eternal laws of morality, he said, was 'not only a truly Christian, but beyond comparison the most useful Method of Preaching'. He attracted large audiences, disturbed Andrews by his unorthodox beliefs (and probably made him jealous), and had to defend himself against charges of heresies tending towards deism. He was suspended, after which he drifted away into obscurity.

HILLSBOROUGH, WILLS HILL, 2nd Viscount (1718–93) Secretary of State for the American Department (1708–73) and for the Northern Department (1779–82). One of the largest landowners in Ireland.

D'HOLBACH, BARON (1723–89) famous atheist and mechanistic philosopher; advanced sociological thinker. Blamed society and bad environment for social ills, and claimed all kings were tyrants. *System of Nature* his most famous work.

HOMES, ROBERT (d. before 1743) husband of Franklin's sister Mary, ship captain in the coastal trade.

HOPKINSON, THOMAS (1700–51) lawyer, came to America before 1731 as agent for London firms; took part in many public activities and held numerous judicial offices; member of the Junto. First president of the American Philosophical Society, and one of Franklin's colleagues in electrical experiments.

HOUDETOT, ELIZABETH-FRANCOIS, Sophie de la Live de Bellegard, Comtesse de, (1730–1813) Franklin, Crevecoeur, Rousseau, and Saint-Lambert were her friends. Kept a high-toned salon, unusually full of writers. Wrote verse. Owned a great estate in Sanois, where she held many fêtes, one of which honoured Franklin.

HOUDON, JEAN-ANTOINE (1740–1828) greatest French sculptor of his time. Travelled to America with Franklin in 1785 to sculpt a statue of Washington.

HUME, DAVID (1711–76) Scottish sceptical philosopher, historian, political economist. Franklin stayed at his home on the occasion of a two-week trip to Scotland in 1771. Hume criticized Franklin's English, but admired his wisdom.

HUNTER, WILLIAM (d. 1761) printer of Williamsburg, Va, and Franklin's agreeable colleague as deputy postmaster general. He published *The Virginia Gazette*, almanacs, and Washington's 1753 journal. Franklin took charge of his illegitimate son's education.

JAMES, ABEL (c.1726–90) prominent Philadelphia Quaker merchant, promoter, with Franklin, of silk culture in Pennsylvania, member of the American Philosophical Society, head of the firm of James and Drinker, which nearly suffered a Philadelphia Tea Party: a consignment was shipped to him in 1773, he hesitated about receiving it, and was 'visited' by angry citizens in a tar-and-feather mood. He guaranteed by his word, his property, and his daughter, that the tea would not be landed. He was one of the executors of Mrs Joseph Galloway's estate, 1782, and it may have been through this means that he came by the first part of Franklin's autobiography.

KAMES, HENRY HOME, Lord Kames (1696–1782) Scots judge and author, lord of session as Lord Kames, 1752.

KEIMER, SAMUEL (c.1688–1742) printer; in London he first joined, then disavowed, the group of religious enthusiasts known as the French Prophets, and spent long terms in prison for debt and for seditious publications. Deserting his wife, he moved to Philadelphia in 1722 and employed Franklin as a journeyman in 1723. Failing in business there, he went to Barbados in 1730, where he was equally unsuccessful. Unconventional in his beliefs and habits and intractable personally, he was nevertheless useful as printer of English works for the American market.

KEITH, SIR WILLIAM Bt (1680–1749) governor of Pennsylvania 1717–26, after previous service as surveyor of the customs for the southern colonies. He was dismissed by the Proprietors for siding with the Assembly, in which he then won a seat. He returned to England, 1728, wrote on colonial affairs, was finally imprisoned for debt, and died in the Old Bailey.

KENNEDY, ARCHIBALD (1685–1763) member of the New York Council, collector of customs; descendant of a noble Scottish family (Cassillis); wrote several important pamphlets on Indian and other colonial affairs. A successful speculator in land, he once owned Bedloe's Island, on which the Statue of Liberty now stands, and sold it to New York City for a quarantine station at a profit of 900 per cent.

KINNERSLEY, EBENEZER (1711–78) ordained a Baptist clergyman but never pastor of a church, master of the English School in the Academy of Philadelphia, lecturer on electricity, Franklin's principal associate in electrical experiments.

KNOX, WILLIAM (1732–1810) Georgia rice-planter who became British government official and served as Under-Secretary for the American Department throughout its existence; a voluminous pamphleteer.

LAFAYETTE, MARIE-JOSEPH-PAUL-IVES-ROCH-GILBERT-MOTIER, Marquis de (1754–1834) orphaned at thirteen, he came into a princely fortune. Major-general in the American army despite age and lack of experience. Lifelong friend of Washington.

LA ROCHEFOUCAULD, D'ENVILLE, LOUIS-ALEXANDRE, Duc de la Roche-Gayon et de (1743–92) Deputy of the nobility to the States General, 1789. Interested in humanitarian causes, especially slavery. Translated the American constitution into French. Honoured Franklin with a eulogy in 1790. Stoned to death, in sight of his mother and wife, by a mob during the Revolution.

LEROY, JEAN-BAPTISTE (1720–1800) physicist. Perfected the lightning rod. Corresponded with Franklin on scientific subjects.

LE VEILLARD, LOUIS-GUILLAUME M. Franklin's neighbour and the mayor of Passy. Travelled with him to Le Havre, and corresponded with him after his return to America. Guillotined during the Revolution.

LOGAN, JAMES (1674–1751) scholar, Quaker statesman, whom Franklin revered, came to Philadelphia, 1699, with William Penn and was for over a half century a leading political figure and the Penns' trusted agent. His intellectual and scientific interests brought him the attention of Linnaeus and other Europeans, and he was the foremost classicist in the colonies. He left his library of 3000 volumes, considered the finest in America, for the benefit of the people of Philadelphia. Franklin was one of the original trustees.

LOUDOUN, JOHN CAMPBELL, 4th Earl (1705–82) major general; he served in Europe and in the suppression of the Rebellion of 1745, before coming to America to succeed Braddock and Shirley as commander-in-chief, 1756. Titular governor of Virginia, 1756–59, but never actually administered the colony. Pitt removed him from his command after the abortive Louisbourg expedition.

MANDEVILLE, BERNARD (1670?–1733) Dutch physician, philosopher, and satirist; MD, Leyden, 1691; practised medicine in London; best known for his *Fable of the Bees,* or *Private Vices, Public Benefits,* 1714.

MANSFIELD, WILLIAM MURRAY, 1st Lord (1705–93) chief Justice of the King's Bench (1756–88); supported British coercive measures.

MARMONTEL, JEAN-FRANCOIS (1723–99) writer and historian. Friend of Voltaire. Translated Pope's *The Rape of the Lock.* Secretary of the Academy. Historiographer of France.

MATHER, COTTON (1663–1728) minister of the second (Congregational) Church, Boston; writer; somewhat more liberal than his father Increase. Interested in science (FRS), he was a pioneer advocate of inoculation against smallpox. Franklin rejected his theological orthodoxy, but accepted the social ethic implicit in the Essays to do Good. His *Magnalia Christi Americana* (1702) is a still useful ecclesiastical history of early New England.

MAUGRIDGE, WILLIAM (d.1766) carpenter, original member of the Junto and Library Co. Related by marriage to Daniel Boone's father, bought his farm, and in 1762 mortgaged it to Franklin, who finally received payment from Maugridge's daughter.

MEREDITH, HUGH (c.1697–1749) printer; fellow employee of Franklin at Keimer's, then his partner; original member of the Junto. Some years after moving to North Carolina he returned to Philadelphia, and Franklin continued trying to help him, but in 1749 noted that he 'went out again with a Parcel of Books, &c. which I trusted him with amounting to about £30. Since which I have not seen him nor received any thing from him.'

MIRABEAU, HONORE-GABRIEL-RIQUETTI, Comte de (1749–91) leader of the French Revolution, finally dying of overwork in its behalf. Close friend of both Cabanis and Franklin. Pronounced funeral eulogy on Franklin's death (1790).

MORELLET, ANDRÉ, ABBÉ (1727–1819) *Manuel des Inquisiteurs* made him famous. Wrote many articles on economics. On a commercial mission to England in 1772, met Franklin at home of Lord Shelburne, and became one of his most esteemed friends. Known for his Swiftian humour, his ability to analyse ideas and as translator.

NOLLET, JEAN-ANTOINE (1700–70), principal electrical scientist of France, FRS, director of the Academie des Sciences, instructor of the Dauphin in science, opponent and detractor of Franklin's theories.

NORRIS, ISSAC (1701–66) wealthy merchant, book collector, non-pacifist Quaker, anti-proprietary leader in the Assembly, speaker, 1750–64; attended the Carlisle Treaty of 1753 and the Albany Congress of 1754 with Franklin.

OSWALD, RICHARD (1705–84) Scottish and West Indian trader who had spent many years in America; acted as intermediary in 1782 between Franklin and Lord Shelburne.

PAINE, TOM (1737–1809) son of stay-maker and small farmer in Thetford; exciseman and radical activist, sailed to America in 1774 with introduction from Franklin; wrote *Common Sense* (1776), *The Crisis* (1777) and *The Rights of Man* (1790–1792); imprisoned in France 1793 but life saved by fall of Robespierre; wrote *Age of Reason* 1794.

PARKER, JAMES (c.1714–70) New York journalist, printer in New York, New Jersey, and Connecticut, one of the ablest in colonial America. He established *The New York Weekly Post-Boy*, 1743, later changing the name to *New York Gazette*. A close and trusted friend of Franklin, who appointed him comptroller of the American postal system before going to England in 1757.

PARSONS, WILLIAM (1701–57) shoemaker, scrivener, surveyor general, 1741–48, and co-founder, with Nicholas Scull, of Easton, 1752, where he held various public offices. He was politically aligned with the proprietary party. He attended Indian conferences, and was a major under Franklin's command on the frontier. In Philadelphia, he was an original member of the Junto and the American Philosophical Society, and librarian of the Library Co., 1734–46.

PEMBERTON, HENRY (1694–1771) physician, writer, FRS, employed by Newton to superintend publication of the third edition of the *Principia*.

PENN, JOHN (1729–95) son of Richard and grandson of William, the founder of Pennsylvania; he resided there, 1752–55, was a member of the Provincial Council and commissioner to the Albany Congress, 1754. Served as governor from 1763 to 1771, when he inherited his father's share of the proprietorship, and again from 1773 to 1776, when proprietary authority ended, but continued to live in Philadelphia until his death.

PENN, THOMAS (1702-75) proprietor of Pennsylvania, resident, 1732-41, absentee thereafter. The son of William the founder, after the death of his brother (1746) he owned three-fourths of the proprietary interest, and his brother Richard, who owned the remainder, took little part in decision making. Thomas departed from Quaker belief and habit, but restored the family fortunes. He was an energetic and often generous administrator, yet alienated the Assembly by his policies and seeming avarice. He and Franklin quarrelled violently over the taxation of proprietary estates and in England became bitter enemies.

PENN, WILLIAM (1644-1718) Quaker founder and proprietor of Pennsylvania, and one of the early proprietors of West New Jersey. He visited Pennsylvania twice, 1682-84 and 1699-1701. Before leaving for the second time he granted the Charter of 1701, which established the political system under which Pennsylvania was governed until the Revolution.

PITT, WILLIAM (1707-78) Secretary of State and in effect Prime Minister, 1756-61; created Earl of Chatham, 1766. Though Franklin first found him 'inaccessible', they both worked desperately in 1774-75 to avoid the break between the colonies and Great Britain. To Franklin, Pitt was 'that truly great Man', and Pitt ranked Franklin 'with our Boyles and Newtons . . . an Honour, not to the English Nation only, but to Human Nature'.

POTTS, STEPHEN (d.1738) Franklin's fellow employee at Keimer's, original member of the Junto, bookseller, later a tavernkeeper, Franklin's ledgers indicate extensive business with him between 1733 and 1757. Upon hearing of his death Franklin noted that he was an odd character, 'a Wit that seldom acted wisely . . . in the midst of Poverty, ever laughing!'

POWNALL, JOHN (1720-95) secretary at the Board of Trade and largely responsible for American policy (1758-76); Under-Secretary of State 1768-76.

POWNALL, THOMAS (1722-1805) AB, Cambridge, 1743, went to New York in 1753 as secretary to Governor Osborne, who committed suicide almost at once. At a loose end, Pownall travelled among the colonies as a sort of unofficial observer for the British government; began a lifelong friendship with Franklin on a visit to Philadelphia; was a guest at the Albany Congress, 1754; and held the nominal office of lieutenant governor of New Jersey, 1755-57. He became secretary to Lord Loudoun, 1756, and was governor of Massachusetts, 1757-60, serving ably and energetically and winning the approval of the popular party. After his return to England he published (1764) and five later editions, *The Administration of the Colonies*, which showed a broad understanding of the colonial point of view. As a member of Parliament he was a friend of the American cause.

PRICE, RICHARD (1723-91) dissenter and philosopher, strongly pro-American.

PRIESTLEY, JOSEPH (1733–1804) Presbyterian clergyman and chemist, librarian to Lord Shelburne (1772–80); FRS. Emigrated to Pennsylvania 1794.

RALPH, JAMES (d.1762) ambitious but undisciplined writer and would-be poet, another of the charming companions and beloved ne'er-do-wells of Franklin's youth. His verse was unsuccessful, but he did collaborate with Henry Fielding as dramatist and journalist and wrote a good history of England. He became so effective a political writer in the interest of leaders out of office that the ministry paid him £300 a year not to write. He and Franklin renewed their friendship in London in 1757, where he helped in Franklin's propaganda activities.

RAY, CATHERINE (1731–94) friend and correspondent of Franklin. Daughter of Simon Ray and his second wife, Deborah (Greene) Ray. Married (1758) her cousin William Greene, later Governor of Rhode Island.

READ, DEBORAH. See Franklin, Deborah Read Rogers.

READ, JAMES (1718–93) lawyer and clerk, Franklin's neighbour and rival bookseller, husband of Deborah Franklin's second cousin. After his failure to replace Franklin as clerk of the Assembly, he moved to Reading, where he continued to hold public office.

READ, JOHN (1677–1724) Deborah's father. Born in London, a carpenter by trade, settled in Birmingham after his marriage in 1701, but had moved to Philadelphia with his wife and one or more children by 1711, when he bought property on Market Street.

READ, SARAH WHITE (1675–1761) Deborah's mother. Born in Birmingham, daughter of Joseph and Deborah (Cash) White, she married John Read in 1701. Of her seven children, only John, Deborah, and Frances attained adulthood.

ROBERTS, HUGH (c.1706–1786) merchant, son of the mayor of Philadelphia, wealthy and well connected. One of Franklin's close friends—they were associated in the Junto, the Pennsylvania Hospital, the Library, American Philosophical Society, the Union Fire Co., and, in 1751–52, in the Assembly.

ROGERS, JOHN potter, married Deborah Read, perhaps bigamously, Aug 5 1725; absconded December 1727, taking with him a Negro lad. His reported death in the West Indies remained unconfirmed in Philadelphia.

SHELBURNE, WILLIAM PETTY FITZMAURICE, Earl of (1737–1805). Associate of Pitt, drafted Proclamation of 1763. Became Prime Minister on Rockingham's death (July 1872–Feb 1783).

SHIPLEY, JONATHAN (1714–88) Bishop of St Asaph, and critic of Britain's American policy; the *Autobiography* was begun at his Twyford home, while Franklin was on holiday there.

SHIRLEY, WILLIAM (1694–1771) London barrister before coming to Boston, where after holding various offices he became a successful governor, serving from 1741 to 1757. His part in the capture of Louisbourg made him something of a popular hero. He was interested, with Franklin, in colonial union, and succeeded Braddock as commander-in-chief until Loudoun, who disliked him intensely, replaced him in 1756. He was governor of the Bahamas 1758–67.

SHIRLEY, WILLIAM, JR. (1721–55) eldest son of the Massachusetts governor; naval officer in Boston, agent for his father in England; and military secretary to Braddock. He was killed in Braddock's defeat.

SLOANE, SIR HANS (1660–1753) physician, antiquarian, botanist, secretary of the Royal Society, successor to Newton as president, 1727; also president of the Royal College of Physicians. Created a baronet in 1716. Sloane bequeathed his natural history and manuscript collections to the nation; these and certain others provided the nucleus of the British Museum in 1754.

SPANGENBERG, AUGUSTUS GOTTLIEB (1704–92) German-born Moravian bishop, lived in America, 1735–62. He organized the Moravian missions in the colonies and was regarded in Europe as the great authority on American missions. Franklin was grateful during his own service on the frontier for Spangenberg's aid in defence.

SPENCER, ARCHIBALD (c.1698–1760) Edinburgh midwife, in America an itinerant lecturer on electricity whom Franklin met in Boston in 1743, where he was giving a Course of Experimental Philosophy. He lectured in Philadelphia the following year and subsequently in the South. Later he was ordained an Anglican clergyman and served a parish in Maryland. His first name has often, but erroneously, been given as Adam.

STEVENSON, MARGARET (c.1706–83) landlady friend, at whose home in Craven Street Franklin stayed through his London years. Her daughter Polly, who married the surgeon William Hewson, became another of Franklin's friends and correspondents, and was with Franklin in Philadelphia when he died.

STORMONT, DAVID MURRAY, Viscount Stormont, 2nd Earl of Mansfield (1726–96). Ambassador in Paris 1772–78.

STRAHAN, WILLIAM (1715–85) Scottish-born but London-settled printer and publisher (of Dr Johnson's *Dictionary*, and of Gibbon, Adam Smith and David Hume, among others); MP.

SYNG, PHILIP (1703–89) came from Ireland in 1714; silversmith (his inkstand was used at the signing of the Declaration of Independence and Constitution), an original member of the Junto, and member of many civic organizations. He engraved the seals for the Library Co., and the Philadelphia Contributionship, and joined with Franklin in electrical experiments.

TURGOT, ANNE-ROBERT-JACQUES, Baron de Laune (1727–81). Leading physiocrat. Lifelong friend of Mme Helvetius (to whom he had proposed before Franklin), Mme Geoffrin, Mme du Deffand, and the Duchesse d'Enville. Also a close friend to Morellet. Many ideas and reforms of the revolution were his.

VAUGHAN, BENJAMIN (1751–1835), diplomat, merchant, agriculturalist. Born in Jamaica, educated in England; his long friendship with Franklin began in London before the American Revolution. He edited the first general collection of Franklin's works, 1779. Sympathetic with the colonies and often employed by Lord Shelburne on confidential missions, he was sent to France (1782) to assist unofficially in the peace negotiations. He became actively interested in the French Revolution, settled in France, escaped from the Terror, and then moved to America (1796), retiring from politics but engaging in writing and in agricultural experiments on his Maine farm.

VICQ D'AZYR, FELIX (1748–94) physician, anatomist, writer. Founded a medical school in Paris. Physician to the king and queen. Franklin was the first foreign associate of the Royal Society of Medicine that Vicq founded in 1776.

VOLTAIRE, FRANCOIS-MARIE-AROUET (1694–1778) one of greatest satirical writers of all time. Lived at court of Frederick of Prussia (1751–1754). Belonged to the same masonic lodge (Neuf Soeurs) as Franklin. Considered the only peer Franklin had, when both met and embraced at the Academy and the audience shouted, 'Behold Solon and Sophocles embrace!'

WATTS, JOHN (c.1678–1763) head of one of the most important London printing houses, located in Wild Court, three-quarters of a mile west of Bartholomew Close where Franklin first worked. Several eminent printers worked there as young men. Watts was also a patron of William Caslon and lent him £100 to make his start as a designer and founder of printing types.

WHITEFIELD, GEORGE (1714–70) strenuous and successful evangelist, joined the Wesley movement while at Oxford, and was ordained an Anglican priest in 1739, soon beginning his open-air preaching in England. He made seven journeys to America, founded an orphanage in Georgia, preached up and down the colonies, attracting unprecedented numbers of auditors wherever he went. He was more responsible than any other one man for starting the 'Great Awakening', the first major religious revival in America. Conservative in doctrine and belief, he was radical and emotional in his methods, and aroused bitter antagonism among many of the clergymen of the chief denominations in both England and the colonies. Though he was never able to win Franklin over to his own religious practices and beliefs, the two remained warm friends.

WHITEFOORD, CALEB (1734–1810) wine-merchant and diplomat, a neighbour of Franklin in Craven Street in London. Visited Passy in 1782 to introduce Oswald to Franklin. Secretary to the British peace delegation at the Paris Peace Conference (1782).

WOLFE, JAMES (1727–50) British major general. Son of an army officer, he was commissioned at the age of fourteen and saw extended active service on the Continent and against the Jacobites in Scotland before he was twenty-one. He commanded the forces sent up the St Lawrence against Quebec, and was killed at his moment of victory over Montcalm on the Plains of Abraham.

INDEX